D0741870

THE HOLOCAUST

THE HOLOCAUST

A Concise History

DORIS L. BERGEN

ROWMAN & LITTLEFIELD PUBLISHERS, INC.
Lanham • Boulder • New York • Toronto • Plymouth, UK

ROWMAN & LITTLEFIELD PUBLISHERS, INC.

Published in the United States of America
by Rowman & Littlefield Publishers, Inc.
A wholly owned subsidiary of The Rowman & Littlefield Publishing Group, Inc.
4501 Forbes Boulevard, Suite 200, Lanham, Maryland 20706
www.rowmanlittlefield.com

Estover Road, Plymouth PL6 7PY, United Kingdom

British Library Cataloguing in Publication Information Available

Library of Congress Cataloging-in-Publication Data

Bergen, Doris L.
[War & genocide]
The Holocaust : a concise history / Doris L. Bergen.
    p.   cm.
Originally published under title: War & genocide.
Includes bibliographical references and index.
ISBN 978-0-7425-5714-7 (cloth : alk. paper)
    1. Germany—History—1933–1945.   2. National socialism.   3. Antisemitism—
Germany—History—20th century.   4. Holocaust, Jewish (1939–1945)—Causes.
5. World War, 1939–1945—Causes.   I. Title.
DD256.5.B3916   2009b
940.53′18—dc22
                                                          2009020406

Printed in the United States of America

∞ ™ The paper used in this publication meets the minimum requirements of American National Standard for Information Sciences—Permanence of Paper for Printed Library Materials, ANSI/NISO Z39.48-1992.

CONTENTS

Preface: War and Genocide: Race and Space   viii

1   Preconditions: Antisemitism, Racism, and Common Prejudices in Early-Twentieth-Century Europe   1

2   Leadership and Will: Adolf Hitler, the National Socialist German Workers' Party, and Nazi Ideology   29

3   From Revolution to Routine: Nazi Germany, 1933–1938   51

4   Open Aggression: In Search of War, 1938–1939   79

5   Experiments in Brutality, 1939–1940: War against Poland and the So-Called Euthanasia Program   101

6   Expansion and Systematization: Exporting War and Terror, 1940–1941   135

7   The Peak Years of Killing: 1942 and 1943   167

8   Death Throes and Killing Frenzies, 1944–1945   215

Conclusion: The Legacies of Atrocity   233

Sources and Suggestions for Further Reading   245

Photo Credits   259

Index   263

About the Author   279

Preface

WAR AND GENOCIDE: RACE AND SPACE

The Holocaust was an event of global proportions, involving perpetrators, victims, bystanders, beneficiaries, and rescuers from all over Europe and elsewhere in the world. Any effort to grasp it in its entirety must begin with recognition of that massive scope.

This book attempts to address the enormity of the Holocaust by situating it in the context of the Second World War, the largest and deadliest conflict in human history. War and conquest delivered into Nazi German hands the Jews of eastern and southeastern Europe—Poland, Ukraine, Belorussia, Hungary, Yugoslavia, Greece, and elsewhere—as well as the smaller Jewish populations of the west: for example, France, Belgium, and the Netherlands. Approximately 95 percent of the Jews killed between 1939 and 1945 lived outside Germany's prewar borders. At the same time, war—in particular the Nazi war of annihilation to Germany's east—exponentially increased the numbers and kinds of victims, as brutal programs of persecution, expulsion, and murder, bloated on carnage, demanded and created even more enemies. Mass killings of non-Jews were also part of the Nazi German war effort, a war launched for the related goals of race and space: so-called racial purification and territorial expansion. War provided killers with both a cover and an excuse for murder; in wartime, killing was normalized, and extreme, even genocidal measures could be justified with familiar arguments about the need to defend the homeland. Without the war, the Holocaust would not—and could not—have happened.

Since the 1960s, the term "Holocaust," from the Greek for "a burned offering," has been used to refer to the murder of approximately 6 million Jews by Nazi Germans and their collaborators during World War II. Sometimes the Hebrew word "Shoah"—catastrophe—is used as a synonym. There is no doubt that hatred of Jews constituted the center of Nazi ideology. Hitler and his associates preached what the scholar Saul Friedländer calls "redemptive antisemitism": the belief that Jews were the root of all evil and that Germany could be saved from collapse only by total removal of Jews and Jewish influence. Jews were the main target of Nazi genocide; against the Jews Hitler's Germany mobilized all its resources: bureaucratic, military, legal, scientific, economic, and intellectual.

Nevertheless, it was not Jews but the mentally and physically disabled who became targets of the first large-scale, systematic killings in Nazi Germany, under the euphemistically labeled "Euthanasia Program." This program, like the assault on European Gypsies (Roma), shared with the genocide of the Jews personnel, methods of killing, and goals of so-called racial purification. At the same time, Nazi Germany persecuted, incarcerated, and killed millions of Slavic people—Polish gentiles, especially members of the intelligentsia; Soviet prisoners of war; and others—and attacked Communists, homosexual men, Jehovah's Witnesses, Afro-Germans, and other people considered unwanted in the "new European order." Whether or not one considers members of any or all of these groups to belong under the label "victims of the Holocaust," their fates were entwined in significant ways with that of the Jews targeted and murdered in the Nazi quest for race and space. This book seeks to identify and explore connections between and among victim groups, not in the interest of establishing some kind of hierarchy of suffering but with the hope of coming to understand how state-sponsored programs of violence and atrocity function and offering at least a glimpse into how they are experienced by those who suffer their ravages.

These are ambitious aims for a short book. Indeed, although this book is concise, it will not necessarily make dealing with the Nazi era, the war, and the Holocaust easy. That history is complex, and I have tried to present it honestly and as fully as possible in a brief survey. Nor do I promise that this small book will resolve the big questions that might be on your mind as you approach this topic: Why did such horrible things happen? If there is a God, how could such atrocities have been possible? What are human beings that they can inflict such agony on other people? Finding answers to those kinds of questions is a lifelong challenge, not something you can accomplish with one book or one class.

Nevertheless, this book will help you address some more modest yet important questions regarding the history of Nazism, World War II, and the

Holocaust. Who was involved and in what ways? What motivated those people to behave as they did? How—through what processes—did large numbers of people, some of them "ordinary," some less so, become murderers of larger numbers of other people? How did the targets of attacks respond, and what strategies did they develop in their quest to survive? If you care enough about the past to try to understand these matters, perhaps you will also discover some insights that help you think about brutality and suffering in our own world.

What follows here is only a brief introduction to a subject so broad and multidimensional that you could probably read for the rest of your life and never get through all that has been written about it. I hope that you will read this book in conjunction with some of the many excellent studies that go into more depth on specific topics. A list of sources for each chapter and some suggestions for further reading are included at the end of the book. Any synthesis such as this relies heavily on the work of other scholars, and I am indebted and very grateful to all of those people whose research and interpretations have shaped and challenged my own.

Many people helped make it possible for this book to appear. My thanks go to Jim Harink and Christine Bergen, who loyally and critically read the first draft. I also appreciate the students and teaching assistants in my courses on the Holocaust at the Universities of Vermont, Notre Dame, and Toronto. Feedback from my class in the fall of 1999 was invaluable, and Kristin Kobes Du Mez provided especially detailed suggestions. Margarete Myers Feinstein, Daniel S. Mattern, Gary Hamburg, Laura Crago, Robert Wegs, Glenda Regenbaum, and Christopher Browning commented on parts or all of the text for the first edition, and C. Paul Vincent, Jürgen Matthäus, Geoffrey Giles, and Francis R. Nicosia provided comments and corrections for this second edition. Uta Larkey and Susan Crane generously shared their students' and their own suggestions, and Gerhard Weinberg gave the book the kind of careful, informed reading of which only he is capable. My friends Linda H. Pardo, Patricia Blanchette, and Catherine Schlegel—a scientist, a philosopher, and a classicist—always came through with insight and encouragement. Emily Elizabeth Fleming and Annamarie Bindenagel read the manuscript for the first edition and gave me useful ideas; I especially appreciated Emily Elizabeth's astute judgments about photographs. Thank you as well to Nicole Thompson for helping prepare the manuscript for press; to Nicole and Karly Bergen for proofreading; and to Janine Riviere and Chris Laursen at the University of Toronto for superb assistance at a crucial juncture. Notre Dame's Institute for Scholarship in the Liberal Arts and the Chancellor Rose and Ray Wolfe Chair in Holocaust Studies at the University of Toronto provided essential funding.

A very special thank-you is due to Sharon Muller and Judith Cohen at the United States Holocaust Memorial Museum Photo Archives. They and the members of their staff were generous, patient, and brilliantly creative in helping me locate photographs for the original edition and this second edition. Steve Wrinn, Mary Carpenter, and Erin McKindley, and subsequently Susan McEachern and Jehanne Schweitzer at Rowman & Littlefield Publishers have been wonderfully supportive, and Donald Critchlow persuaded me to tackle the project in the first place.

Without my two scholarly mentors, Annelise L. Thimme and Gerhard L. Weinberg, I would never have come to work in this field in the first place. They have influenced me in ways that continue to surprise me, and I am deeply grateful to them both. Of course, all errors and shortcomings in the book are my own responsibility.

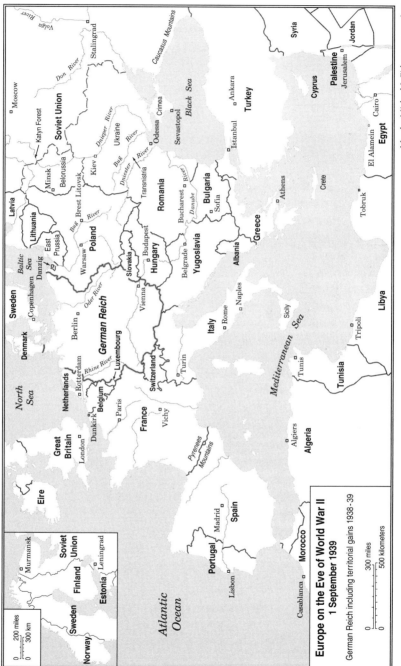

Map by Michael J. Fisher, cartographer

Europe on the Eve of World War II
1 September 1939

German Reich including territorial gains 1938-39

0   300 miles
0   500 kilometers

1

PRECONDITIONS

Antisemitism, Racism, and Common Prejudices in Early-Twentieth-Century Europe

In order for a house to burn down, three things are required. The timber must be dry and combustible, there needs to be a spark that ignites it, and external conditions have to be favorable—not too damp, perhaps some wind. Hitler's Nazi regime in Germany provided the spark that set off the destruction we now call the Holocaust, and World War II (1939–1945) created a setting conducive to brutality. However, without certain preconditions—the dry timber—mass murder on such a scale would not have been possible. People had to be prepared to accept the identification of other members of their society as enemies. In other words, a substantial part of the population had to be ready to consider it desirable, acceptable, or at least unavoidable, that certain other people would be isolated, persecuted, and killed.

Hitler and his National Socialist German Workers' Party, now commonly referred to as the Nazis, came to power in Germany in 1933 and remained in place until the military defeat of Germany in 1945. More than half a century later, Nazism has become synonymous with the mass murder of millions of innocent people: Jews, above all, and also disabled people, Gypsies, political opponents, and others.

In their choices of target groups the Nazis reflected and built on prejudices that were familiar in many parts of Europe. Hitler and the Nazis did not invent antisemitism—hatred of Jews—nor were they the first to attack Sinti and Roma (Gypsies) or people considered handicapped. Their hostilities

1

toward Europeans of African descent, Slavic people, Jehovah's Witnesses, and homosexuals were not new either. The Nazis were extremists in the lengths to which they went in their assaults, but they were quite typical in whom they attacked.

Long-standing hatreds alone did not cause the Holocaust. Sadly, the world is full of old prejudices; fortunately, only rarely do they erupt in genocide. Leadership, political will, and manipulation of popular sentiments are needed to fan hostility into organized killing. Widespread negative attitudes on their own do not create a holocaust, but they are a necessary condition for mass persecution—that is, the rest of the population must regard certain groups as legitimate targets in order for them to participate in or tolerate open assault. Nazi leaders could not simply have invented a category of enemies—for example, people between the ages of 37 and 42—and then have expected the majority of the population to turn against them. Such a group would have been incomprehensible to most people. The identities of those targeted for destruction during World War II were no coincidence; these people were already victims of prejudice.

This chapter surveys some of the widespread attitudes toward Jews and other groups in Europe prior to the Nazi rise to power in Germany in 1933. It outlines some ideas already in place in Europe by the early twentieth century that provided the ground in which the Nazi ideology of race and space— "racial purification" and territorial expansion—could take root and grow.

A NOTE ON VOCABULARY AND SOME WORDS OF WARNING

The Holocaust originated in Nazi Germany, but it was by no means uniquely German in terms of its perpetrators, victims, bystanders, beneficiaries, or heroes. They came from all over Europe and even farther away, swept into the deadly force field of developments with worldwide repercussions. By the same token, many of the ideas and attitudes that fed into the Holocaust had roots and branches outside Germany, particularly elsewhere in Europe. Although much of the discussion in this chapter focuses on Germany, it is important to keep in mind that scholarship, publications, opinions, and prejudices flowed freely across national borders throughout the modern era; most Germans of the 1920s and 1930s were more typical than they were atypical for Europeans in their time.

Discussing the Nazi era raises some thorny problems of vocabulary.

Should one say "Nazis" or "Germans" when referring to the people of Hitler's Germany? Some scholars have argued that using the term "Nazis" in this general way is misleading. It implies that Hitler's supporters were not themselves Germans and that the "real Germans" were somehow untouched by Nazism. On the other hand, simply saying "Germans" suggests that all Germans marched in step behind Hitler. That was not the case either. German Jews were excluded from the Nazi movement by definition—that is, they were not permitted to join the Nazi Party or its affiliates—and the same was generally true of Germans deemed handicapped, Gypsies, and other outsiders. Nevertheless, those people too were Germans. Moreover, some Germans also opposed the regime and tried to distance themselves from it. Throughout this book, I try to be as precise as possible in my use of terms, while recognizing the impossibility of avoiding overgeneralization.

A final introductory word of caution: prejudices always reveal more about the people who hold them than they do about those at whom they are directed. You will not learn much useful information about Judaism or Jews by studying antisemitism, but you can learn quite a lot about antisemites, their insecurities, and their fears. By the same token, examining the lives of Jews in Europe before World War II is important in its own right, but it will not answer the question as to why antisemites hated Jews any more than studying African American history will explain why white supremacists hate black people. Prejudices are habits of thought; they are not reasoned responses to objective realities. When you read the descriptions of common prejudices that follow, keep in mind that these attitudes were based on imaginings about people rather than on who those people really were.

To illustrate this point, it is useful to observe that Nazi prejudices against all of the target groups followed similar patterns. Proponents of Nazi ideas focused their attacks on people who were already suspect in the eyes of many Germans. They then echoed and enlarged familiar hatreds and linked them to current anxieties and concerns. For example, in the 1920s and 1930s, many Germans were distressed by Germany's defeat in World War I. So, no matter which of their supposed enemies they described—Jews, homosexuals, Communists, Jehovah's Witnesses—Nazi propagandists accused them of causing Germany to lose the war. Similarly, many Germans in Hitler's time were worried about decadence, criminality, and supposed racial degeneration. Nazi thinkers charged every enemy group with promoting immorality, spreading crime, and polluting the bloodstream. Whether they were talking about Slavic people, Gypsies, Jews, Afro-Germans, or homosexuals, Nazi propaganda used similar slurs.

ANTISEMITISM

Why begin a discussion of preconditions with the topic of antisemitism? Hatred of Jews was the center of Nazi ideology. Nazi propagandists labeled all of Germany's supposed enemies as "Jews" or judaized: they depicted Jews as deformed and criminal and compared them to disabled people and Gypsies, whom they also described as monstrous and dangerous. Nazi ideologues linked Communists, capitalists, and liberals with a purported Jewish conspiracy; they described homosexuals, eastern Europeans, the British, and the Americans as nothing but cover groups for alleged Jewish interests. So by studying the history of antisemitism and Nazi uses of it, we can begin to get a sense of how other Nazi ideas functioned and built on older traditions.

The term "antisemitism" was coined in the 1870s by a German journalist who wanted to contrast his supposedly scientific hatred of Jews with religious forms of anti-Judaism. As a label, "antisemitism" is misleading, because the adjective "Semitic" describes a group of related languages, among them Hebrew, Arabic, and Phoenician, and the people who speak them. Often you will see the word written with a hyphen—"anti-Semitism"—a spelling I avoid in this book. Use of the hyphen implies that there was such a thing as "Semitism," which antisemites opposed. In fact, no one who used the term in the nineteenth century (or since) ever meant it to mean anything but hatred of Jews.

Antipathy toward Jews in Europe dated back much further than the 1800s—as far as the ancient world. Roman authorities worried that Jewish refusal to worship local and imperial gods would jeopardize the security of the state. At times such unease, coupled with political conflicts, turned into open persecution and attacks. In 70 C.E. the Romans destroyed the Jewish temple in Jerusalem, the focal point of Jewish life up to that time; sixty years later they dispersed the Jews of Palestine, scattering them far from the region that had been their home.

The rise of Christianity added new fuel to anti-Jewish sentiments. Christianity grew out of Judaism—Jesus himself was a Jew, as were the apostles and important figures such as Paul of Tarsus. Nevertheless, early Christians tried to separate themselves from other Jews, both to win followers from the gentile (non-Jewish) world and to gain favor with Roman imperial authorities. Some early Christians also stressed their loyalty to the state by pointing out that the Kingdom of God was not of this earth and therefore did not compete with Rome. Such efforts paid off: in less than four hundred years, Christianity went from being a persecuted branch of Judaism to being the dominant religion of the Roman Empire. It is significant that some early Christian accounts blamed Jews for Jesus's death even though crucifixion was a specifically Roman form of punishment commonly practiced during Jesus's time. The version of events that had Jewish mobs demanding Jesus's death while the Roman governor Pontius Pilate washed his hands allowed later Christians to emphasize their difference from Judaism and downplay the hostility that Roman authorities had shown toward Christianity in its early stages. All of the false accusations against Jews associated with the Roman imperial period—that Jews were traitors and conspirators, that they killed Christ—remained familiar in Europe into the twentieth century.

In many ways the Middle Ages—from around the ninth to the sixteenth centuries—were difficult times for Jews in Europe. Often crusades against Muslims and Christian heretics started off or ended up with violent attacks on Jews. Such attacks, which later came to be known as pogroms, a word derived from Russian, were also common responses to outbreaks of plague or other disasters. For example, in many parts of Europe, the Black Death of 1348 sparked brutal pogroms, as Christians blamed Jews for somehow causing the epidemic of bubonic plague. Mobilized by such accusations, Christian mobs—sometimes spontaneously, sometimes urged on by state and church leaders—attacked Jewish homes and communities, plundering, destroying, and killing. The scale of pogroms varied wildly, from brief local incidents to weeklong massacres that swept through entire regions. In their wake they left among Christians a habit of using Jews as scapegoats, and among Jews, a sense of vulnerability and a repertoire of defenses, such as paying protection money, sticking together, and keeping a low profile.

In addition to sporadic waves of violence, Jews faced harassment and restrictions of various kinds from governments across Europe. In some cases, regulations forced Jews to live in certain areas or ghettos; sometimes Jews were required to wear identifying badges; elsewhere, state authorities drove Jews out of their territories altogether. Between 1492 and 1497, for example, King Ferdinand and Queen Isabella of Spain expelled all Jews and Muslims from the Iberian Peninsula except those who agreed to convert to Christianity. Throughout the Middle Ages, Jews everywhere in Europe faced limitations on the occupations in which they could engage as well as the kinds of property and titles they could hold.

Some church leaders and secular rulers tried to convince or coerce Jews to abandon their religion and convert to Christianity. But even conversion did not necessarily solve the problems of intolerance. Converts from Judaism to Christianity in sixteenth-century Spain found that they were still viewed with deep suspicion and regarded as somehow tainted by supposed "Jewish blood." So even the notion of Jewishness as a "race" was not entirely original to the Nazis.

The Protestant Reformation did not improve the lot of European Jews. At first its leader, the German monk Martin Luther, hoped that his break with what he considered the corrupted church of Rome would inspire mass conversions of Jews to Christianity. When the anticipated wave of baptisms did not occur, Luther turned against the Jews, whom he derided as stubborn and hard-necked. In 1542 he wrote a pamphlet called *Against the Jews and Their Lies.* That tract, with its vicious characterization of Jews as parasites and its calls to "set their synagogues and schools on fire," would later be widely quoted in Hitler's Germany. Other medieval images—the association of Jews with the devil; charges that Jews used the blood of Christian children for ritual purposes—also survived into the modern era. Even those Nazi leaders who hated Christianity and mocked it for its historical ties to Judaism found it useful to invoke these powerful, traditional notions about Jews. In other words, Nazi antisemitism was different from older religious forms of anti-Judaism, but its proponents still drew on those traditional hostilities. Ancient associations of Jews with deadly evil gave modern antisemitism a virulence that set it apart from other prejudices.

Antisemitism after the Emancipation of European Jews

In the seventeenth, eighteenth, and nineteenth centuries, European society became more secular, but bigotry toward Jews did not disappear. Instead, social, economic, and political prejudices grew alongside and sometimes in place of older religious resentments. Enlightenment thinkers in eighteenth-century Europe favored religious toleration and mocked the rigidity of institutionalized Christianity. But even such a self-consciously progressive thinker as the French writer Voltaire labeled Jews with contempt as "vagrants, robbers, slaves, or seditious." In the nineteenth century, Napoleon and other rulers introduced legislation to repeal old restrictions on Jews in Europe. This process is usually referred to as the emancipation of the Jews. Nevertheless, formal and informal limitations often remained in place.

Like every minority group striving to better its position while hampered by obstructions, European Jews ended up overrepresented in some occupations and underrepresented in others. Hostile non-Jews made much of the fact that in Germany by around 1900, the field of journalism included a higher percentage of Jews than did the population as a whole. However they never mentioned the fact that Jews were almost completely excluded from the higher ranks of the government bureaucracy and the military. By the late 1800s, political parties that openly championed antisemitism had sprung up in various parts of Europe. Vienna's popular antisemitic mayor Karl Lueger would make a deep impression on the young Adolf Hitler. In particular Hitler noticed how Lueger played on widespread anti-Jewish sentiments to whip up enthusiasm in the crowds he addressed and to boost his own support.

Modern antisemites claimed that their views were scientific, based on the biological "facts" of blood and race. In reality hatred of Jews was no more scientific than were European attitudes of superiority toward Africans, Asians, or native peoples in the Americas. Moreover the notion of "Jewishness" as a race was invented, as were the concepts of "blackness," "whiteness," and "Orientalism" that became so central to how many Europeans and North Americans viewed the world. Still, Social Darwinist ideas about struggle between rival "races" and survival of the strongest provided fertile ground, not only for Nazi notions about Jews but for an entire, interlocking system of prejudices against people deemed inferior. Sexual anxieties and sexualized stereotypes fed the racist mind-set in powerful, pernicious ways. Notions about Jewish and black men as sexual predators insatiable in their lust for white women coexisted with charges that Jews and men of color were feminized weaklings incapable of soldierly honor. In medieval Europe, religion had served to legitimate and justify hatreds. In the modern era science and pseudoscience played a comparable role.

THE DIVERSITY OF JEWISH LIFE IN EUROPE

Never more than a small minority—at most 1 or 2 percent of the entire population of Europe—Jews existed alongside Christians for centuries. Judaism was and is a religion and a living community. Despite pogroms, massacres, and expulsions, Jews survived in Europe. They thrived as individuals and as a community in different places at different times—in Spain before the Inquisition, later in the Netherlands, at times in Poland and Germany. Ever since ancient times the Jewish contribution to European life has been enormous.

European Jews, like European Christians, were and are a diverse group. It is important not to oversimplify or let studies of persecution distort our understanding of Jewish history. By the early twentieth century many were highly assimilated; neither from appearance, habits of daily life, nor language could they be distinguished from their gentile French, German, Italian, Polish,

Greek, or other neighbors. Some attended religious services several times a year; others, never. Some maintained a strong sense of Jewish identity; others, very little or none at all. Many Jews were intermarried with Christians; often Jews in intermarriages converted to Christianity, and usually they raised their children as Christians. Karl Marx, the founder of Communism, is frequently described as a Jew, but in fact he was the son of a couple who converted from Judaism to Christianity. Nazi law would not recognize such conversions but considered converts to Christianity, as well as the children and in some cases grandchildren of converts, to be Jews.

In Europe in the early 1900s there were also more visible kinds of Jews. In some parts of eastern Europe many Jews lived in small communities known as shtetls. Forced by the Russian tsars to remain in an area in the west of the Russian empire called the Pale of Settlement, these Jews developed a lifestyle of their own based on shared religious observance, the Yiddish language, a diet following kashrut—the Jewish dietary laws—and predominance of certain occupations. For example, many were small traders and craftspeople. Those lines of work did not require them to own land, something from which they were restricted and in some places prohibited altogether.

Jews in southern and southeastern Europe tended to come from what is called the Sephardic tradition and to speak a language called Ladino rather than the Yiddish of the Ashkenazic Jews of northern and central Europe. By the twentieth century, there were many strands of European Judaism. Some Jews were strictly Orthodox, so that their mode of dress, adherence to dietary laws, and other religious observances set them apart from the gentiles around them. Others were Reform, part of a branch of Judaism that emerged out of early-nineteenth-century Germany and emphasized adapting rituals and practices for modern times. Some Jews embraced the tradition of Hasidism, a movement that started in Poland and emphasized joyous mysticism; others were more austere. Some dressed distinctively, with the adult men wearing beards and earlocks; other Jewish men might be distinguishable only by the physical marking of circumcision.

In short, there were wealthy Jews in Europe around 1930 as well as middle-class and very poor Jews. There were Jewish bankers and Jewish shopkeepers, and Jewish doctors, nurses, actors, professors, soldiers, typists, peddlers, factory owners, factory workers, kindergarten teachers, conservatives, liberals, nationalists, feminists, anarchists, and Communists. Nazi propaganda would create the category of "the Jew," a composite based on myths and stereotypes. Nazi persecution then reified that gross generalization, as violence and destruction rendered obsolete distinctions of age, sex, class, and national origin among

Jews, all of whom were slated for destruction. In reality there was no such thing as "the Jew," only Jews who often differed as much, and in many cases much more, from one another than they did from the Christians around them.

Three Jewish Lives in Prewar Europe

Perhaps the best way to capture the diversity of Jewish life is to look at several individuals who experienced the assault of Nazism as young people in Europe. One example comes from a memoir by Peter Gay called *My German Question*. Gay was born in Berlin in 1923 to a middle-class family named Fröhlich, which means "happy" in German. (After moving to the United States, the name would be changed to the English translation "Gay.") Peter's father bought and sold glassware; his mother worked part-time as a clerk in her sister's sewing notions store. Committed atheists, Fröhlich's parents officially left the Jewish community. They had their son circumcised but showed few other signs of Jewish identity.

Fröhlich's father fought in World War I and was wounded and decorated. An avid fan of all kinds of sports, Fröhlich Sr. had many close friends who were not Jewish. Young Peter was one of a handful of Jewish boys at his school; he

A group of religious Jews goes on a kayaking excursion in Poland in the 1930s. In the middle of the rear kayak, holding a child, is Tsvi Majranc. Mr. Majranc died of dysentery during the war in the Lodz ghetto.

does not remember ever being ridiculed or harassed. He and his family considered themselves thoroughly German. Gay and his parents managed to get out of Germany before the Second World War began in 1939. Gay eventually moved to the United States, where he became an important historian of modern Europe and a professor at Yale University.

As a young girl in Hungary, Aranka Siegal lived a rather different Jewish life in Europe before the Holocaust. She describes it in her book, *Upon the Head of the Goat*. Siegal, whose name at the time was Piri Davidowitz, was an observant Jew like her parents and her four sisters. Born in 1931, she went to a public school, where her friends included Catholic, Protestant, and Russian Orthodox as well as Jewish children. Some of her fondest childhood memories are of the months she spent each summer on her grandmother's farm. It was from her grandmother that Piri learned the most about Judaism. With her grandmother she lit the Sabbath candles, recited the blessing for the new year on Rosh Hashanah, and prepared traditional foods.

Siegal's grandmother also taught her about Jewish history. Old enough to have vivid memories of pogroms in Ukraine and Hungary in the 1910s and 1920s, she told her granddaughter how Christians had often used Jews as scapegoats in times of trouble. She also warned the little girl about a "madman" called Hitler, who was terrorizing Jews in Germany and Poland. Aranka Siegal's grandmother was right to be afraid. Almost everyone in the family would be killed in the Holocaust. Miraculously Piri and one sister survived being sent to the Nazi killing center of Auschwitz. After some time in Sweden, Aranka Siegal moved to New York. She speaks to many students every year about her experiences during and after World War II.

A third, very different Jewish life is that of Jack Pomerantz, which is recorded in his memoir *Run East*. A native of Radzyn, a small town near Lublin in Poland, Pomerantz was born in 1918 during a pogrom, a violent attack on the Jewish community by their Christian neighbors. His mother was hiding in a barn when she gave birth to Yankel, one of eight children. (He would later anglicize his first name to "Jack.") Yankel's father was a peddler; he wore a long beard, dark clothing, and often a prayer shawl. Although the family was desperately poor, Yankel's mother still always tried to have a special meal for Shabbat, the best day of the week. Like all married Orthodox women she wore a wig. For the Jewish holidays most of the women in the shtetl made wonderful food, but sometimes Pomerantz's mother had nothing to cook. She would boil rags just to steam up the windows of their shack and create the impression that they too were preparing a feast.

Pomerantz spoke Yiddish at home and was very conscious of himself as a

Jew. His town was about half Jews and half Polish Christians, and there was considerable tension between the two groups. As a boy Yankel heard people say they hated Jews because they "killed Christ." Once, in a fight, a Polish Catholic boy cut Yankel's cheek with a knife, right through into his mouth. Pomerantz was no stranger to antisemitism.

Like Peter Gay and Aranka Siegal, Jack Pomerantz survived the war and came to the United States, where he worked as a builder and contractor in New Jersey. He died a few years after publishing his memoir. Gay, Siegal, and Pomerantz are only three of millions of examples of the immense range of living situations experienced by European Jews before the Holocaust.

EUGENICS AND ATTITUDES TOWARD
PEOPLE DEEMED HANDICAPPED

When one considers the long history of anti-Jewish attitudes and actions in Europe and the dramatic, destructive ways that Nazi antisemitism disrupted the lives of people like Peter Gay, Aranka Siegal, and Jack Pomerantz, one might conclude that Jews must have been the first targets for systematic murder in Hitler's Germany. That, however, was not the case. Instead, the first category of people slated for mass killing were individuals deemed handicapped. Perhaps Nazi leaders believed they would encounter less opposition to attacks on that segment of the population; perhaps they thought it would be easier to keep such a program secret. Certainly initiatives came from within the scientific and medical communities, whose members played key roles in carrying out the killings. These are all matters open to research and discussion. What is clear is that attitudes toward people with disabilities in Europe developed in a manner rather different from what we have seen with regard to antisemitism. Nevertheless, here too Nazi ideology and practice built on existing prejudices in ways that were extreme but not unique.

It is hard to know exactly how the majority of the population regarded people with mental and physical handicaps in medieval and early modern Europe. Christianity, like Judaism, out of which it grew, taught compassion for the afflicted, and church as well as state law provided some protections for those who could not protect themselves. But there is also evidence, including many literary accounts, that the able-bodied often ridiculed, took advantage of, and abused those weaker than they were. Nevertheless it seems that in various ways society found places for those with mental and physical disabilities. The village idiot, court dwarfs, fools, beggars, and cripples were all familiar characters. They showed that, although life might not always be fair or good to those with handicaps, at least everyone recognized their existence and assumed that they, like the poor, were a permanent part of society.

By the nineteenth century the assumption that the disabled would always be present had begun to change, at least for many people in Europe and elsewhere. Scientific and medical advances together with Social Darwinist notions led to the idea that society could be engineered so that only the supposedly healthiest elements would reproduce. This way of thinking, and the pseudoscience that grew up around it, is often referred to as eugenics.

Eugenics became popular all over Europe and North America in the early twentieth century. Many places introduced programs to sterilize people considered undesirable. Even though the proponents of such plans claimed to be objective and scientific, they tended to identify people already viewed as outsiders as the least desirable "breeding stock" and to label them "feebleminded" or "degenerate." For example, eugenics programs in some parts of the United States disproportionately targeted African Americans; elsewhere in North America native people were prime subjects. Europeans often focused on Gypsies and other itinerant people, and everywhere poor people came in for the closest scrutiny. In the wake of the First World War, many political leaders, interested in boosting the size and health of their populations—and their armies—promoted eugenics programs. Meanwhile, perennial problems such as crime seemed solvable to people who believed that criminal tendencies were inherited and that their carriers could be identified by physical characteristics.

Even many scientists, medical experts, and social workers who considered themselves progressive reformers supported programs to attempt to "raise" the quality of the population by "selective breeding," with or without the consent of those involved. For example, in the 1910s and 1920s the British sex reformer Marie Stopes helped thousands of men and women learn about birth control and gain access to necessary technologies and supplies. One of Stopes's arguments in support of legalizing birth control was the assumed need to curb the reproduction of people considered burdens on society. When a deaf man wrote to ask Dr. Stopes a question about reproductive rights she fired back an angry letter demanding to know why someone like him would even consider having children. Of course such efforts to "improve" humanity, even at the expense of those considered inferior, were different from attempts to build a Nazi-style "master race" that would rule the world. Still, by the 1920s, as notions about building a "better race" became mainstream, they served to legitimate more extreme schemes of exclusion, manipulation, and domination.

A look at one influential publication illustrates the radicalization of eugenic ideas after World War I. In 1920 Karl Binding, former president of Germany's highest court, and Alfred Hoche, a German professor of psychiatry, wrote *Permission for the Destruction of Worthless Life, Its Extent and Form*. Binding and Hoche believed that World War I (1914–1918) had produced a marked increase in the number of "mental defectives." As a result, they said, Germany was weighed down with people they called "living burdens." They expressed shock at the tremendous care that was devoted to inmates of mental hospitals at a time when the country had lost so many young men in war. In their view the mentally ill were "completely worthless creatures."

Binding and Hoche did not explicitly say that people who wanted to live should be killed, but their ideas still had radical implications. According to them, every human being's worth could be measured in terms of contribution to the community and the nation. Some people, they suggested, did not really have any value. Although Binding and Hoche's book was controversial, the mentality it expressed was widely shared in Europe and North America in the decades before World War II. Given this background, it is perhaps no surprise that Hitler's regime would begin its program of mass murder with attacks on people deemed mentally or physically handicapped.

PREJUDICES TOWARD SINTI AND ROMA (GYPSIES)

Hitler and his followers intended to wipe out the Gypsies of Europe, whom they associated with criminality and degeneracy. The Jews, people deemed handicapped, and the Gypsies were the groups toward which the Nazis most consistently followed a policy of annihilation that included murdering even babies and old people. Anti-Gypsyism, like antisemitism, was an old, familiar hatred in Europe, so with regard to the Gypsies too, Nazi Germany could draw on long-standing prejudices.

The origins of the European Roma remain somewhat contested, but many scholars agree that they moved into Europe from India during the Middle Ages. The English word "Gypsy," often applied as a pejorative term or insult, developed from the mistaken idea that the people in question originated in Egypt. The German term for Gypsies is *Zigeuner*, but it too has taken on negative connotations, so that many people now try to avoid using that label. Instead they prefer to speak of "Roma," "Rom people," or "Roma and Sinti." The Sinti are a group of Gypsies primarily based in German-speaking Europe. It is hard to pin down whether Roma/Gypsies are a racial, ethnic, or social group, that is, whether they are defined by family relationships with one another, language and traditions, or lifestyle. Perhaps that difficulty itself is an apt reminder of how arbitrary such categories are. It is probably most useful to think of Gypsies as a group that includes elements of all those criteria.

When Gypsies first arrived in medieval Europe, they encountered hospitality from some European courts. Soon, however, they became targets of hostility from Europeans who were suspicious of these newcomers. Whether from habit or because of coercion, many Gypsies were itinerant, and their mobile lifestyle further roused the antagonism of others. The rest of European society labeled them thieves and tricksters who used their musical abilities and physical charms to lure the unsuspecting to their ruin.

A number of common attitudes toward Roma in the medieval period echoed anti-Jewish notions. Non-Jewish Europeans falsely accused Jews of stealing Christian children in order to use their blood; likewise non-Gypsies charged Gypsies with kidnapping children for evil purposes. Like Jews, Gypsies were easy scapegoats in times of disaster, such as plagues or earthquakes. Their opponents claimed that they poisoned the wells, practiced magic, and consorted with the devil. European folklore did not accuse Gypsies of killing Jesus, but because the Roma were known for their skills as metalworkers, it charged them with forging the nails that pierced his flesh.

According to European myths, Gypsies, like Jews, had been condemned by God to wander the earth without ever finding a homeland. One popular version of events held that while still in Egypt, the Gypsies had tried to prevent Joseph, Mary, and the baby Jesus from gaining refuge from King Herod, and God punished them with eternal homelessness. Probably by the twentieth century few Europeans would have accepted such myths as the literal truth. Nor would most non-Gypsies have realized that in some parts of southeastern Europe, Roma had been enslaved until the mid-nineteenth century. Nevertheless what remained was a widespread sense that Roma were somehow evil outsiders who did not merit the respect or protection awarded to other members of society.

Nineteenth- and twentieth-century notions about heredity and criminality also contributed to attacks on the Roma in Europe. If criminality was inherited and Gypsies were criminals, "experts" reasoned, then one could fight crime by preventing Gypsies from having children. Social scientists, medical specialists, and criminologists tended to regard Roma as if they were some kind of disease, as evident in references to the "Gypsy plague." Public authorities introduced all kinds of restrictions on where Gypsies could reside and what activities were permitted them, and police all over Europe were especially diligent when it came to enforcing such laws and "controlling" Gypsies. Years before Hitler came to power in Germany, Sinti and Roma in that country were required to carry photo identification cards and to register themselves with local police. France, Hungary, Romania, and other European countries had anti-Gypsy measures of their own.

It is even harder to make meaningful generalizations about the lives of people considered handicapped and the Gypsies in Europe prior to World War II than it is about Jews. There is certainly much less published about members of these two outsider groups. Many disabled people were not in a position to leave written records. For that matter, many probably did not think of themselves as members of a special group whose particular experiences should be preserved. Romany tradition, it seems, has always been more connected to the present than the past, more oral than written, and centuries of persecution produced a tendency to be secretive with people outside the immediate group.

Even something that seems as obvious as the numbers of people in these categories cannot be pinned down with any precision. Who was considered handicapped, mentally or physically, could vary enormously from place to place and time to time. For their part, Gypsies were skilled at evading such formalities as government censuses. Experience with various bureaucracies had taught them that they had little to gain and much to lose by being counted.

The European officials who introduced restrictions on Gypsies and the police who enforced them were often unclear about who exactly was a Gypsy. Non-Gypsies tended to assume they could recognize Gypsies by their appearance: many Roma had darker hair, skin, and eyes than most people in northern, western, and eastern Europe, but by no means were there always physical markers. In some areas Gypsies were associated with certain trades, such as working with metal or leather. Most Europeans thought all Gypsies were wanderers who made a living from fortune-telling, music, dancing, and theft. In fact, not all Roma were itinerant, and many held regular jobs, for example, as civil servants. Nor were all wandering people in Europe Gypsies in any sense of the word. Sometimes, however, police and other authorities treated people who were not ethnic Roma at all as if they were Gypsies, because they fit the stereotype of homeless, petty thieves.

Just as Nazi ideologues invented the category of "the Jew," as if all Jews were somehow the same, they created the stereotypical, deformed "life unworthy of living" and the monolithic "Gypsy." In actuality people deemed handicapped represented the full range of European society: they were Christians, Jews, Gypsies, women, men, children, rich, poor, beautiful, dependent, self-reliant, and anything else you might add. As for Roma, they too varied considerably from one another in terms of religion, lifestyle, language, appearance, name, and occupation. Many were Christians; some intermarried with non-Gypsies. Some spoke a language known as Romani, which linguists believe is linked to languages on the Indian subcontinent; others spoke the languages of the people around them. As would be the case with European Jews, the shared experience of Nazi persecution created a degree of commonality among Gypsies that would not have existed otherwise.

IMPERIALISM AND RACISM

European imperialism, especially its nineteenth-century forms, was also indirectly part of the preconditions to the Holocaust. Through the experience of ruling over subject peoples in their overseas colonies and other conquered territories, Europeans gained habits of behavior and thought that lent themselves to developing hierarchies among peoples within Europe. From their experiences in Africa, Asia, and elsewhere, Europeans learned methods and technologies for oppressing and enslaving large groups of people. Ways of thinking about subject peoples whom Europeans considered inferior to themselves were also transferred onto targets of abuse within Europe, such as Jews. The notion that humanity was divided into races that struggled with one another for survival and dominance was in large part a product of the colonial experience.

Over the course of the nineteenth century, Europeans divided almost the entire continent of Africa among themselves. The British and French had large colonial holdings in Africa, as did the Portuguese, Belgians, Italians, and Germans. These and other European powers already dominated vast territories around the world. In Asia, the British controlled India, for example, and the Russians, Central Asia. The Dutch held Indonesia, and various Europeans had colonies in the Pacific, the Caribbean, and the Americas. The rule of law and protections of citizens' rights that had been introduced in many European jurisdictions by the late 1800s usually did not apply in the colonies, so missionaries, entrepreneurs, administrators, and military men often had very few limits on their behavior once they were overseas. They could and did use flogging, torture, and even death for offenses committed by native peoples that could never have been punished so severely at home. In the Belgian Congo, for example, European rubber magnates sometimes ordered that the hands be cut off of Africans whose production did not meet certain quotas.

Europeans' technological and military advantage enabled them to carry out such acts more or less with impunity. A massacre known as the Battle of

Omdurman provides a graphic illustration. In 1898, a small group of British military on an expedition south of Egypt encountered resistance from local Sudanese tribesmen. The British, armed with machine guns, opened fire. The Sudanese, mounted on horseback and equipped with swords and other weapons for hand-to-hand combat, rode wave after wave into the barrage. The British killed an estimated eleven thousand Sudanese and lost only twenty-eight of their own men. Such events must have contributed to a sense among many Europeans that human life—at least the lives of people they considered inferior—was extremely cheap. Notions of racial superiority were by no means unique to Germany.

Nevertheless, Germans did engage in their own atrocities overseas during the imperial era. Since 1883, Germany had a protectorate over Southwest Africa, the modern-day country of Namibia. By 1904 white pressure on native lands led to a revolt of the largest tribe in the area, the cattle-herding Herero. A smaller group called the Nama joined the rebellion. It took some fourteen thousand German soldiers three years to crush these uprisings. By 1907, fifteen hundred German men had died in the Southwest African conflict, half of them from illness.

But the Herero and Nama suffered far more. In what developed into an act of genocide, the Germans slaughtered more than fifty thousand Herero and ten thousand Nama. They shot many, especially adult men; hunted women, children, and old people into the desert, where they died of thirst and starvation; and forced others into concentration camps, where disease, inadequate food, and horrendous conditions took a terrible toll. In the end, between 75 and 80 percent of all Hereros died; among the Nama the death rate was over 45 percent. This carnage was not ordered by German authorities in Berlin but evolved out of specific military goals: a demand for "total victory" and a drive to annihilate the enemy in order to prevent any possibility of resurgence. German accusations that the Africans were irregular combatants who shot from concealed positions, used women and children as warriors, and mutilated the bodies of their victims served to legitimate ruthless acts of "retaliation" that treated soldiers and civilians with equal viciousness. Such practices left a brutal legacy that would be evident in both the First and the Second World War.

Anti-Black Racism in Germany before the Nazis

Many Nazi ideas about what a race was grew out of ways of thinking about people of color that were common among white Europeans—and Americans—in the early twentieth century. An obvious illustration of some of these ideas comes from Germany in the 1920s. After World War I, the French occupied the Rhineland, an area in the western part of defeated Germany. The occupation forces included some indigenous troops drawn from France's overseas territories in Africa and Asia. Many Germans were horrified at the presence of these men of color on German soil.

Stereotypes about African men as sexual predators on white women were widespread in Europe, and German racists and nationalists played on such fears and fantasies to stir up resentments against the French occupation. Judging from the hysteria in the German press in the early 1920s, one might have thought that hordes of Africans were raping and pillaging all over Germany. In fact there were at most about five thousand black men stationed in the Rhineland at any given time between 1919 and 1923 and perhaps another twenty thousand nonwhite forces. Among these men of color were Senegalese and a small number of Sudanese; Frenchmen, Arabs, and Berbers from Morocco; Malagasies from Madagascar; Annamese from Indochina; and others. They seem to have gotten into no more trouble than any other French units. Nevertheless, Nazi propagandists would return to this topic in the 1930s in their own efforts to whip up German anxieties about supposed racial defilement.

Some of the French African troops in Germany in the 1920s became involved with German women, and in some cases those liaisons produced children. These few biracial individuals—who in 1924 may have numbered only seventy-eight—also attracted a great deal of attention. Fanatical German nationalists and racists of various kinds referred to these people as the "Rhineland bastards." Throughout the 1920s some Germans claimed that the existence of those biracial individuals proved there was a vast conspiracy—controlled by the French, the Jews, or simply the unnamed enemies of Germany—to befoul German blood and weaken the German nation. It is no surprise that once in power, Hitler and his Nazi regime would take steps against Germans of African background, too.

ANTI-SLAVIC ATTITUDES

Hindsight, they say, is twenty-twenty. Looking back on European history more than half a century after World War II, it is clear that certain widespread German attitudes toward eastern Europeans, especially the Slavic peoples—Poles, Russians, Ukrainians, Czechs, Serbs, and others—were also a precondition for the atrocities of the Second World War.

The origins of these negative ideas are hard to identify. Certainly nineteenth-century German nationalists commonly contrasted what they considered their culture's unique achievements with the supposed primitivism and barbarism of their neighbors to the east. Even the German language included slurs against Slavs. For example, a common German expression for a chaotic situation was a "Polish economy." In general many twentieth-century Germans considered Slavic people to be backward, uneducated, slovenly, brutish, and childlike. The fact that eastern European industrialization lagged behind that of the west seemed to confirm those stereotypes for many Germans who conveniently ignored the artistic, cultural, and scientific achievements of their eastern neighbors.

Developments in the early twentieth century added new dimensions to German notions of superiority over the Slavs. After World War I, for the first time since the late 1700s, an independent Polish nation was established. Until the war, territories in which many Polish people lived had been ruled by the German, Austro-Hungarian, and Russian empires. With the defeat of Germany and the collapse of the old Habsburg empire in Austria-Hungary in 1918, the way was cleared for creation of an independent Polish state. Many Germans resented this new neighbor and the loss of territories formerly under German control to Polish rule.

Instead of disbanding at the end of World War I, some German soldiers reformed themselves into units called the Freikorps (Free Corps) to fight Communists and others they considered Germany's enemies. Freikorps activities included attacks on Poles both inside Germany and across the border in Poland. During the decades before Hitler came to power, Germans inside Germany also encouraged the ethnic Germans who lived in Poland to provoke clashes with Polish authorities.

A similar situation existed with the German minority who lived in Czechoslovakia. Like Poland, Czechoslovakia was a newly created state after World War I. Politically and economically weak, it was no match for its powerful German neighbor. Some members of Czechoslovakia's German-speaking population were happy enough to live in a country where they were far fewer in number than Czechs and Slovaks, but others resented their minority status. Here too Nazi agitators in the 1930s would find fertile ground for their notions of German superiority and their plans to rearrange the borders of Europe in Germany's favor.

Developments in Russia also added a new dimension to German suspicion of Slavs. Germany won some of its most dramatic victories during World War I against Russia. In fact, the Russian military effort collapsed in 1917, and as soon as Lenin and the Bolsheviks had claimed control of the country, they sued for peace with Germany. It was all the more humiliating for the Germans a few months later in 1918, when, still flushed with their successes in the east, they had to concede defeat in the west and abandon all claims to the territories they had won from Russia.

The Russian Revolution of 1917 and the civil war that followed were extremely violent. Accounts of the bloodshed reached Germany and, at least for some, seemed to add more reasons to fear and hate Russians. After World War I, many Germans believed they were surrounded by enemies who conspired for Germany's destruction. The fact that Communist ideology called for world revolution and the existence of a very visible Communist party in Germany itself after 1918 seemed proof that such a conspiracy was indeed under way.

Antisemitic Germans often linked their fear of the Soviet Union with their hatred of Jews. They pointed to some prominent Communists who were Jews or had Jewish names as evidence that Jews were somehow responsible for the Russian Revolution. Of course there were some Jewish Communists, but there were also many non-Jewish Communists as well as many anti-Communist Jews. Sometimes antisemites imagined or invented Jewish identities for powerful individuals, such as Lenin, who was often described as Jewish but in fact came from a Russian Orthodox family. This tangled web of prejudices toward Slavs, Communists, and Jews would emerge in a more massive and violent but still recognizable form in Hitler's Germany.

COMMON PREJUDICES TOWARD HOMOSEXUALS, JEHOVAH'S WITNESSES, FREEMASONS, AND SO-CALLED ASOCIALS

Historians often fail to mention some of the additional groups persecuted by the Nazi regime. In some cases, such as the Jehovah's Witnesses and Freemasons, their relatively small numbers make them easy for outsiders to forget or ignore. In other cases, such as homosexuals, the persistence of prejudices against them long after collapse of the Third Reich may have blocked recognition of their suffering at Nazi hands. As for people who came under the vague label of "asocial," they have been criticized and attacked so often that their victimization is sometimes almost taken for granted. Study of the Nazi era, however, demonstrates that assaults on such people also grew out of a particular ideology.

Nazi officials created a category called "asocials" into which they put all

German wartime propaganda, showing interconnected Nazi hatreds. Parts of the text read: *"'Onward Christian Soldiers!' sang the hypocrites Roosevelt and Churchill, as they gave Stalin and his Bolshevik hordes new promises of help. This is how they look, the 'Christian Soldiers.' Their bestial deeds of murder fill the world with disgust and rage! But the German military is destroying the Bolshevik enemy. No pharisaical false piety will help you now, Mr. Roosevelt and Mr. Churchill!"*

kinds of people they considered problematic: Gypsies, the homeless, criminals deemed incurable, people with certain mental disorders, or those accused of sexual perversions. One did not have to be a Nazi in twentieth-century Europe to be afraid of "asocials." Explosive population growth in the nineteenth century and rapid urbanization in many parts of Europe in the twentieth century contributed to a perception among many people that the world was becoming a more dangerous place, full of bizarre and threatening people. In the decade before Hitler came to power in 1933, the Nazi Party in Germany played on such anxieties to present itself as the force that would "clean up" a society supposedly degenerating into lunacy. Propagandists and, after 1933, Nazi policymakers, used the catchall label "asocial" to stigmatize people who did not fit the national ideal. The unemployed became criminal "shirkers"; women suspected of sexual improprieties—lesbian relations, promiscuity, prostitution—became vulnerable to incarceration as "asocials."

Attitudes toward Homosexuals

Pre–World War II prejudices against homosexuals are hard to summarize, because scholars disagree as to when the category of "homosexual" even became recognizable in Europe. It seems evident that in the ancient world certain forms of intimacy between people of the same sex did not carry any stigma or preclude sexual relations with members of the opposite sex. By the modern era, it seems, much of this flexibility was gone, although even the supposedly prudish society of Victorian England showed considerable tolerance for at least some kinds of same-sex intimacies. For example, many people considered sexual experimentation among boys in boarding schools to be a normal part of development; loving relationships between women who often became lifelong companions were not uncommon either.

Nevertheless, by the late nineteenth century many parts of Europe had introduced laws against homosexuality. The German criminal code of 1871 explicitly forbade sexual relations between men. The state prosecuted some cases, and public interest in such "scandals" ran high. For example, it was an enormous sensation when Prince Eulenburg, a member of the inner circle of

A scene from around 1929 in the Eldorado, a gay club in Berlin's Motzstrasse. During the Weimar Republic, Berlin developed a vibrant gay scene that many conservatives detested. Attacking homosexuals was one way the Nazi regime sought to curry favor with elements of the German public.

the German Kaiser Wilhelm II (1888–1918), was charged with homosexual activities and forced from public life. Somewhat paradoxically, an increased openness around the subject of human sexuality in the decades after World War I served to make homosexual men and women more visible in Europe and to increase the panic some heterosexuals felt about them.

Political changes in Germany after World War I made it possible for the first time for Berlin to develop a gay scene that included clubs, restaurants, and bathhouses frequented by homosexual men. Lesbians, it seems, tended to attract less public attention, although there were also some clubs popular with homosexual women. Laws against sex between men were still on the books in Germany's first democracy, the Weimar Republic, but enforcement was slacker than it had been before World War I, especially in the major cities. Many heterosexual Germans, however, disapproved of what they considered their overly permissive society.

Magnus Hirschfeld (1868–1935), a sex reformer and homosexual rights leader in Berlin, made an international reputation for his research in sexology, the new field of studies of sex and sexuality. Hirschfeld regarded homosexuality as the "third sex," a natural and legitimate variant between masculine and feminine. Homosexuals, he pointed out, looked and behaved normally and should be treated accordingly. For many people the work of researchers and activists such as Hirschfeld offered new possibilities for human freedom. For others it seemed to represent the decadence of a society that had abandoned its traditional values. Hitler's Nazis capitalized on such fears as well; they forced Hirschfeld out of Germany, and his research institute was one of the first casualties of their new regime.

Attitudes toward Jehovah's Witnesses

As European outsiders, the Jehovah's Witnesses were relative newcomers. Founded in the United States in the late 1870s, the Jehovah's Witnesses, or International Bible Students, as they were initially called, were not a large group. By the early 1930s they had about twenty thousand members in Germany.

A number of beliefs and activities important to Jehovah's Witnesses made them stand out in European society. Because Jehovah's Witnesses considered themselves citizens of Jehovah's Kingdom, as a principle they did not swear allegiance to any earthly government, nor did they serve in any nation's military. The world, they believed, would soon enter a peaceful, thousand-year

„Wir wollen kein Königreich Gottes Jehovas! Wir haben unsere Kirche u. unsern Führer!"

Johannes Steyer, a German Jehovah's Witness, spent ten years in Nazi concentration camps, prisons, and forced labor units. During the 1970s he depicted his experiences in a series of watercolors. Here Steyer, preaching under surveillance, is told: "We do not want Jehovah God's Kingdom! We have our church and our Führer!"

heavenly rule, but not until it had gone through the battle of Armageddon. In order to teach others and prepare for the end times, Jehovah's Witnesses emphasized door-to-door preaching and distribution of literature. Such efforts made them publicly visible in large German cities and even some smaller towns to an extent far out of proportion to their numbers.

Jehovah's Witnesses were not popular with mainstream European society in the early decades of the twentieth century. Members of the established Protestant and Catholic churches labeled the Jehovah's Witnesses a "sect" or a "cult" and discounted their interpretations of Christian scripture. Some critics considered the Jehovah's Witnesses' emphasis on the Old Testament suspect and intimated that they might be somehow connected with Judaism. Many people found their proselytizing efforts and handing out of tracts to win converts annoying or offensive. Public officials were suspicious because most Jehovah's Witnesses refused to serve in the military or acknowledge state authority if it clashed with their understanding of God's commands. The group's international ties and connections to the United States were also suspect to some ardent nationalists in Germany and elsewhere. Jehovah's Witnesses would be easy targets for the Nazis, who made them the first religious group to be out-lawed in 1933.

Attitudes toward Freemasons

Nazi authorities were also hostile to members of the Freemasons, a European association dating back to the eighteenth century and devoted to the

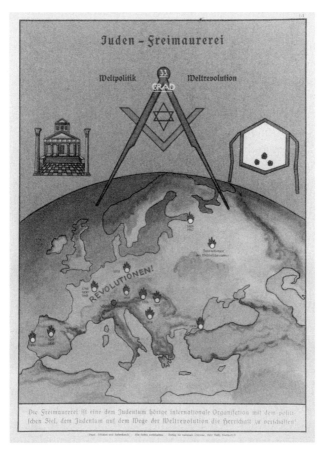

A 1933 poster depicting the Nazi view of Freemasonry and its purported links to a Jewish world conspiracy. The temple, apron, square, and compass are all Masonic symbols. The text reads: "Jews—Freemasonry. World Politics—World Revolution. Freemasonry is an international organization beholden to Jewry with the political goal of establishing Jewish domination through worldwide revolution."

ideals of the Enlightenment: progress, freedom, and tolerance. Many well-known Europeans in the age of the French Revolution and afterward belonged to the Freemasons. Mozart was an enthusiast, for example, and he incorporated some of the ideas and rituals of the Masons into his opera *The Magic Flute.*

Over the years the Freemasons had developed some secret rites, and the air of secrecy that surrounded the group made it seem all the more threatening in the eyes of its critics. Especially in central and eastern Europe, conservatives and nationalists regarded the Freemasons with suspicion, accusing them of spreading atheism, liberalism, and disobedience to authority. People fearful of Freemasonry associated it with the "decadent" West, especially France, and with French traditions of secularism and anticlericalism. There were rumors of bizarre sexual rituals, too. Not surprisingly, opponents of the Freemasons also often hinted that the organization was run by Jews as part of some supposed international Jewish conspiracy. When they attacked the Freemasons too, the Nazis chose a familiar target.

In fact, the number of Freemasons in twentieth-century Germany was always very small, and the organization neither wielded any significant power nor posed a threat to the state. Nevertheless, after 1933, under Nazi rule, men who belonged to the association would face a whole range of discriminatory measures. Some lost their jobs; others ended up in prisons and concentration camps.

WORLD WAR I AND THE CHEAPENING OF HUMAN LIFE

It is important to conclude this survey of some common attitudes in Europe with reflections on the influence of the First World War (1914–1918). This cataclysmic event had a profound impact on Europe and on the world as a whole. In significant ways it too formed part of the preconditions that set the stage for the Nazi era, World War II, and the Holocaust.

The connections between the First World War and the horrors of the Nazi era, however, are rather different than is often claimed. You may have read that the victorious French and their allies imposed such a humiliating peace on the defeated Germans after 1918 that the Germans had no choice but to seek the restoration of national honor at any price. You may also have read that the victors in World War I, in particular the French, forced the Germans to pay crushing reparations, thereby sparking hyperinflation in the 1920s and destroying the German economy. According to this line of argument, the desperate Germans turned to Hitler to rescue them and turned on the Jews as a scapegoat for their suffering.

Both of these common sets of assumptions are deeply flawed. The Germans did lose the war—in fact, it was their military leaders Generals Paul von Hindenburg and Erich Ludendorff in October 1918 who convinced the civilian government that it was necessary to sue for peace. And the Germans did have to accept the terms of the Treaty of Versailles in 1919, without having been part of the negotiations that drew up that accord. Still, the treaty was not exceptionally harsh. In fact, if you compare it to the Treaty of Brest Litovsk, which the Germans had imposed on the defeated Russians just a year earlier, you might almost call it generous.

In March 1918 the Germans had demanded that the Russians cede about 30 percent of their territory, including much of their agricultural, industrial, and mineral wealth. Under the terms of the Treaty of Versailles the Germans lost about 10 percent of their territory, much of it fairly recently acquired: Alsace and Lorraine, for example, taken in 1870 from France. Contrary to what is often said, the Treaty of Versailles did not blame the Germans for the war itself. Article 231, often referred to as the "war guilt clause," was in fact not a moral judgment but a general, legal statement stipulating that Germany was responsible for paying for damages in the places outside Germany where most of the fighting had occurred. A similar clause appeared in the treaties with Germany's former allies Austria, Hungary, and Turkey.

As for reparations, the Germans paid only a very small amount of the bill originally presented to them, which was repeatedly adjusted downward. The victorious nations, above all the British and the French, had neither the ability to make Germany pay nor the will to risk another war after all the suffering and loss they had experienced between 1914 and 1918. Certainly the payments that were made imposed hardships on the Germans, and especially in the aftermath of a devastating war, the notion of reparations itself was psychologically harsh. All of Europe, however, faced terrible economic problems after what had been an extremely costly war, and the Germans were by no means alone in their difficulties, although admittedly the knowledge of widespread hardship probably provided little comfort to anyone.

The First World War did not cause Nazism or the Second World War in such direct ways. Its impact was both less obvious and more insidious. Although the Germans ended World War I in better shape economically than many of the actual victors, they cultivated a politics of resentment that promoted a bitter sense of humiliation and poisoned the chances for the new German democracy formed in 1918. Refusal to accept the reality of defeat led many Germans to search for people to blame for what they perceived as a betrayal. That climate of scapegoating, in turn, created a kind of open season on many familiar outsiders. For example, old accusations that Jews had crucified Jesus dovetailed with the popular stab-in-the-back myth that blamed treacherous Jews for Germany's loss of the war. Communists, homosexuals, and hostile neighbors were blamed too, especially by German military leaders who falsely claimed that their forces had been undefeated in the field.

World War I brought tremendous bloodshed and disastrous implications that extended far beyond Germany. An estimated 20 million Europeans died in the war and the epidemics and deprivations that followed in its wake; the war wiped out almost an entire generation of young men. Those who made it home again included many wounded, crippled, and shell shocked. In addition to combat, blockades, food shortages, and disease took their tolls. From the Russian steppes to Belgium, from England to Serbia, by 1918 there would be scarcely a European family without casualties.

In many cases, soldiers, their families, and their political leaders emerged from four years of carnage with a deep fear of ever risking another war. In other cases, however, they took away different, and more dangerous, lessons: the notion that only in warfare could a man prove himself a real man; the conviction that the sense of camaraderie between fighting men was the most perfect form of human communion possible; the belief that sheer force was in the end the strongest thing in the world.

Perhaps most importantly, the Great War, as it was called at the time, seemed to many Europeans to prove that human life was cheap and expendable. It sparked a cult of violence that flourished in the brutality of the revolution and civil war in Russia, in the paramilitary groups that sprang up around Europe in its wake, and in the nihilistic pessimism of so many Europeans in the 1920s and 1930s. World War I did not lead inevitably to either the rise of Nazism, the outbreak of World War II, or the Holocaust. However, the massive legacy of death and suffering it left behind did constitute one of the preconditions that made possible an unprecedented explosion of violence just two decades later.

2

LEADERSHIP AND WILL

Adolf Hitler, the National Socialist German Workers' Party, and Nazi Ideology

The previous chapter described some preconditions for developments in the Nazi era: historical antisemitism, eugenics, racism, negative German attitudes toward Slavs, and the cheapening of human life after World War I. If historical prejudices made the timber of European and German society combustible, Hitler lit the match that set the house on fire. This chapter examines the leadership provided by Adolf Hitler and the National Socialist German Workers' Party. Who was Hitler, and what was his view of the world? How did he come to power in Germany?

ADOLF HITLER

Any discussion of Adolf Hitler (1889–1945) raises both general and specific questions about the role of the individual in making history. Do personalities shape events? Would the Nazi era, or World War II, or the Holocaust have occurred without Hitler? Certainly common wisdom assumes that Hitler was central to the shaping of those sets of events. There is no denying that Hitler has caught the popular imagination like no other tyrant—the evidence is ubiquitous. Fascination with Hitler seems to cut across all kinds of lines: nationality, age, gender, level of education.

Is so much interest in Hitler justified? Scholars in fact disagree about just how crucial Hitler was. One group, often referred to as intentionalists because they emphasize Hitler's intentions and consider the Holocaust the result of long-term planning, describes Hitler as the mastermind of mass murder. These scholars point to the consistency of Hitler's views from the early 1920s right down to his final testament in 1945. They emphasize the direct, hands-on way he made the major decisions in Nazi Germany.

Others, sometimes called functionalists because they describe the Holocaust as a function of other developments, especially during the war—something that evolved over time in an improvised way—downplay the role of Hitler. Some functionalists argue that Hitler was actually a weak dictator, more a pawn swept along by forces outside his control than the orchestrator of colossal events.

Scholars influenced by Marxism have also tended to pay little attention to Hitler. In their interpretations, Nazism was an extreme form of capitalism that had much more to do with broad, economic structures than with the ideas or actions of any one individual.

These debates about Hitler have moral as well as historical implications. Some people criticize the intentionalist stance because they think it focuses too much on Hitler and lets everyone else off the hook. Others attack the functionalist and Marxist positions for depersonalizing the past. They say that functionalists, who describe the Holocaust and other crimes of Nazism as the result of developments or events, draw attention away from the people who in fact made the decisions and took the actions involved in genocide. Still other people reject both the intentionalist and the functionalist positions and argue that we should pay less attention to the perpetrators altogether and concentrate instead on the victims of Nazi crimes.

In this book I proceed on the assumption that in order to understand the causes of Nazi crimes we need to study those who initiated and carried them out. With regard to Hitler I take what might be called a modified intentionalist position. Hitler was an essential factor in Nazism and the genocide it produced. He did not have complete power—even dictators depend on popular support—and a program as massive as the crimes of Nazism required many accomplices. Nonetheless, Hitler's leadership was essential in setting the agenda. Hitler was no mere opportunist; he operated from a consistent view of the world. He could be flexible, pragmatic, and responsive to the situation "on the ground," but he took the initiative and provided much of the drive and the will that proved crucial in setting Germany on the path to war and genocide. Without Hitler, Nazism, World War II, and the Holocaust would have taken very different forms, if they had occurred at all.

A Brief Biography

Adolf Hitler was born in 1889 in the small Austrian border town of Braunau am Inn. Not much is known with certainty about Hitler's childhood, because the most detailed source—his autobiographical book *Mein Kampf* ("My Struggle")—was a work of propaganda intended to depict him as someone who had been marked from his earliest days for greatness. In fact, Hitler's early life seems to have been fairly typical for a middle-class boy in late-nineteenth-century central Europe.

Adolf was the fourth child of an Austrian customs official and his third wife, but the first to live past infancy. The family was comfortable although not wealthy and did well enough to afford a cook and a maid. Adolf's father, Alois, was a strict, authoritarian man with a bad temper, who seems to have taken little interest in his family. For reasons now unknown, Alois changed his last name from Schicklgruber to Hitler, more than a decade before the birth of the son who would make the new name notorious. Alois Hitler died in 1903, when Adolf was still an adolescent.

Adolf's mother, Klara, was much younger than her husband, whom she met when she worked as a maid in his household. According to the account of her doctor, Klara Hitler was a gentle, pious woman devoted to her children, especially her one surviving son. Adolf returned the affection and later wrote in *Mein Kampf,* "I had honored my father, but loved my mother." Other than his mother, Hitler does not seem to have been close to anyone in his family.

Even decades after his death the rumor persists that Hitler had "Jewish blood." That claim is false. It is true that Hitler did not know the identity of his paternal grandfather, because his father, Alois, was born to an unmarried woman. Alois was baptized into the Roman Catholic Church, as his son Adolf would be, too. In the 1920s and later, rumors circulated that Adolf Hitler's grandmother had been a maid in a Jewish household and had become pregnant by one of her employers' sons. Those allegations were unfounded. In fact there were no Jews in the town where Hitler's grandmother lived, because Jews were prohibited from living in that part of Austria at the time.

What is the significance of this rumor? First of all it shows the extent to which people in Hitler's time became obsessed with issues of blood and race. In Nazi Germany, accusations of so-called Jewish blood were a sure way to discredit someone. It is no surprise that similar rumors circulated about many top Nazis and about other people, too.

The persistence of such a rumor may also tell us something about our own society. What would it actually explain even if the rumor of Hitler's

"Jewish blood" were true? Obviously nothing, just as it would explain nothing if there were any truth to the claims that Hitler was secretly homosexual or that he had only one testicle. (Both of those common allegations, to the best of anyone's knowledge, are false as well.) Such claims reflect a desire to find easy explanations for historical processes that in fact have many complicated causes. Rumors of that kind also reflect a widespread tendency to blame the victims for their misfortunes, as if someone who was "part Jewish," or "secretly homosexual," or in some way physically deformed might somehow be expected to initiate programs to murder Jews, persecute gay men, or kill people deemed handicapped. An honest understanding of history requires a critical—and self-critical—response to such simplistic notions.

As a child Hitler was a mediocre student. Later, in *Mein Kampf*, he would claim that he led his class in geography and history. That was not the case, although he did better in those subjects than in some others, where he received failing grades. When he was sixteen he dropped out of school. Young Hitler spent the next two and a half years in the Austrian city of Linz, idling, dreaming, drawing, and redesigning the city on paper. He always had a penchant for grandiose plans.

In 1907 Hitler relocated to Vienna, where he planned to study art. He failed to get into art school, however, a fact he concealed from members of his family and even close friends for as long as possible. Hitler's many drawings, paintings, and architectural sketches showed some technical ability but little creativity. It is not surprising that years after his death an ambitious forger would have no trouble cranking out many convincing fakes. Hitler later made much of his dire poverty during his years in Vienna, and he did face some hard times when he could not afford lodgings and had to live in a men's shelter. His means of support included selling cards on which he painted local scenes. During most of his young adult years in Vienna, however, Hitler received funds from his family that enabled him to live quite comfortably without ever being employed. For example, he could afford to see Richard Wagner's opera *Lohengrin* and other favorites over and over again.

While in Vienna Hitler picked up on many ideas and currents around him. He was interested in Pan-Germanism—the conviction that Germans should be unified in one state instead of dispersed throughout central and eastern Europe—as well as in ultranationalism and antisemitism. He admired Karl Lueger, mayor of Vienna from 1895 to 1910 and a member of the antisemitic Christian Social Party. Lueger's use of propaganda particularly impressed Hitler.

In Vienna Hitler began to fuse his ideas into a worldview and to get acquainted with political extremists of various kinds. He became enthusiastic about Social Darwinist theories that described life as a struggle between races. His reading consisted mostly of popular tracts about mythology, biology, and even the occult. Hitler preferred to read summaries and pamphlets rather than the actual writings of people such as the philosopher Friedrich Nietzsche. Enthusiasm for the operas of Wagner encouraged Hitler's tendencies toward a grandiose style. If you have seen or heard any of Wagner's operas you know something about their huge casts, imposing music, exaggerated passions, and powerful depictions of Germanic myth; all of those elements inspired Hitler as he developed his own vision of politics and power.

In 1913 Hitler left Vienna for Munich. He crossed the border from Austria to Germany in violation of Austrian law, which required him as an able-bodied young man to perform military service for his homeland. Hitler's motivations for moving are not known for certain, but he had never made a secret of his contempt for the Austrian government and his conviction that the future lay with Germany.

In Munich Hitler's self-education was interrupted by the outbreak of war in 1914. He volunteered for the German army, where he reached the rank of corporal. Wounded in action during World War I, he served with distinction as a runner who relayed messages from the rear to the front. It was a dangerous job, although not exactly the combat role Hitler would later imply he had played, and he received an Iron Cross for his bravery. Nevertheless, a report by one of his superiors—in hindsight tinged in irony—commented that Hitler lacked leadership qualities.

It is not completely clear when and how Hitler developed his fanatical antisemitism. He certainly came into frequent contact with antisemites in Vienna, although he also had acquaintances, associates, and even what might be called friends who were Jewish. In any case, Hitler's experience of Germany's defeat in World War I deepened and hardened his hatred of Jews, or at least he would later claim that his conversion to antisemitism came in 1918. To his mind, the Jews were somehow to blame. That reaction was completely unfounded; German and Austro-Hungarian Jews had fought and died loyally alongside fellow citizens in their countries' armies. But as he would do with every disappointment he faced throughout his life, whether it was failing to get into art school or losing a war, Hitler considered the Jews at fault.

In 1919, a year after the war ended, Hitler got involved in a political organization called the German Workers' Party. It would soon change its name to the National Socialist German Workers' Party. The German acronym was NSDAP. English-speakers commonly use the abbreviation "Nazi," taken from the first two syllables of the German pronunciation of "National." Within a year Hitler had become a full-time agitator and extremely popular speaker for the group.

On 9 November 1923, Hitler and a group of coconspirators that included the war hero Erich Ludendorff launched what became known as the Beer Hall Putsch in Munich. They intended to overthrow the government of Bavaria in order to install a regime that would be the beginning of a national revival in Germany. Poorly planned and disorganized, the Putsch failed; Hitler was captured and sentenced to five years in prison for high treason. He served only thirteen months in Landsberg Prison, where he was treated like a celebrity by most of the staff and many of his fellow inmates. So many admirers flocked to visit him that he eventually stopped receiving them in order to have time to write the book he had begun. By the time Hitler was released in 1925, he had written and published *Mein Kampf,* a combination memoir and propaganda tract. The book did not become a best seller until Hitler became chancellor of Germany in 1933.

In this earlier phase of his career, Hitler was still relatively obscure, part of the fringe elements that proliferated in German society after the First World War. Most Germans outside Bavaria knew little about him and did not take him seriously. His modest background, his relatively unremarkable military career, and his lack of education and experience with the wider world all made him seem almost laughable to some of the people he encountered. For example, one German aristocrat, a Bavarian baron called Fritz Percy Reck-Malleczewen, described his early impressions of Hitler with contempt. He once saw Hitler in a deserted restaurant in the early 1930s, Reck-Malleczewen recorded in his diary, later published as *Diary of a Man in Despair.* Reck-Malleczewen had a pistol in his pocket and could easily have killed the future dictator. "But I mistook him for a cartoon character," the baron said, looking back on the event, "and I did not shoot."

Because of the tremendous fascination with Hitler, the person, we know quite a bit about some details of his daily life. He was a vegetarian who loved animals and hated cigarette smoke. He liked to watch movies, especially comedies, and enjoyed reading Westerns, like those by the popular German writer Karl May. May, like Hitler, never set foot in the Americas. Hitler's most intense emotional attachment after the death of his mother seems to have been his relationship with his niece Geli Raubal, the daughter of his half sister Angela. Hitler had invited Angela to live with him to supervise his household in Munich.

Evidence points toward some kind of affair between Hitler and his much

Hitler on vacation, pictured with Helga, the daughter of propaganda minister Joseph Goebbels and his wife, Magda. Photographs of Hitler with children were used to promote a kindly, avuncular image of the Führer. In April 1945, Helga Goebbels, together with her brothers and sisters, was killed by her parents before they committed suicide in the bunker with Hitler.

younger niece. Proud of the vivacious young woman and possessive of her time and attention, Hitler was often seen with her in public. Geli seems to have chafed under the control of her domineering uncle, and some observers later claimed she was trying to get away from him. In 1931 Geli died under suspicious circumstances. The official verdict was suicide, but rumors of foul play persisted for years. The young woman was found in her uncle's Munich apartment, shot with his pistol. Stories circulated—Geli was pregnant, people whispered; she had a Jewish lover, some hinted; her jealous uncle had her killed, people speculated. Given the few documents and witnesses available and the years that have since passed, it is unlikely that we will ever get to the bottom of events surrounding Geli Raubal. Scandalous and intriguing as the whole affair is, it does not seem to have played a major role in shaping Hitler or his view of the world.

Indeed, none of the details of Hitler's life that can be found have managed to provide the clue needed to explain the strengths of his obsessions or his ability to realize his convictions. The magnitude of the crimes he initiated remains oddly out of proportion to the banality of his person and his life.

Hitler's Worldview

It is impossible to talk about Nazi ideas without borrowing Nazi terminology, most of which, even translated into English, is offensive, nonsensical, or both. Words like "Aryan," "race," and "blood" had particular meanings within the Nazi system of thought, but those terms do not describe objective realities. However, once Nazi ideology became enshrined in laws and regulations and implemented in practice, such labels would take on very real implications of life and death.

The main elements of Hitler's ideology developed during his years in Vienna, his time in Munich, and his years with the German army during and immediately after World War I. Those ideas remained remarkably constant from the beginning of his political career in the early 1920s to his death in 1945.

Hitler's core ideas can be summed up in the phrase "race and space." Hitler was obsessed with two notions: that humanity was engaged in a gigantic struggle between "races," or communities of "blood"; and that "pure Germans," members of the so-called Aryan race, needed space to expand, living space that Hitler called by the German term *Lebensraum*. For Hitler, these two notions of race and space were intertwined. Any race that was not expanding, he believed, was doomed to disappear. Without living space—land to produce food and raise new generations of soldiers and mothers—a race could not grow. Hitler saw the potential living space for German "Aryans" to Germany's east, in the territories of Poland and the Soviet Union. The "races" that he considered prime threats to the survival and dominance of his "Aryans" were the Slavs who occupied that land and the Jews, who, in his theory, sought to infiltrate, weaken, and destroy German strength.

What was an "Aryan"? Like all races the category "Aryan" was an invention, a social construction rather than a physical fact. Hitler did not coin the term "Aryan" but borrowed it from eighteenth- and nineteenth-century European racial theorists who used various labels for the categories into which they divided humanity. The word "Aryan" originally referred to a group of people in ancient India. Hitler drew on vague theories that these people, supposedly taller and lighter skinned than their neighbors, were a superior group who somehow ended up in Europe, where they continued to be the bearers of all cultural creativity. Hitler and other Nazi writers tended to be rather vague when it came to the details of their theories, and they were not troubled by internal contradictions. Thus Hitler considered the ancient Greeks to have been Aryans; so, at least in his mind, were the best elements in ancient Rome as well as the Germanic tribes that finally destroyed Roman power.

Using the term "Aryan" to describe his supposed master race gave Hitler a degree of flexibility that proved very useful. Had he simply preached the "German" master race he would have had to find some way to exclude German Jews, many of whom were certainly as German as their fellow citizens in terms of language and ethnicity. Had he drawn exclusively on terms like "Nordic," which tended to describe physical appearance rather than less visible qualities of blood and character, he might have had some explaining to do with regard to the inclusion of many loyal Nazis in the privileged category. As it was, Germans would tell jokes during the Nazi years about the less-than-perfect specimens who were their leaders: "What does the ideal Aryan look like? As tall as Goebbels, as slim as Göring, as blond as Hitler." In fact, propaganda minister Joseph Goebbels was short and had a clubfoot. Hermann Göring, commander of the German air force, was a fat man, and Hitler had dark hair.

In general the label "Aryan" combined the ring of scientific authority with the vague, elastic quality of a new invention. It could be and was redefined as needed to fit the imperatives of race and space. The only reliable constant was the claim that "Aryan" was the opposite of "Jew."

By the early 1920s, hatred of Jews was a fixed point in Hitler's ideology. No mere opportunist, he maintained until his death a fanatical antipathy to anything he considered Jewish. Hitler's antisemitism incorporated all of the strands of previous generations. It had religious and metaphysical dimensions: he regularly spoke of Jews as evil enemies of virtue and honor. It was political, too: his theory of a Jewish conspiracy extended in every direction. At various times Hitler described Communism, capitalism, liberalism, anarchism, atheism, Christianity, Great Britain, the United States, and France as parts of some international Jewish plot. There were cultural elements to Hitler's antisemitism: he considered jazz, abstract art, and many other forms of modernism somehow degenerate and "Jewish," because, in his view, they distorted reality and lured people away from racial purity. Of course, Hitler's hostility included familiar social and economic resentments. He shared all the stereotypes of Jews as greedy bankers, legalistic pedants, lecherous males, and seductive, destructive females. "Jewish" to him meant everything he considered negative, the antithesis of the supposedly perfect Aryan. Hitler regarded Jewishness as a race, a biological fact that could not be altered by any change of religion, name, or habits. The sheer multidimensionality of Hitler's antisemitism gave it a kind of mass appeal. Many Germans could find something in it they shared, even if they did not buy the whole package.

Hitler drew on old forms of antisemitism, but he combined them in ways that produced something new. The historian Saul Friedländer has labeled Hitler's particular strain of hatred "redemptive antisemitism." By this phrase Friedländer means that Hitler combined a murderous rage with an idealistic goal. Hitler, and the hard-core Nazis who accepted his views, had a religious fervor, a fanatical conviction that attacks on Jews were necessary to save the world for Aryan Germany. Hitler stated his faith at the end of the second chapter of *Mein Kampf:* "Today I believe that I am acting in accordance with the will of the Almighty Creator: by defending myself against the Jew, I am fighting for the work of the Lord."

Hitler's view of "the Jew" was full of internal contradictions. He called Jewish men effeminate and weak yet also characterized them as sexual predators. He denounced Jews as inferior idiots yet believed they had a cunning intelligence, which made them a diabolical threat to the supposedly superior "Aryans." Certain images enabled him to reconcile these contradictory accusations, at least rhetorically. One of his favorites was that of the germ. A germ or a parasite, Hitler was fond of pointing out, was very small, even invisible, and yet it had an incredible, superhuman ability to kill. He claimed that Jews were similar: they might seem few and weak, but according to Hitler's paranoid view, they had enormous powers of destruction.

Another important feature of Hitler's ideology was its sense of urgency. According to Hitler, time was running out: it was five to midnight for the Aryan race, he warned, and the clock was ticking. The race was already dangerously polluted, he insisted; if it were not saved immediately it would perish. That notion of impending doom added an apocalyptic dimension to Hitler's thought. His belief in the necessity—and desirability—of war gave that mythical struggle concrete form. Only war would redeem the Aryan race, Hitler maintained: war in the name of racial purity and in the quest for living space.

Other traits of Hitler's worldview were also connected to his key notions of race and space. Hitler was passionately anti-Communist, although once in power he would show himself willing to make at least temporary concessions toward Communism in favor of his more central goals. Hitler blamed German Communists as well as Jews for the loss of World War I. By the late 1920s he regularly linked Communism and Bolshevism with Jews, and he accused Jews of creating Communism as part of a plot to destroy Germany. During World War II, Hitler would return repeatedly to the idea of some diabolical Jewish-Communist plot in order to rally Germany against the Soviet Union. One of Hitler's typical terms of derision was "Bolshevik Jewish internationalists."

Hitler's ideas about women and men also fit into his worldview. He claimed that he would restore women to what he called their rightful place in the home. He regarded women's bodies as important to the state, because they produced new generations of soldiers and breeders. But women's bodies in Hitler's view could also be the floodgates to racial impurity, the means through which supposed pollutants entered the Aryan bloodstream. Some German women found such theories appealing, because they seemed to offer women a powerful position as mothers and guardians of the master race. Others recognized the misogyny inherent in Nazi ideas.

Hitler's sexism and antisemitism were mutually reinforcing. He used anti-woman images and vocabulary to belittle Jews and other so-called enemies. At the same time, he equated feminists with Jews and derided Jewish men as defilers of Aryan womanhood and champions of homosexuality and other supposed perversions. Such sexual images caught the attention of Hitler's audiences and played on many of their own anxieties.

Hitler endorsed a position that he and other National Socialists referred to as the "Führer principle." The German term *der Führer* means "the leader" in English. Hitler would later take that title for himself. The Führer principle meant commitment to uncontested leadership. When individuals in the Nazi organization grew powerful enough to pose a potential threat to Hitler's position, he found ways to clip their wings, even if it meant temporarily weakening the Nazi Party's base of support. Hitler believed power had to be focused in order to be effective; the crucial focal point, in his view, was himself.

As Führer, Hitler demanded total loyalty from his followers. One of his most devoted associates turned out to be Joseph Goebbels, later minister of propaganda, who wrote in his diary: "I love you, AH." Hitler rewarded faithful subordinates with privileges, powers, and, in special cases, access to him and his inner circle. Admittedly, spending time with the Führer had disadvantages even for the most dedicated Nazis: his impromptu speeches, lectures, and dinner diatribes could last for hours and often put his listeners to sleep. Nevertheless, the Nazi focus on Hitler as leader gave the movement and subsequently the entire system a powerful dynamic that the historian Ian Kershaw calls "working toward the Führer." Once his position and power were assured, Hitler did not need to issue specific orders in most cases. It was enough to let his wishes be known in general terms and his underlings would rush to fulfill and even anticipate them, in the hope of winning his favor and advancing their own careers. In the words of one Nazi functionary: "It is the duty of every single person to attempt, in the spirit of the Führer, to work towards him."

The Führer principle was also linked to the goals of race and space. Hitler was convinced that he needed unquestioned power to complete his historic mission. Democracy, he claimed, was a product of Jewish-Bolshevik liberal internationalism; in his opinion, democratic institutions obstructed the work of "great individuals." Hitler's Führer principle was both a means to achieve his policies of race and space and an end in itself.

Adolf Hitler was not a brilliant, original thinker. There was nothing really new about his ideas nor even about the way he combined them. His ideology was a mix of nineteenth-century racial theories, Social Darwinism, post–World War I resentments, antisemitism, antimodernism, and sexism dressed up in familiar symbols drawn from nationalism, mythology, and even Christianity, although Hitler and many of his closest associates simultaneously professed and detested Christianity, which they considered a religion for the weak. What was different was the intensity with which he held his views and his ability to captivate large audiences in such a way that many who heard him speak felt he gave voice to their own feelings and beliefs. Above all, what differentiated Hitler from the many other demagogues and ideologues in Europe between the wars was the tremendous power he achieved after he became chancellor of Germany in 1933. From that position he was able to harness an entire government—its military, diplomacy, and bureaucracy—behind implementation of his notions of race and space.

Old Fighters and "True Believers"—The Inner Circle

Hitler neither rose to power alone nor developed his ideas in a vacuum. A rather motley crew of men formed his inner circle. Three individuals who stuck with Hitler throughout his political career were Hermann Göring, Joseph Goebbels, and Heinrich Himmler. All of them would play key roles in the Nazi regime.

Hermann Göring (1893–1946) was a hero of World War I who rose through the air force to become commander of the famous Richthofen Squadron. Somewhat at a loss after the war ended with Germany's defeat and massive demilitarization, he joined the Nazi Party in 1922. One of Hitler's oldest associates, Göring had the distinction of having been wounded at the Beer Hall Putsch in 1923. Nazi lingo reserved the label "old fighters" for those of the faithful who had been members before the failed Putsch.

Hitler often presented Göring as one of Nazism's more respectable figures. Göring's father had been a judge and consular official, and he had ties with conservative and nationalist circles. Göring senior had even served as resident minister plenipotentiary in German Southwest Africa, site of the German genocide of the Herero and Nama people in 1907. In fact there is a street

Hermann Göring delivers a speech at the District Party Day rally in Weimar in April 1931. Notice Hitler standing beside the car.

named after him in Windhoek, the capital of Namibia. Throughout the 1930s Hitler showered appointments on Hermann Göring: when the Nazi Party became the largest party in the German parliament, Göring became president of the Reichstag (as the German parliament was called). Göring established the Gestapo, a political police force, and was named commander in chief of the Luftwaffe (air force). In 1936 Hitler chose Göring to head the Four-Year Plan to prepare Germany for war. A swaggering, flamboyant individual who relished luxury and excess, Göring was also an ambitious schemer and a vicious infighter.

Joseph Goebbels (1897–1945) was a rather different kind of Nazi. A journalist and writer, he had a Ph.D. and wrote a novel called *Michael*, although it remained unpublished until the Nazi Party press picked it up in 1929. Goebbels first came into contact with members of the Nazi Party in 1924; by 1928 Hitler had made him head of propaganda. In 1933 Goebbels became minister for popular enlightenment and propaganda. He kept that post throughout the entire Third Reich, although his ambitious, energetic nature meant that he was always trying to find ways to play even bigger roles.

Goebbels was a master propagandist who excelled in stirring up hatred and orchestrating gigantic extravaganzas, such as the annual Nazi Party rallies. He was the only one of Hitler's early associates who stayed with him right to the end. When Hitler committed suicide in 1945, Goebbels did so, too: he and his wife, Magda, had their children poisoned before he had her and himself shot. Goebbels's extensive diaries, large parts of which have been published, reveal him to have been a "true believer," committed to Hitler as a person and to realization of his ideas.

Heinrich Himmler (1900–1945) would become, next to Hitler, the most powerful man in the Third Reich. Head of the elite Nazi guard known as the Schutzstaffel (SS) from 1929 to 1945, by 1936 he had also become chief of all German police. In these positions he presided over a vast network of offices and agencies that implemented terror and mass murder all over German-occupied Europe.

Himmler was neither flashy like Göring nor educated like Goebbels. Awkward and homely as a young man, he read voraciously and had developed his own conspiratorial view of the world even before he met Hitler in 1926. Like Hitler, Himmler feared and hated Jews and believed in the superiority of the so-called Aryan race. Himmler too was convinced that Germany had to expand to the east. Dogged and capable of meticulous attention to detail, Himmler involved himself directly in projects that targeted homosexual men and Gypsies as well as Slavs and Jews. With justification the historian

Richard Breitman and others have labeled Himmler the "architect of genocide."

There were no women in Hitler's inner circle, nor did any women wield direct political power. The closest was Gertrud Scholtz-Klink (b. 1902), national women's leader from 1934 until 1945. A true believer in Hitler's worldview, Scholtz-Klink described herself as fighting for Hitler's cause with the weapons of a woman. According to Scholtz-Klink, the crowning achievement of a Nazi woman was motherhood. Her own three marriages produced eleven children.

By catching Joseph Goebbels off guard, renowned photographer Alfred Eisenstaedt captured something of the propaganda minister's sinister character. Of this image Eisenstaedt said, "This picture could be titled 'From Goebbels with Love.'"

Hitler referred to Scholtz-Klink and her Nazi women's organizations when it suited him to do so, but he did not consult her or for that matter seem to take her seriously. Like many women in the Third Reich, Scholtz-Klink played the role of the enthusiastic supporter and beneficiary of Nazism.

THE NAZI RISE TO POWER

How did Hitler come to power in Germany? It is important first to outline some of the common—and mistaken—answers to this question. Hitler's rise to power was not inevitable. It was neither an automatic product of Germany's defeat in World War I nor the unavoidable result of the Great Depression. Hitler was not swept to power by a stampede of German voters hypnotized by his oratorical skills, nor did he seize power in an illegal coup d'état. The road that brought Adolf Hitler into the chancellor's seat by 1933 was both less direct and more mundane than these standard interpretations suggest. Briefly put, it was a combination of difficult circumstances, political maneuvering, luck, treachery, and miscalculation on the part of many people that catapulted Hitler into power.

The Weimar Republic

What was the situation in Germany prior to Hitler's rule? In the wake of military defeat in 1918, Germans introduced a form of government new to them: a republic based on a democratic constitution. It has become known as the Weimar Republic, after the city of Weimar, which served as its temporary capital until the situation in Berlin was stable enough for the government to set up shop there.

In hindsight it is easy to dismiss the Weimar Republic as a failed experiment in German democracy, nothing more than a chaotic prelude to Nazism. In fact, although novel in many ways, the Weimar Republic built on long-standing political parties, legal and bureaucratic structures, and even electoral practices in Germany. Moreover, it lasted two years longer than the Nazi regime Hitler and his followers promised would be a "Thousand-Year Reich." The Weimar Republic persisted in some form for fourteen years, from its proclamation in November 1918 to Adolf Hitler's appointment as chancellor in January 1933.

The Weimar Republic witnessed considerable achievements in the political and cultural spheres as well as in foreign policy and the economy. Antidemocratic Germans often complained that the victorious powers of World War I had forced democracy on a defeated Germany. The Weimar Republic, however, was able to build on liberal and democratic tendencies within Germany that predated the war. Under the Weimar Constitution of 1919, Germany became the first major European power after Russia to give women the vote. Weimar Germany produced the most modern, innovative film industry in the world at the time, and it returned Germany to international respectability with the country's incorporation into the League of Nations in 1926. In short, the existence of the Weimar Republic by no means made Hitler's rise inevitable.

It may come as a surprise that Weimar Germany had the strongest economy in continental Europe for most if not all of its history. Its postwar recovery was eased by the fact that very little of the fighting in World War I had taken place on German soil. As a result Germany's infrastructure and industry remained mostly intact. In contrast, Germany's neighbors to the west—France and Belgium—had been demolished by the war. They sought reparations, but the Germans managed to avoid paying most of the sums charged, by negotiating the amounts downward, by falling behind on payments, and eventually by ceasing payments altogether. To the east, the territories of Poland and the Soviet Union had been on the whole less industrialized than Germany already before 1914. The enormous costs and devastation of years of war put their struggling economies even further behind the Germans.

Of course Weimar Germany faced very real economic problems itself, the most dramatic of which was inflation. In 1923 inflationary tendencies spiraled into a hyperinflation that saw the value of the German Mark plummet to impossible levels. The situation got so bad that people needed enormous quantities of bills merely to buy a loaf of bread or a glass of beer. Images of desperate Germans demanding their pay hourly before it could become worthless and moving their petty cash in wheelbarrows have become standard features in histories of the Weimar years.

The hyperinflation of 1923, however, was not simply the result of crushing reparations payments, as is often assumed. Instead it was irresponsible fiscal policies on the part of the German government during the war and an attempt to thwart French and Belgian efforts to seize reparations directly from Germany afterward that destroyed the value of the German currency. Moreover, all of Europe experienced inflation after the war, although the months of massive inflation in Germany in 1923 were especially dramatic.

As in any inflation, some Germans lost a great deal. Those on fixed incomes, such as pensioners, and people who had loaned out money were particularly hard hit. Yet there were also big winners in 1923, as is true of every inflationary situation: people with property in forms other than money, speculators, and above all debtors who can pay back what they owe in currency worth a fraction of its value when they borrowed it. Currency reform in 1923 halted the hyperinflation and began a period of economic stabilization in Germany that lasted until the end of the decade. By the time Hitler came to power, the hyperinflation of 1923 was ten years in the past.

Weimar Germany's situation in terms of national security was also much stronger than is often recognized. The old Habsburg Empire, once Germany's rival for power in central Europe, disappeared completely in the war, leaving a small, weak Austria as Germany's neighbor to the south. Before World War I, the Habsburg Empire had ruled large parts of central and eastern Europe, including territories that lie in modern-day Austria, Poland, Hungary, the Czech Republic, Slovakia, Croatia, and other countries. After the war, those lands were organized as much smaller, independent countries that often had reasons to focus their animosities on one another rather than competing with or challenging German power in Europe.

After World War I, Germany's former rival to the east, the once formidable Russian Empire, was gone too, replaced by Lenin's new Soviet Union. Racked by civil war until the early 1920s, the Soviet Union was in no position to threaten German interests. In any case, the postwar settlement in Europe meant that Germany no longer shared a border with Russia, because the creation of an independent Poland created a buffer between the two larger nations. After 1918, Germany's immediate neighbors included Poland in the east and Czechoslovakia in the southeast—tenuous, new nations engaged in their own struggles for stability.

In short, all of Europe faced enormous economic, political, and social challenges in the 1920s. Even Great Britain, with its massive empire, was weakened after years of war. The British retained wartime rationing of bread longer after hostilities ended in November 1918 than did the Germans. The Weimar Republic had as good a chance to survive as did most of its European counterparts. Being surrounded by neighbors poorer and weaker than itself gave it some significant advantages.

World War I and the Myth of a Stab in the Back

But what about the shame of defeat? Many textbooks argue that Germans who wished to return their nation to greatness naturally turned to Hitler to lead them out of humiliation. This view is oversimplified. Military defeat need not usher in tyranny and destruction. In fact it can generate reassessment and reform, as was the case after 1806, when Prussia's defeat at Napoleon's hands led Prussian reformers to introduce remarkable changes to their country's military, bureaucracy, and system of education. Likewise, it was Russian defeat in the Crimean War of 1853–1856 that prompted the tsar to free the serfs. In Germany after 1918, however, such positive change was blocked by a widespread refusal to accept the reality of defeat.

In the fall of 1918 Germany's military leadership—Generals Paul von Hindenburg and Erich Ludendorff—had insisted on suing for peace. Germany simply did not have the resources to fight on, its top generals realized. Even before the armistice was concluded, however, they began to spin the account of events to save their own reputations. It was not the military but the German civilians who had lost their nerve, they claimed. It was the disloyal, revolutionary home front, they accused, that had stabbed the fighting men in the back and betrayed them to their enemies.

The myth of a stab in the back spread quickly. Many Germans needed an explanation for defeat in a war that their military leadership had never let on it was losing. The fact that the war ended with almost no foreign troops on German soil lent credence to the idea of betrayal from within Germany. And the notion of an undefeated military fit with comforting myths about national greatness. In the eyes of many Germans, their new, democratic government symbolized the civilian weaklings who had supposedly betrayed Germany's fighting heroes. This perception in turn undercut the authority of the Weimar Republic.

Hitler would later capitalize on the stab-in-the-back myth. He was able to do so because, by the time he appeared on the national scene, the idea had been propagated within Germany for more than a decade: by military leaders who refused to take responsibility for defeat; by nationalist professors, schoolteachers, and clergy; and by antidemocratic politicians and publicists who found it easier to live in a glorified past than to face the challenges of the present. Defeat in World War I did not make Hitler's rise to power inevitable, but the way that many Germans chose to respond to the challenges of defeat weakened the base of support of their own government and prepared the way for even more extreme manipulation of public opinion.

The National Socialist German Workers' Party in the 1920s

From its beginnings, the Weimar Republic faced a crisis of legitimacy. Its critics on the left wanted a revolutionary, Communist regime instead of a liberal, democratic republic. Conservatives and those further to the right considered the whole idea of democracy to be weak, ineffective, and non-German. Beset by extremists of all kinds, Weimar authorities tended to crack down hard on the left but treat the right with leniency.

The new government in 1918 had not purged the judiciary or the civil service, so the republic's judges, lawyers, and bureaucrats were the same people who had served the German kaiser before World War I. Many of them were less than enthusiastic about the democratic constitution they supposedly upheld. When faced with illegal actions or revolutionary efforts by Communists, they dealt out long prison terms and imposed death sentences. Right-wing extremists charged with criminal acts or caught in plots to overthrow the government received much lighter penalties. Critics of the Weimar system often fault its liberal constitution for tolerating antidemocratic movements such as the National Socialists. But there were laws that might have curbed the growth of Nazism; they were simply not enforced.

Hitler's early career is a case in point. In 1923 he was arrested for his role in the Beer Hall Putsch and charged with high treason. Instead of being a setback, the trial gave Hitler a chance to gain national publicity. He was sentenced to five years—a rather light term for someone caught in the act of trying to overthrow the government—and served a total of only thirteen months. Communists in the Weimar Republic charged with similar offenses regularly received much harsher treatment: life terms and death sentences were not uncommon for them.

Hitler spent the decade after the failed Putsch building his party. He presided over a two-pronged approach. On the one hand was the paramilitary, street-fighting wing of the movement: the SA (Sturmabteilung), or Stormtroopers. On the other hand was the legal, political party, the National Socialist German Workers' Party (NSDAP). The brown-shirted Stormtroopers, modeled after Benito Mussolini's Fascist Black Shirts in Italy, brawled with Communists and Social Democrats, harassed and attacked Jews and homosexuals, and generally used terror tactics to intimidate the public. At the same time, the existence of the Nazi Party allowed for legal actions: collecting funds, organizing local support, putting forward candidates for election, and hosting rallies and other events.

Until 1929 the NSDAP was just one of many splinter political groups vying for the attention of voters. That year brought electoral breakthroughs in local and state elections, most notably in Thuringia, and a dramatic increase in Party membership. Evidence of national popularity preceded the Great Depression; it was not simply economic hardship that brought some Germans to support the NSDAP, although hard times certainly brought some new voters and activists. Indeed a general climate of political polarization meant that all parties at the extremes—Nazis and ultranationalists on the right, Communists on the left—gained at the expense of the moderate middle. Over the course of the 1920s, the NSDAP became a genuine mass party with voters in all social classes: workers, members of the lower middle class, students, academics, clergy, the wealthy, women as well as men.

The 1930s and the End of Democracy in Germany

The U.S. stock market crash of 1929 was felt all over the world, not just in Germany. It is with good reason that the depression associated with that event has been called a world depression. Germany faced growing unemployment as did much of the industrialized world. German farmers, like their counterparts elsewhere, faced falling commodity prices and shrinking markets. Economic hardship did not make the rise of a Nazi dictator inevitable, but it did add to the challenges of the Weimar Republic.

By early 1930 economic difficulties had brought Germany into a political crisis. High taxes, increased tariffs, cuts in government spending, and deflationary policies did nothing to ease the situation. In the midst of that misery and strife, few people even noticed the evacuation of the last French troops from German soil in June 1930.

The chancellor, Heinrich Brüning, was unable to get the backing of the Reichstag for his measures. So he convinced the German president, the old war hero Paul von Hindenburg, to invoke Article 48 of the constitution. Article 48 allowed the president to govern by decree in a state of emergency. Brüning had no problem convincing Hindenburg. Never a fan of democracy, Hindenburg had long believed that parliamentary government was too chaotic. By 1930 he was an old man—some say he was senile. A joke made the rounds: one aide to another, "Don't put your sandwich paper down in front of the president. He might sign it!"

From 1930 until the end of 1932, Hindenburg and his various chancellors ruled by decree rather than relying on the democratically elected Reichstag. Democracy was essentially dead in Germany, but there were still alternatives to Hitler: some people awaited a military coup; others expected some kind of conservative, authoritarian rule.

In that climate Hitler and the Nazi Party ran in a number of important elections. In one, the presidential election of 1932, Hitler lost his bid for the presidency to the aged Hindenburg. In another, in July 1932, the Nazi Party won 37 percent of the votes cast, its highest return in a free election ever.

Although some Germans later would claim that no one could resist the mag-
netic force of Hitler's oratory, more than 60 percent of German voters had no
trouble doing so in 1932. Some of them are on record as having found his style
braying, annoying, low class, and offensive. Nevertheless, the July election
brought the Nazis more seats than any other party in the Reichstag.

In the third election, in November 1932, support for the Nazis dropped,
and the party lost 2 million votes. With 196 seats, it was still the strongest party
in the Reichstag, but the Communists, with 100 seats, were not far behind.
Some observers thought the Nazis had peaked. In his disappointment Hitler
contemplated suicide and wondered whether he had missed his opportunity.

Hitler was saved, not by his own ingenuity but by the miscalculation of
his rivals. Former chancellor Franz von Papen, a conservative and nationalist,
convinced Hindenburg to name Hitler chancellor. Papen reckoned that giving
Hitler the post would buy popular support for his own cause—he planned to
make sure it did so by getting himself named Hitler's vice chancellor. From
that position, he told Hindenburg, he and others loyal to the president would
be able to control the Nazi upstart.

Other conservatives and some industrialists backed Hitler as well. They
hoped to defuse discontent among workers and prevent any increase of Communist strength. Hitler could not do much harm, they told President Hindenburg, as long as he was surrounded with members of the cabinet who were not
Nazis. Hitler for his part said he would accept the chancellorship only if he
could name two of the Nazi Party members of the Reichstag as government
ministers. Hindenburg agreed, and on 30 January 1933 Hitler became chancellor of Germany. Like all the members of his cabinet he swore an oath to the
constitution. A photograph widely distributed in the German press showed
him shaking hands with President Hindenburg. The Bavarian aristocrat Reck-
Malleczewen described the look on Hitler's face as that of "a headwaiter as he
closes his hand around the tip." Hitler did not need to seize power. It was
handed to him.

3

FROM REVOLUTION TO ROUTINE

Nazi Germany, 1933–1938

Looking back it is easy to forget that half of the Nazi era occurred before World War II began. Those first six years proved crucial. Between 1933, when Hitler became chancellor, and 1939, when German forces invaded Poland, Nazi rule revolutionized Germany. During those same years, the "Third Reich" or third empire, as Hitler and his followers called their new Germany, became routine for many Germans. This chapter examines those two phases of Hitler's rule: first, the Nazi revolution, and second, the routinization of Nazism that followed. How did Hitler begin to implement his ideas of race and space during the peacetime years of Nazi rule? How did the German public respond, and what was life like for Germans under the Nazi system?

The previous chapter outlined Hitler's worldview and described how he came to be chancellor of Germany. Throughout that discussion you might have noticed an imbalance between the ordinary aspects of Hitler's life and the extraordinary impact he had. There was nothing so unusual in Hitler's background, nor were his ideas original. Even the factors that brought him to power—misfortune, opportunism, miscalculation—were unsensational. And yet the destructive role that Hitler would play was far from ordinary. Even today, when asked to name one individual who has dominated the past millennium, many people say "Adolf Hitler."

That same dichotomy or gap between the extraordinary and the ordinary is evident throughout the entire Nazi period. On the one hand, Hitler revolutionized Germany, but on the other hand, the ways in which he did so seemed undramatic to many participants and observers at the time. Between 1933 and 1938, Nazism became everyday and ordinary for many Germans, but that routine normalized terror and legalized extraordinary persecution.

PHASE I: THE NAZI REVOLUTION, 1933–1934

Hitler's appointment as chancellor in January 1933 was in itself unspectacular. Since 1918, Germany had seen many chancellors from a range of political parties, and many of their governments had been short lived. Yet that seemingly unremarkable event on 30 January 1933 marked the beginning of a revolution that would transform German politics and society. The new chancellor lost no time in attacking the elements of the population he despised, but he did so in ways that expanded his own power even as he isolated his enemies.

Political Revolution

Hitler's political position in early 1933 was not that strong. His party's support had dropped from its July 1932 peak, and even then it had received only 37 percent of the votes cast. The Nazi Party faithful themselves were divided into factions with very different visions for Germany's future. Some favored a social revolution that would redistribute wealth and property in radically egalitarian ways; others wanted to bolster traditional elites. Meanwhile, Hitler's cabinet included only two members of the Nazi Party besides himself: Hermann Göring and another longtime associate, Wilhelm Frick, as minister of the interior. The rest of the cabinet posts were assigned to conservatives and nationalists, members of the Catholic Center Party, and military men who thought they could control their inexperienced new chancellor. Instead he proved skilled at manipulating them.

Hitler made his first major move in early 1933 against the Communists, a target he chose with care. Communism could have posed a real threat to Nazi power. Like the Nazi Party, the Communist Party had local cells throughout Germany. It was well represented both in the Reichstag and in the streets, where its men had fought the Nazi Stormtroopers for more than a decade. The Communists, however, were an ideal first target for another reason as well; Hitler was guaranteed to have allies against them. Precisely those elements in German society that had helped Hitler into the chancellor's seat— conservatives, nationalists, industrialists, and military men—hated and feared

Communism. They were unlikely to protest any anti-Communist measures, no matter how unconstitutional or harsh.

On 27 February 1933 the Reichstag—the German parliament building—burned down. The Reichstag fire gave Hitler the opportunity he wanted. His spokespeople insisted that Communists had torched the building, and the German press, relying on information from Nazi sources and reluctant to speak against the new regime, echoed those accusations. At the time some non-Nazi Germans assumed that Hitler's own people had started the fire, but they could do little except grumble in private, unless they were willing to risk being accused of sympathizing with the Communists. For a long time, research seemed to indicate that the blaze was the work of a lone, Dutch arsonist named Marinus van der Lubbe, who was linked to neither the Communist nor the Nazi party. Subsequent work, however, points back to the Nazis as the instigators.

Hitler ordered massive reprisals against the German Communists in response to the fire. He had thousands arrested, tortured, and beaten; hundreds were "shot while trying to escape." That phrase was a euphemism or indirect way of saying that police or soldiers had shot them in the back. Thousands more fled into exile. Shortly after the Reichstag fire, in March 1933, German newspapers announced the opening of the first official concentration camp—at Dachau, near Munich. Among the first prisoners sent there were many Communist men.

With the actions of late February 1933, Hitler crippled Communist power in Germany. That assault was only the beginning: by the end of the Nazi regime, about 150,000 German Communists would be arrested, and many of them would be killed by 1945.

The Reichstag fire gave Hitler a pretext to dismantle what was left of Germany's democratic institutions. Pointing to the supposed risk of disorder and to his now proven ability to act decisively, he convinced the members of the Reichstag to pass the Enabling Law of 23 March 1933. The Enabling Law allowed Hitler to put through any measure without approval from the Reichstag. He no longer even needed to have the president declare a state of emergency or sign a decree. Social Democratic representatives opposed the Enabling Law, but they were the only mainstream party to do so. In effect the Reichstag was now defunct; its own members had voted it out of existence. Their reasons for doing so varied: quite a few welcomed the new regime they thought would replace the cumbersome parliamentary system they hated with authoritarian order; others felt intimidated by Nazi attacks on Communists and

Social Democrats; some hoped to curry favor with Hitler and his people by proving how willing they were to cooperate.

By the end of the summer of 1933, Hitler had used his authority to dissolve or outlaw all political parties except the NSDAP—the National Socialist German Workers' Party, or the Nazi Party. Even the facade of German democracy was gone. Hitler's political revolution was not without violence, but he established his dictatorship through means that were, at least in a narrow sense of the word, legal.

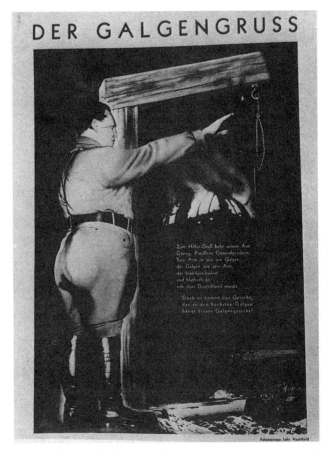

The German artist John Heartfield created this photomontage in response to the Reichstag fire in February 1933. The text, titled "The Gallows Greeting," reads: "He raises his arm for the 'Heil Hitler,' Göring, Prussia's General Policeman. His arm is like a gallows, the gallows like his arm, which blackened by fire and flecked with blood, stretches itself across Germany. But the judgment is coming that will hang this gallows-face on the highest gallows."

Social Revolution—Testing the Waters

The Nazi revolution had immediate effects on those groups Hitler had described as enemies for years. It was not only political opponents like the Communists who felt early blows; homosexuals, Jehovah's Witnesses, German Jews, people considered physically or mentally handicapped, and Afro-Germans all experienced attacks within the first year of Nazi rule.

Hitler and his associates in the new German leadership struck in dramatic, decisive ways, but they always tested the public response to each move before proceeding further. This mixture of boldness and caution would be typical of Nazi tactics throughout the Third Reich, from its inception in 1933 to its collapse in 1945. Public opinion was very important to Hitler. A firm believer in the stab-in-the-back myth, he was convinced that a disgruntled German public had lost Germany the First World War. He was determined to avoid a repeat of that situation under his rule, during the war he intended to wage.

In *Mein Kampf* Hitler had made it clear that he planned to "deal with" the Jews. He started his social revolution, however, with attacks on a group that was even less likely to receive public support: homosexual men. In the 1920s and early 1930s, Berlin and other major German cities had become centers of a small but vibrant gay culture. Even before the Nazis came to power, police had sometimes harassed men known or suspected to be homosexual; many Germans regarded homosexuality as deviant and decadent and urged their government to crack down by imposing what they considered moral and sexual order.

Since 1871, Paragraph 175 of the German criminal code had outlawed sexual relations between men: "A male who indulges in criminally indecent activities with another male or who allows himself to participate in such activities will be punished with jail." The prohibition did not mention sexual acts between women. Hitler built on this law in early 1933 to ban homosexual rights organizations in Germany. According to National Socialist teachings, homosexuals were an abomination because they opted out of the reproduction of the so-called Aryan master race. Moreover, according to Himmler and others, homosexual men in public positions of any kind were dangerous because they were always vulnerable to blackmail. Antagonistic Nazis focused on gay men; they seemed for the most part not to see lesbians or bisexual women as posing a particular threat, because women did not exercise public power by serving in the military or at high ranks of the bureaucracy. In any case women, some Nazi activists presumed, could always be forced to bear children for the German Volk, regardless of their own sexual orientation. Nevertheless, in some individual cases lesbians were persecuted as so-called asocial elements.

Leadership from above prompted initiatives by people acting out their own hostilities. In 1933, Nazi Stormtroopers and other thugs raided gay bars and clubs in German cities and forced many of them to close. A few managed to remain open longer—some intermittently until the end of World War II—but under constant threat of raids and violence. In May 1933, a group of Nazi students stormed and destroyed the Institute for Sexual Research in Berlin. Its director was the gay rights activist Magnus Hirschfeld. For the most part the German public was indifferent or cheered such offensives.

There was likewise no protest within Germany in the spring of 1933, when Nazi regulations banned the Jehovah's Witnesses. In fact, leaders of the official German Protestant and Catholic churches actively encouraged state measures against a religious group they considered a dangerous cult. Many mainstream Christians in Germany disliked Jehovah's Witnesses for their efforts to win converts; German nationalists inside and outside the churches found Jehovah's Witnesses suspect because they neither swore allegiance to the state nor in many cases served in the military.

Most Germans were just as unlikely to complain when the new regime used existing laws and conventions to bear down hard on Gypsies. Stereotyped as shiftless wanderers, Roma and Sinti had suffered police harassment and public prejudice for decades, even before Hitler came to power. Nazi persecution in its early stages hardly seemed new.

Germans of African descent were easy targets as well. They were few in number—probably only hundreds in the early 1930s—and vulnerable in their visibility; those with dark complexions stood out in a nation of white people. Some had come from Germany's former colonies in Africa—territories in modern-day Cameroon, Namibia, Burundi, and Tanzania—or were children of colonials. Some were the offspring of African soldiers or other men of color stationed in the Rhine area after 1918 as part of the French occupation forces. Many Germans had responded with panic to the appearance of black troops in their midst, and the children some of them left behind seemed to many racist Germans to be living examples of Germany's humiliation. Even before he came to power Hitler had spoken of his desire to see all Germans of African descent—people he, like others, called the "Rhineland bastards"—sterilized. The early months of Nazi rule brought attacks, official as well as spontaneous, on these people as well. Compulsory registration of all Germans deemed "half-breeds" revealed 385 such individuals, 370 of whose fathers had been part of the French occupation. In 1937 most of those 385 people were sterilized.

One German woman named Doris Reiprich recalls how her landlord evicted her and her African father, white German mother, and sister from their

Baſtarde zwiſchen Hottentotten und Weißen
(links oben Hottentottin)
Aus „Siemens, Vererbungslehre"

Schulz, Lichtbilder=Vorträge.   Vortrag II, Karte 5.

These portraits of the offspring of a union between an African woman (upper left) and a white man (not pictured) come from a set of slides illustrating a 1934 lecture on race and heredity by a researcher at the SS Race and Settlement office. The heading reads, "Bastards between Hottentots and Whites."

apartment after Hitler came to power. She lost her job, and fellow students tormented her sister, Erika, in school. Teachers were no better; they forced Erika to take part in a course on "race" and listen to such statements as "God made all whites and blacks; half-breeds come from the Devil." The authorities tried to convince the girls' mother to divorce their father, but she refused.

Both Afro-German sisters would make it through the war by acting in movies. They recount their experiences in the book *Showing Our Colors: Afro-German Women Speak Out*. German filmmakers needed a few people of color to make movies promoting German colonialism in Africa. Throughout the Nazi years most Afro-Germans had no such protective positions. Like Doris Reiprich and her sister, they suffered a whole range of indignities and abuses, and many of them experienced even harsher treatment—sterilization, incarceration, and death.

The Nazi Revolution and the Jews

Of course the Nazi revolution also meant assault on German Jews. In 1933 Germany's Jewish population was small: about half a million people, less than 1 percent of the total population. New regulations in April banned Jews from the German civil service. That same month the Nazi Party organized a boycott of Jewish businesses throughout Germany, although the boycott was not the success its planners had anticipated.

Hitler's Nazis used a combination of intimidation and legislation to create a mood of hostility toward Germany's Jews, a kind of open season for abuse. During the boycott Stormtroopers stood outside Jewish businesses to frighten potential customers. Some Jewish children experienced vicious harassment in school from teachers as well as fellow students. Nazi activists staged public humiliations of Jews and friends of Jews. Especially singled out for attack were German Jews and non-Jews who were involved in intimate relationships. In one case, for example, they forced a gentile woman and her Jewish boyfriend to stand in the street wearing sandwich boards. Hers read, "I am the biggest pig in the place and go around only with Jews." His said, "As a Jewish boy I only take German girls to my room."

The civil service ban and the boycott were less successful for Hitler's new regime than Nazi activists had hoped. For one thing, there was no concrete definition of who exactly counted as a Jew. So it was not always clear to whom the ban applied. Given Hitler's sensitivity to public opinion, it was important not to antagonize potential "Aryan" supporters by mistaking them for Jews. Moreover, by April 1933, German Jews had not yet been isolated from the rest of population. The Nazi government did not dare impose measures against Jewish veterans of World War I, for example, or against Christian spouses of Jews. There was also uncertainty around how to regard people who had converted from Judaism to Christianity. Outraged German Jews who did not yet know how far the regime would go in attacks on them deluged authorities with petitions and requests for exceptions, and sometimes non-Jews supported their efforts.

Some non-Jews, however, went even further than the civil service law

This snapshot shows a woman emerging from a Jewish-owned business in violation of the April 1933 boycott. Such photographs, circulated and displayed, were used to denounce individuals and intimidate members of the German public into compliance with anti-Jewish measures.

to introduce anti-Jewish measures on their own. Some gentile spouses quietly divorced "undesirable" Jewish mates. In many universities, gentile administrators fired scholars who were not in fact targeted by the law, for example, Christian men with Jewish wives or people whose parents had converted from Judaism to Christianity. Removing such individuals made those supervisors look especially eager to cooperate with the new government. Students and the other professors were not too likely to complain, because they hoped to benefit from the situation. After all, professorial positions were in high demand in German society, with its many educated people, high level of unemployment, and great respect for academics.

In the Protestant church, pro-Nazi clergy who belonged to a group called the German Christian Movement tried to expel from the pulpits any pastors who had converted from Judaism to Christianity or who were the children or grandchildren of such converts. Only a handful of clergy actually fell into those categories. Uneasy as to how Protestant church people inside Germany and abroad would respond, Nazi government authorities decided in 1933 not to back that scheme. Public opinion was still more important to Hitler than complete thoroughness. There would be time to widen the net later. Meanwhile, individuals and organizations were free to develop anti-Jewish initiatives that suited their own purposes. German municipal governments, strapped for cash, found it expeditious to drop Jewish recipients of public support from their welfare lists, before authorities in Berlin had even thought of the idea.

As for the anti-Jewish boycott of April 1933, it did not really catch on. Some German gentiles complained that the ban on Jewish businesses disrupted their lives and created public disorder. Many continued to frequent Jewish shops out of habit or convenience. Outside Germany there was considerable negative publicity around the anti-Jewish measures. In the United States, Britain, and elsewhere, Jews and people who generally opposed abuses of human rights threatened to organize a counterboycott of German goods to pressure the German government into curbing antisemitic behavior. Aware that the anti-Jewish boycott was damaging his public image at home and abroad, Hitler ended it.

Nazi leaders learned some lessons from these early anti-Jewish experiments. First, they realized that it was easiest to attack people who were already marginalized. Second, they learned that members of the general public were more likely to participate in or at least tolerate attacks on minorities if they stood to gain rather than to lose from such initiatives. In any case, leading Nazis found out that unanimous approval was not required. Indifference of the majority was all that was needed to carry out many plans.

German Jewish Responses

How did German Jews respond to Nazi attacks? Like Communists and homosexuals, some left the country. Departure, however, was not a simple proposition, especially for people with families and deep roots in Germany. There had been Jews in German territory for some sixteen hundred years; many Jews were at home in German society in ways that made leaving almost unfathomable. Moreover, some of the people who antisemites considered Jews did not regard themselves as Jewish at all. Over the centuries Jews had intermarried with Christians and some had converted to Christianity, but because Nazi ideology was based on the notion of blood, its adherents claimed all such people were still Jews.

Unlike Communists, who could (mistakenly) expect a haven in the Soviet Union, there was no obvious place for Jews to go. No State of Israel existed yet in the 1930s, and the traditional countries of immigrants—the

United States, Canada, Australia—all had very restrictive immigration policies. Economic problems linked to the Great Depression and a climate of nativism made governments and public alike hostile to immigrants, especially those who were not Christian or did not come from western Europe.

Many German Jews tried to find new ways to pull together within Germany. They organized self-help efforts and sought to combat social isolation by providing educational and cultural opportunities for themselves. To these ends, in September 1933 a group of Jewish leaders created the Reich Representation of the German Jews to unify attempts to preserve Jewish religious life and offer practical assistance to Jews from all over Germany. The group's president, Berlin Rabbi Leo Baeck (1873–1956), would steadfastly refuse to leave even when he had opportunities to do so. As long as any Jews remained in Germany, Rabbi Baeck believed, he belonged with them.

Once German officials began deporting German Jews to the killing centers in late 1941, the Reich Representation of the German Jews lost its already very limited ability to do anything to help its members. Its leaders too were sent to camps and killing centers. In 1943 German police sent Rabbi Baeck to the ghetto and transit camp at Theresienstadt, also known as Terezin, near Prague. Rabbi Baeck survived the war and moved to London.

In 1933 some German Jews joined Zionist associations. The Zionist movement had emerged in the late nineteenth century. Its members believed that Jews were not only a religious group but a distinct people who deserved a country of their own. Zionists took their name from the biblical name "Zion," the hill in Jerusalem on which the Jewish temple had stood. They worked to establish a Jewish national homeland, and some even moved to Palestine. Before the 1930s Zionism had been rather unpopular among German Jews, but Nazi measures made many Jews in Germany think it was their only alternative. After Hitler came to power, some German Zionist leaders who promoted immigration to Palestine found ways to work out arrangements with Nazi authorities who wanted Jews out of Germany. Others continued to wait and hope that somehow the storm would pass.

The Nazi Revolution and the Disabled

The Nazi revolution advanced on all fronts in its drive for so-called racial purity. In May 1933 Hitler introduced a law to legalize eugenic sterilization, that is, sterilization to prevent reproduction by people deemed unworthy on the basis of mental or physical conditions. More radical legislation followed just two months later.

In July 1933 Hitler proclaimed the Law for Prevention of Hereditarily Diseased Offspring. It ordered sterilization of people with certain physical and psychiatric conditions. The list included people characterized as severe alcoholics, epileptics, schizophrenics, and a number of other loosely defined categories such as the "feebleminded." Roma and Sinti were targeted too, as "asocials." Nazi minister of the interior Wilhelm Frick went so far as to suggest that 20 percent of the population should be sterilized. Ultimately the number of Germans sterilized under this law would come to less than .5 percent of the German population, but that still meant destroying the reproductive capabilities of some 400,000 people without their consent and in many cases against their wills.

There was some criticism of the sterilization law, especially from Catholic clergy. Nevertheless proponents of the measure also found a few Catholic theologians who were willing to endorse it. Meanwhile enforcement required the participation of many people: lawyers who drafted the legislation; medical and social workers who reported people to be sterilized to the authorities; bureaucrats who handled the paperwork; doctors, nurses, and aides who performed the procedures. As the Nazi regime established and reinforced its power, it involved ever larger numbers of people, who in turn developed a stake in its continuation. Through this dynamic, Nazi ideas gained acceptance, even among people who might earlier have opposed them.

The Policy of Coordination

The Nazi revolution brought rewards for those who cooperated as well as attacks on those deemed undesirable. Many Germans of all ages enjoyed participating in an exciting, dynamic movement that welcomed them as long as they were "the right kinds of people."

In 1933 Hitler and his accomplices introduced a process called *Gleichschaltung*, which means "coordination," literally "shifting into the same gear." In the name of national unity, new Nazi organizations swallowed up other, independent groups and clubs. For example, the Nazi-run German Labor Front replaced the old trade unions. Nazi organizations of farmers, women, boys, girls, writers, and artists absorbed associations of people in those categories. These new groups had monopolies over their clienteles and did not tolerate competing organizations.

Local cooperation and leadership were essential to the success of "coordination." So was a bombardment of propaganda from party-controlled news-

Members of the League of German Girls (Bund Deutscher Mädel, or BDM) take children from large families to the park while the mothers of the infants are busy elsewhere. Founded in the late 1920s, the League of German Girls aimed to prepare young "Aryans" to serve the Reich as mothers.

papers and publicists enthusiastic about the "national awakening." For at least some Germans the surge of group activities provided an exciting sense of belonging. Melitta Maschmann, a teenager in 1933, later described how she loved being part of the Nazi League of German Girls. It gave her a chance to assert independence from her parents, she said, and to feel like someone important, part of dramatic new developments. Testimonials collected from Nazi Party members in the 1930s by the American social scientist Theodore Abel echoed those sentiments: joining the Nazi movement empowered many Germans.

Hitler's government introduced all kinds of programs to win favor with the majority of the population. Enormous publicity was devoted to job creation and massive public works programs. Many people still claim that Hitler "saved" Germany from the depression, and indeed, Nazi policies did accelerate the process of economic recovery. At the same time, many of Hitler's schemes continued what his predecessors had begun, and in any case, by 1933, the depression seemed to have bottomed out in Germany. Of course Hitler took credit for all improvements, and the Nazis even set up an agency called Strength Through Joy to organize workers' leisure activities and plan holiday trips. Strength Through Joy set up package tours, such as cruises to the Mediterranean or Scandinavia or short trips within Germany. It also sponsored mass production of the "people's cars"—Volkswagens—and set up savings plans so that workers could arrange to buy them. Even fun was to appear to be a gift of the Führer.

Terror and Pageantry

The Nazi revolution claimed to restore order, but from the beginning it was enforced with terror. In March 1933, not even two months after Hitler became chancellor, Nazi authorities opened the first official concentration camp. Located at Dachau, just outside Munich, its initial prisoners were political—Communists arrested in the wake of the Reichstag fire—but it also held men charged with homosexuality and common criminals. Dachau Concentration Camp was no secret. To the contrary, the Nazi press covered its opening in detail, on the theory that merely knowing it existed would serve as a public deterrent.

Dachau and the network of similar camps that followed were under the control of Heinrich Himmler, one of Hitler's longtime associates, and the SS, Nazism's elite force. By July 1933 German concentration camps held an estimated twenty-seven thousand people in what was euphemistically called "protective custody."

Violence itself served the Nazi regime as a form of propaganda. In May 1933, Hitler's minister of propaganda, Joseph Goebbels, organized public book burnings, which presented intimidating spectacles of Nazi force. Thousands of pro-Nazi students proved especially eager to participate. They and other Nazi supporters made huge bonfires of books by Jewish authors such as Albert Einstein and the satirist Kurt Tucholsky. They also burned works by Communists and others associated with left-wing positions—for example, the playwright Bertolt Brecht and the writer Heinrich Mann; liberals such as Thomas Mann; and foreigners, including the American Jack London. Such scenes must have communicated a clear threat to outsiders and critics of Nazism.

Pageantry was the flip side of Nazi terror, another show of strength. The first months of Hitler's rule featured endless torchlight parades with columns of marching men. Observers after the fact often interpret footage of those

Himmler speaks to an inmate at Dachau during an SS inspection of the camp in 1936. Opened with fanfare in 1933, Dachau was Nazi Germany's first official concentration camp and remained a major site of detention, torture, and death until April 1945.

events as evidence of the unanimity of Germans behind Hitler. It would be probably more accurate to see those demonstrations as efforts on the part of the new regime to create an image of unanimity that itself worked to prevent opposition. It must have been a lonely and terrifying experience to be on the outside of a torchlight march looking in. What chance would one feel one had against that monolith of power?

The columns of Nazis often sang as they marched. Supporters adapted old songs and wrote reams of new ones, everything from sentimental folk songs to outright vicious fighting songs, with lyrics about "Jewish blood" spurting from German knives. The most famous Nazi song was the "Horst Wessel Lied." It was named after its lyricist, a young Nazi Stormtrooper who had been killed in a brawl with a Communist in 1930. Set to a familiar folk tune, Horst Wessel's lyrics extolled the Nazi flag, called for unity against the foe, and praised the comrade-heroes who had died for the cause. During the Third Reich the Horst Wessel song became part of Germany's official national anthem. It was always sung with the right arm outstretched in the "Hitler salute."

A Revolution in Foreign Policy

As he had at home, Hitler used a combination of boldness and caution to bring about a revolution in foreign policy. He was a master of making his aims look safely conventional, even while his intentions were dangerously radical. Hitler railed against the Treaty of Versailles, but so had almost all German politicians since the war. He talked about restoring German boundaries to their "rightful" location; so had many German nationalists. Hitler's plans, however, were far more ambitious, and he wanted nothing short of world domination. Nevertheless, in the first stage of his rule he used diplomacy to work toward achieving his goals.

In this regard too Hitler chose his priorities carefully. His first major foreign policy success came in July 1933, shortly before announcement of the new sterilization law. That month Hitler's representatives signed an agreement called the Concordat with the Vatican in Rome. In exchange for recognition of his regime's legitimacy from the pope, Hitler promised to respect the rights of Catholics and the Catholic Church in Germany. The pope, for his part, hoped to protect Catholic interests within Germany and to use Hitler's Nazi regime as a defense against Communism all over Europe. For Hitler the Concordat turned out to be an extremely effective way to buy support both at home and abroad.

Germany's population in 1933 was almost 40 percent Roman Catholic, and Hitler himself was raised in the Catholic Church. Nevertheless many German Catholic clergy were initially suspicious of Nazism. They saw Nazi ideas as anti-Christian, especially the emphasis on race and blood and the obvious disrespect for human life. Before the Concordat, some priests in Germany had refused to administer the sacrament of communion to church members in Stormtrooper or SS uniforms.

The Concordat pulled the rug out from under potential Catholic opposition in Germany. How could parish priests criticize a chancellor who had been recognized by their pope? What possibility remained for a united Catholic front against the sterilization program? Meanwhile, abroad the Concordat added to the prestige of Hitler's new regime. Even if the pope no longer wielded much political power, he still had moral authority with Catholics all over the world.

Other foreign policy successes followed. By January 1934 Hitler's diplomats had negotiated a Non-Aggression Pact with Poland that was supposed to last for ten years. Hitler had no intention of keeping that promise, but such deals bought precious time. Meanwhile, Germany withdrew from all its multilateral arrangements; most notably, in October 1933, it left the League of Nations.

Under Hitler Germany actively began to rearm. Because the Treaty of Versailles restricted German military power, rearmament at first had to be secret. In 1933 Hitler's government set up a phoney initiative called the Agricultural Tractor Program, which was a cover for a project that in fact built tanks. By 1934 Germany was producing explosives, ships, and aircraft in quantity. In 1935 Hitler dropped even the pretense of secrecy. Germany had become a military power once again, with an air force, a navy, and an army based on conscription.

The Nazi revolution was difficult to oppose because it occurred with a mixture of subtlety and force. The regime did not snap into place in January 1933 as a full-blown totalitarian prison. There was still room for Germans—at least those who were not considered handicapped, Jewish, or otherwise unwanted—to maneuver, even to criticize. Precisely those mainstream members of society, however, were the least likely to recognize the revolutionary nature of the new regime. Many of them stood to gain from the measures it introduced, and others were apathetic. What did any of it have to do with them? Sadly it was exactly those in the most vulnerable positions—Nazism's targets—who were the first to recognize what was at stake. They, however, had little power to do much about it, other than to warn people like them, who often preferred to hope for the best instead of heeding alarmists, or to try to convince a busy and often hostile world of their impending doom.

A Telling Incident

An incident recounted by a German waiter and recorded in Bernd Engelmann's book *Inside Hitler's Germany* captures the dynamics of the early months of Nazi rule. In early 1933, the man worked at a restaurant in a small town. One day a group of Nazi enthusiasts came in. The editor of the town's Nazi newspaper was there, so were the chief Stormtrooper and the local party leader. At another table all alone sat an elderly, Jewish lawyer who had lived in the town all his life.

The group of Nazi functionaries got louder and drunker. Suddenly they summoned the waiter, a young man at the time, to their table and told him to deliver a note to the lawyer. Afraid to refuse, the waiter complied, but as he put the note down on the table he saw that it said something like: "Get out, you Jewish swine."

The lawyer read the note and began trembling with rage and shame. He stood up at his table and addressed the three men. How dare you, he challenged them: "I am a veteran of the World War. I risked my life for this country." The restaurant became deathly still. No one at any of the other tables spoke or even seemed to breathe. The waiter remembered being able to hear the sound of pots and pans in the kitchen.

The three Nazis broke the silence. They taunted the lawyer again and turned back to their beers. The lawyer summoned the waiter and, still shaking, handed him money to cover his meal, then left the restaurant.

Later the waiter realized that the man had given him far too much money for his bill. He went to the lawyer's home to return the extra. There he found the man dressed in his hat and coat with a suitcase in his hand. He was leaving, he told the waiter, because there was no future for him in Germany.

What would have happened to any of the other Germans at that restaurant if they had spoken in defense of their Jewish neighbor? At that point, in early 1933, probably very little. The aggressors were drunken bullies new to their roles. The observers likely knew them personally, as they did the lawyer. So why did they say nothing? Perhaps they did not want to risk an unpleasant, embarrassing scene. Maybe they would have taken the chance for someone else, a woman, say, or a Christian clergyman. In any case, they were silent, and their silence emboldened the ruffians. All over Germany the silence of others like them sent a message back up to Hitler: it was safe to keep pushing.

The Night of Long Knives and the End of the Revolutionary Phase

The end of Nazism's revolutionary phase can be marked with reference to a specific event—the so-called Night of Long Knives, also known as the Röhm Putsch, of 30 June 1934. Ernst Röhm (1887–1934) had been Hitler's associate since the early 1920s, when he had been instrumental in building up the Stormtrooper organization. By 1934 Röhm was head of 2.5 million Stormtroopers. A veteran of World War I, Röhm and his Stormtroopers had played a powerful role in destabilizing the Weimar Republic and consolidating Hitler's new regime. After some professional setbacks and personal scandals, Röhm immigrated to Bolivia in 1928, but Hitler brought him back to Germany in 1930 to reorganize the Stormtroopers.

After Hitler became chancellor, he began to view the Stormtroopers as a liability. Restless for action and disgruntled with what seemed a slow pace of change, many of them thought Hitler had sold out their movement's ideals for the sake of respectability. The SS, or Schutzstaffel (protective staff), Nazism's elite guard headed by Himmler, had grown more powerful and wanted the upper hand over its rival organization, the Stormtroopers. Meanwhile the army and Hitler's new conservative friends considered the Stormtroopers disreputable thugs who disrupted the public order.

Hitler had to choose. Would he cast his lot with the SS and the army or be loyal to his old brown-shirted Stormtrooper allies? He decided to move against the Stormtroopers. On the night of 30 June 1934, on Hitler's orders, the SS struck.

It is often said that a revolution devours its own children. Hitler's revolution was no exception. In a bloody rampage, SS men fanned out to kill Röhm, other old allies of the Führer such as the Nazi ideologue Gregor Strasser, and Hitler's rivals, including former chancellor General Kurt von Schleicher and, for some reason, Schleicher's wife. In general, Hitler and SS leader Himmler used the purge to get rid of people they found problematic. The list of dead even included a Catholic priest who had helped write *Mein Kampf* when Hitler was in prison. Perhaps that man was a victim of mistaken identity, or Hitler may have thought he knew too much to be trusted.

The total number of people killed is unknown. Some place it as low as 150; others estimate it in the thousands. At least eighty high-ranking Stormtroopers were shot. The numbers of more lowly individuals killed on local initiatives, that is, not on direct orders from Hitler or Himmler, may have been much higher. Hitler did not dismantle the Stormtroopers completely after the purge, but he clipped the organization's wings and subordinated it directly to his authority.

Hitler dressed the bloodbath in the guise of conventional morality. Ernst Röhm was openly homosexual. Hitler had known about Röhm's sexual preferences for years and never seemed to have considered them a problem. Now, however, in his bid for legitimacy, Hitler publicly reviled Röhm. The killings, Nazi press reports contended in lurid detail, were part of a cleanup of the movement, a necessary measure against decadence and perversion.

How did the German public react? You might expect shock or horror. In fact there was little of either expressed in Germany, at least in public. President Hindenburg sent Hitler a telegram of congratulation for restoring order, and German military leaders likewise praised what they considered appropriate measures in the interest of public safety. Members of Hitler's cabinet declared the purge retroactively legal. Many observers believed that now the Nazi regime had become an ordinary government, its dangerous, extremist days behind it.

Victor Klemperer, a German professor of Jewish background in Dresden, had a different opinion. After such blatant criminality, he was certain that the regime of brutes had to fall. Surely the old German elite would come to its senses and throw out the upstarts, he hoped, but Klemperer was wrong. The Night of Long Knives left Hitler stronger than ever.

PHASE II: ROUTINIZATION, 1934–1937

June 1934 marked a turning point in the Nazi regime. By no means did it signify the end of brutality, but it did usher in a new phase of routinization. Instead of uncontrolled, revolutionary shows of force, Nazi authorities concentrated on systematizing violence and normalizing coercion. They did so by centralizing power in the hands of a few and passing laws to make their measures at least look respectable. Inventing rituals and convincing people to police their own behavior in keeping with Nazi regulations were also parts of the process.

Centralization of Power

One component of routinization was centralization, which took many forms. One of the most significant was the centralization of police power under Heinrich Himmler and the SS. The Night of Long Knives brought the Stormtroopers under Himmler's control. In 1934, Himmler, along with his associate Reinhard Heydrich, who ran the intelligence office known as the Security Service, took over all political police, known in Germany as the Gestapo. By 1936 Himmler had pulled the criminal police into his orbit as well, so that the head of the SS and the concentration camps was now in charge of all police forces in Germany.

Himmler and his tens of thousands of SS men were crucial to the Third Reich. Unlike the German military, the SS was officially linked to the Nazi Party organization, not to the government of Germany. Throughout the Third Reich, the Nazi Party retained its own separate hierarchy with headquarters in the Brown House in Munich. Its status as attached to the party gave the SS an unprecedented degree of independence from any kind of authority that pre-dated Hitler's rise to power. The SS was an ideologically dynamic organization that combined the functions of a conventional, repressive political police with a drive to implement the "Führer's idea." Himmler saw his goal as defending "purity of the blood" and persecuting those who he believed threatened it: Communists, Freemasons, Jehovah's Witnesses, homosexuals, Jews, Gypsies, and others.

In August 1934 President Hindenburg, the man who had appointed Hitler chancellor of Germany, died. In another act of centralization, Hitler united the offices of president and chancellor in his own person. That change did not substantially alter Hitler's actual duties, nor did the president's death remove a major obstacle to the expansion of Hitler's power. Hindenburg had done little to check Hitler's activities in the first year and a half of Nazi rule. Nevertheless, for some Germans the death of the old man Hindenburg meant the end of any hope that Hitler and Nazism would be stopped.

There were also practical repercussions to the uniting of the offices of chancellor and president in the person of the Führer. According to the German constitution, still officially in force, the president was the supreme commander of the German armed forces. Hitler now claimed that position for himself and used it to require members of the military to swear an oath of personal allegiance to him.

Legalization

A second component of routinization involved legalizing Nazi measures. The goals of Hitler and the Nazi "true believers," as we have seen, were two-fold: "racial purity" and spatial expansion. In this phase of development after the Nazi revolution of 1933–1934, pursuing those goals meant revamping German law. Members of all professions—teachers, journalists, doctors— served the Nazi cause, but lawyers and judges played an especially important role in giving the regime and its measures a veneer of legitimacy that was important to international observers and at least some Germans. As he consolidated and expanded his power, Hitler had to operate within the prevailing view of Germany as a state governed by law.

The first minister of justice under Hitler, Franz Gürtner, was not a Nazi, although he supported authoritarian rule. Gürtner was prepared to sanction the blatant illegalities of the revolutionary phase, including attacks on Communists and the Röhm Putsch massacre. Justice Minister Gürtner also presided over laying the legal foundations for what would become mass murder of people considered handicapped and of Jews.

The key pieces of legislation when it came to attacks on Jews were the Nuremberg Laws, passed in the fall of 1935. The laws had two parts. First was the Law for Protection of German Blood and Honor, which forbade marriage or sexual relations between Jews and "Aryan" Germans. Jews could not fly the German flag nor employ German gentile women under age forty-five in their households. Such measures were intended to isolate German Jews from the rest of the population and stigmatize them as disloyal, destructive outsiders.

The second component was the Reich Citizenship Law of November 1935. This legislation defined, for the first time, who was to count as a Jew in Nazi Germany. According to Nazi ideology, Jewishness was a racial trait, but in fact there was no way to measure distinctions of blood, because they did not actually exist. In other words, there were no reliable markers of appearance, blood type, or any other physical traits that Nazi "experts" could use to separate Jews from "Aryans." Instead the Nuremberg Laws fell back on religion as the only way to define Jews.

Under the law it was not one's own religion but that of one's grandparents that mattered. People with three or more grandparents of the Jewish faith counted as Jews. Most Germans defined as "Jews" under the law lost the rights associated with German citizenship.

The Nuremberg Laws considered people who had two grandparents of the Jewish faith to be *Mischlinge,* or "mixed bloods," a category that would remain in dispute throughout the entire Third Reich. Mischlinge who were Jewish by religion or who married people categorized as Jews also counted as Jews. Some Mischlinge who had no contact with Judaism or Jews likewise ended up being treated as Jews, perhaps because they looked stereotypically Jewish or had especially hostile neighbors or coworkers. There were, however, Mischlinge who managed to continue living in German society throughout the Nazi period, and a few of them even served in the German military in World War II. The law did not address people with one Jewish grandparent, but in practice some of them would also face disadvantage and discrimination of various kinds.

The Reich Citizenship Law offered no definition of "Aryan" other than the implied opposite of "non-Aryan" or "Jew." Thus, by default, Germans with four grandparents who were baptized into a Christian church were generally assumed to be "Aryans."

Most non-Jewish Germans gave little thought to the Nuremberg Laws. They seemed just one more bureaucratic measure that would have little direct impact on their lives. Nor did the international community regard the laws as especially significant. After all, every nation reserved for itself the right to determine who counted as its citizens, on what basis, and what rights they received.

Their mundane appearance notwithstanding, the Nuremberg Laws proved to be a crucial step toward the destruction of Germany's Jews. All kinds of attacks on Jews were now directly sanctioned, even mandated, by law. Moreover, once Jews were defined, it would be much easier to isolate, rob, deport, and eventually kill them.

Although focused on Jews, the Nuremberg Laws had repercussions for other target groups as well. Regulations that followed meant that under certain conditions, Gypsies, as "alien to the Aryan species," could also lose the rights of German citizens. They too faced prohibitions on marrying so-called Aryan

Germans. Eager German racists applied measures described in the Nuremberg Laws to Afro-Germans as well. One woman remembers how as a small girl she was sent home by a teacher who forbade her, as a "non-Aryan," to march behind the German flag.

The phase of routinization also brought increased measures against homosexuals. In June 1935, Paragraph 175 of the German criminal code was revised to expand the definition of "criminally indecent activities between men." Now sexual relations did not have to be established; any physical intimacy assumed to lead to sexual arousal could be grounds for prosecution. It became easy for denouncers to lay charges of homosexuality, and the courts used their power to impose a crackdown that brought thousands of men accused of homosexual behavior into prisons and concentration camps.

Meanwhile, Nazi sterilization developed its own routines, and new regulations extended the assault on those considered handicapped. For example, a 1935 law required any pregnant woman who should have been sterilized under the 1933 law but had not been to have an abortion. The laws and regulations already introduced against people deemed handicapped routinized worsening conditions in institutions and hospitals around Germany. What kind of treatment would you expect health-care workers to mete out toward people whose government labeled them "useless eaters" and "unworthy lives"?

Ritualization

In addition to centralization and legalization, a third component of Nazi routinization was ritualization. After the first year, Nazi pageantry developed a ritualized rhythm. The largest event was the annual Party Rally, held each year in the southern German city of Nuremberg. It was an enormous spectacle, choreographed by propaganda experts to the smallest details. As with the early torchlight marches, these imposing shows of strength were supposed to create a sense of unanimity and invincibility so that any opponents of the system would feel isolated and helpless. In 1934 the German director Leni Riefenstahl filmed the rally and released it under the title *Triumph of the Will*. It has become one of the most famous propaganda movies of all time.

Later some Germans would describe their participation in these Nazi extravaganzas as among the high points of their lives. In particular children seemed very impressed. Alfons Heck, a member of the Hitler Youth from a small town near the French border, described his trip to the Nuremberg Party Rally in 1935 in his book *A Child of Hitler,* which he wrote many years later. Heck was awed by the pageantry, the uniforms, and the scale of the whole affair. No doubt those sensations contributed to his own devotion to the Nazi cause and his desire to share in such amazing power.

Of course, for others inside Germany Nazi spectacles brought other kinds of routines—predictable harassment and the drudgery of confinement. In preparation for the 1936 Olympics in Berlin, an event that Nazi organizers used to showcase the "new Germany" in all its splendor, police forced about six hundred Gypsies out of Berlin into detention in a camp near a sewage dump and the cemetery in the nearby suburb of Marzahn. Guarded by police and their dogs, the camp had only three water pumps and two toilets. Under those conditions, contagious diseases ran rampant. Otto Rosenberg, a Sinto from Berlin, had just turned nine when police shipped him, his granny, a teenaged aunt, and a brother and sister to Marzahn. The smell of sewage was terrible, he recalled, and people lived in huts knocked together from sheet iron they scrounged for themselves. The glories of the Third Reich looked rather different from the vantage point of what amounted to an overcrowded, filthy, open-air prison.

Self-Coordination

A fourth important aspect of routinization might be called self-coordination. In the years between 1934 and the beginning of the war, Nazism lost much of its momentum. Some people became disillusioned or bored with the new system, but most of the population, even those who were not overly enthusiastic, fell into the habit of going along with the regime. They grumbled in private, perhaps, or expressed their criticism in ineffective forms, such as jokes. In either case they posed no real threat to Nazi control.

One popular joke that poked fun both at Hitler's pretensions and at public gullibility went as follows. Hitler and Goebbels were driving through the German countryside when their car struck a dog. Hitler, who loved animals, was devastated. "Go and find the masters of that loyal German dog," he ordered his minister of propaganda. "Apologize to them in the name of the Führer." Some time later Goebbels returned, beaming and bearing all kinds of gifts: bread, sausage, and beer. "What happened?" Hitler demanded. "Were they unhappy?" "Not at all, mein Führer," Goebbels answered. "All I said was 'Heil Hitler! Der Hund ist tot' [The dog is dead], and they began to celebrate."

Self-coordination also involved self-policing. Since 1933 a law called the Malicious Practices Act had banned remarks that offended or subverted Nazi authority. Such prohibitions can only be effective if people report one another, and they did so in Nazi Germany. Throughout the 1930s denunciations poured into the offices of the Gestapo, the political police in charge of crimes against the state. Some people denounced others in order to demonstrate their own loyalty to the Nazi cause. Others sought to better their positions, attack outsiders, or just carry out old grudges. The prevalence of denunciations and police raids inspired German wits to invent two new national "saints," Maria D'enunciata and Marie Haussuchung—that is, Holy Mary the Denouncer and Mary of the House Searches.

Fear of denunciation led people to develop what became known as the "German glance"—the quick look over the shoulder before one spoke to see who might overhear. The SD or Security Service employed an elaborate network of infiltrators and informers whose job it was to report in detail on the public mood across Germany. Nazi routinization depended on consensus and co-option as well as coercion.

Nevertheless Nazi Germany cannot simply be characterized as a "police state." Indeed, as the historian Robert Gellately has shown, there were in fact relatively few police per capita in Germany in the 1930s. A high level of cooperation from the general public, not an unusual number of men in uniform, made Nazi control possible. Smooth functioning of the system did not require all Germans—or even most—to share every tenet of Nazi ideology. Enough enthusiasts could always be found to stage enormous public shows of support, such as the annual Nuremberg Party rallies. On a day-to-day basis, the Nazi regime only needed most people to obey the law, try to stay out of trouble, and promote their own interests as best they could under the current circumstances.

Preparations for War

Even during the period of routinization Hitler did not lose sight of his goals of race and space. In various ways he presided over Germany's preparation for war. After two years of secret rearmament, in 1935 Hitler's government went public. It reintroduced conscription and revealed its new military machine to the world.

No one had altered the Treaty of Versailles, but German contravention of its terms had become routine under the Nazis. The victors of World War I were not in a position to risk a new conflict in order to check German violations. Impoverished by the war and the difficult years that followed and faced with their own problems at home, the British and the French had no desire to play the role of international police. The United States had retreated into isolationism, and most of its people opposed its government involving them again in the turmoil of European affairs.

In 1936 Hitler took his biggest foreign policy gamble so far. Under the Treaty of Versailles, the westernmost part of Germany along the Rhine River had been demilitarized to provide a buffer zone for France. A year after reintroduction of conscription, rumors began to circulate that Hitler intended to reoccupy the Rhineland with Germany's new military. For some months he seemed to waver, waiting until the Winter Olympics in Berlin had ended and collecting the views of his inner circle, Germany's diplomats, and military leaders. By the beginning of March, he had made his decision and prepared to act.

Hitler made the announcement in a speech on 7 March to the Reichstag and, by radio, to the people of Germany. It was a lengthy and in places emotional speech, which denounced Versailles and railed against Communism. Hitler saved the punchline for the end. "In the interest of the primitive rights of a people to the security of its borders and safeguarding of its defense capability," he proclaimed, "the German Reich government has therefore from today restored the full and unrestricted sovereignty of the Reich in the demilitarized zone of the Rhineland." The six hundred deputies in the Reichstag, all in Nazi uniform, went wild, stretching out their arms in the Nazi salute and screaming "Heil!"

Meanwhile, German troops were approaching the Hohenzollern Bridge across the Rhine River in the city of Cologne. Propaganda minister Goebbels had arranged for planeloads of journalists to be on hand to record the event, and thousands of Germans crowded into nearby streets to cheer the soldiers as they crossed into the demilitarized zone. Even in this moment of national euphoria, Hitler and his advisers retained some caution. They made sure that the forward troops were instructed to withdraw and fight if they met military resistance from the French. As Hitler had expected, the French did not respond by sending in their own troops. Instead the gamble paid off by giving Hitler's prestige at home its most enormous boost yet.

Even as he publicly pledged his commitment to European peace, Hitler announced to his inner circle in 1936 that Germany must be ready for war within four years. To that end he named his old associate Hermann Göring head of a "Four-Year Plan" to prepare the German economy and military for war. Göring took over economic planning, and the old minister of the economy resigned.

In the winter of 1937–1938, Hitler completed the routinization and consolidation of his rule by dumping the old elites who had been so instrumental in bringing him to power. Those old-fashioned conservatives had been useful throughout the phases of Nazi revolution and routinization. They had lent respectability to the regime when it needed it and had provided expertise and continuity as it consolidated its power. Now, as Hitler prepared to move to a more aggressive phase, they had become a burden.

In November 1937 Hitler met with leaders of the German army, navy, and air force. It had been two years since Germany had announced its rearmament. Since 1936 German forces had been involved in the Spanish Civil War on the side of General Francisco Franco and the enemies of the Spanish Republic. Hitler had pushed German intervention even though many Germans opposed it. Because the Soviet Union backed the Republic in Spain, support of Franco gave Hitler a way to attack Communism. Moreover, Mussolini was actively behind Franco as well. So Spain offered a chance for Germany and Italy to practice cooperation in the spirit of their leaders' mutual admiration. For the Germans the Spanish Civil War was also an opportunity to try out new military equipment. In particular they broke in their new air force by bombing Spanish towns and cities. Now Hitler was ready to risk more.

Hitler gave those gathered at the November meeting a lengthy harangue on Germany's need for more space. They were skeptical. How could Germany be ready for war? Hitler's response to their misgivings was typical. In early 1938 he launched a purge of the military leadership, replacing old conservatives with men more amenable to Nazi plans. He retired fourteen senior generals, replaced or pensioned approximately sixty others, and assumed command of the armed forces as minister of war.

Hitler made a clean sweep of all positions directly related to his plans for war. He replaced the conservative foreign minister Constantin von Neurath with the loyal Nazi Joachim von Ribbentrop. The Nazi general Walter von Brauchitsch became head of the army in place of Werner von Fritsch. There were new Nazi ambassadors to Rome, Tokyo, and Vienna.

Hitler's methods in early 1938 were quite different from those he had used to purge the Stormtroopers less than four years earlier. This time he employed less violent means, in keeping with the stature of the individuals involved and the spirit of routinization rather than revolution. But the tactics were no less vicious for all their bloodlessness. For example, Hitler disposed of the war minister Werner von Blomberg by stirring up a scandal around his new wife. She was a former prostitute, the Nazi press claimed; how could a man thus compromised hold a position of such responsibility? The fact that both Hitler and Göring had served as witnesses at the wedding was conveniently omitted, and Blomberg went abroad in disgrace.

Two years earlier, rumors of homosexual activities on the part of Fritsch, the head of the army, had been ignored. Now Fritsch had to go, and the old charges provided the perfect means to force him out. He, like the others, had served his purpose; he had supported Hitler's regime in its early stages and helped provide it with a veneer of legitimacy by linking the new system to familiar, experienced military leaders. After four full years in power Hitler had consolidated his position, and preparations for war were under way. Fritsch, Blomberg, and the others had outlived their usefulness to Hitler, and it was no problem to find replacements eager for their positions. Meanwhile those members of the military elite who kept their jobs fell into line with barely a murmur. It would become much more difficult to challenge Nazi rule now that not only the police but the military was firmly in hand.

Contrary to the image presented by Nazi propaganda—Germans marching in massive columns, their arms raised as one in the salute to Hitler—not all Germans fell into line. Friedrich Thimme, a trained historian and fervent German patriot who had headed the Foreign Office's division on the so-called War Guilt Question in the 1920s, railed in his private and not-so-private correspondence against Hitler and his henchmen and refused to break ties to his Jewish friends. Thimme's daughter Annelise, a teenaged schoolgirl in Berlin in the early years of the Third Reich, announced to her classmates that obviously the Nazis had lit the Reichstag fire themselves, and she scoffed at Nazified teachers who preached the party line in the classroom. With a group of high-spirited schoolmates, Annelise once played a trick on one of the worst offenders. One at a time the girls rode by the teacher, who was on her own bicycle, calling out "Heil Hitler" so that the woman repeatedly had to raise her right arm in salute until she lost her balance and fell. In a small way, that youthful prank reveals the continued presence in Hitler's Germany of people who for all kinds of reasons—family ties, personal loyalties, religious and moral principles, political allegiances—remained skeptical and even critical of their government and its actions.

In early 1938, however, most Germans were not thinking about challenging Nazi rule. Looking back on his youth in Germany, Alfons Heck can see some of the factors that made him an enthusiastic Nazi. There was the indoctrination in school and in the Hitler Youth, for example, and the unrelenting propaganda. But there were also concrete ways that Nazism benefited him. It promised action, rewards for his ambition, power, a chance to be an insider, and a role in something enormously successful. Heck, like many of Hitler's German supporters, was no brainwashed automaton. He was just one of millions of "ordinary people" who, for all kinds of ordinary reasons, endorsed and accepted a brutal system.

4

OPEN AGGRESSION: IN SEARCH
OF WAR, 1938–1939

By early 1938, Nazi rule had become a familiar routine for most Germans. For some, such as the eager young Hitler Youth member Alfons Heck, it was a comfortable yet exciting existence. Ambitious and enthusiastic, Heck could expect to realize his goal of becoming an airplane pilot. After all, was not Germany becoming richer and stronger? Its new air force beckoned him from its triumphs in Spain; his teachers and the books and newspapers he read assured him the future was his. Born in 1927, Heck could hardly remember the Nazi revolution. The normalization of Nazi power coincided with his development of political and social awareness. It was really the only world he knew.

Born the same year as Alfons Heck, the Gypsy boy Otto Rosenberg also grew up with the Nazi system. By 1938 he knew all the miseries of the Marzahn "lot" and had mastered some ways around them. Often hungry, he pulled beets for nearby farmers in exchange for pennies and food: Belgian buns with icing, coffee with milk. He became used to seeing the riot squad beat people with sabers and haul them off to what was known in local parlance as the "concert-camp." In 1938, he watched police round up the young men of Marzahn and drive them away in trucks to Sachsenhausen. Still, when his mother, who had arrived in Marzahn after him, was ordered to report to police in Berlin, Rosenberg waited for her to return. Instead she was sent straight to the women's concentration camp at Ravensbrück.

For others, such as Victor Klemperer, professor of French literature in Dresden, routinization of Nazi rule meant an ever-tightening trap. The university dismissed Klemperer in 1935, even though he was both a convert from Judaism to Christianity and a veteran of World War I. One insult and deprivation followed another. Klemperer was forbidden to publish. He lost borrowing privileges at the library, and eventually library staff refused even to let him use the reading room. Over the years Nazi regulations robbed Klemperer of his car, his house, his driver's license, even his pets. If the years from 1933 to 1938 seemed to fly on magical wings for the young Nazi boy Heck, for the middle-aged "non-Aryan" Klemperer they crawled by, an endless drudgery of discouragement and abuse. The years ahead would be even worse.

Beginning in early 1938, Hitler's Germany entered a third stage of its development. After the euphoric phase of revolution and the consolidating phase of routinization, Hitler and his inner circle took off the gloves and began actively seeking war. For Hitler war was more than military conflict; it was to be a decisive step toward realizing his ideas. By 1938 he had already prepared the ground by rearming, isolating target groups, and appointing loyal supporters in key positions. Now, open aggression would characterize developments in Nazi Germany even before the invasion of Poland in September 1939.

This chapter outlines some of the key events of that turbulent period in 1938 and 1939: annexation of Austria in March 1938; the Czech crisis later that year; the so-called Kristallnacht pogrom in November 1938; the Hitler-Stalin Pact; and the beginnings of a program to kill Germans deemed handicapped. In dramatic ways, Hitler began to realize his goals of race and space even before he got the war he wanted.

SKEPTICISM AND SUCCESS

Contrary to the stereotype, most Germans were not foaming at the mouth, eager for war, in 1938 and 1939. In fact, the German public as a whole, including many people who were enthusiastic about aspects of the Nazi domestic program, would greet with skepticism many of the moves that Hitler and his Nazi elite would make in this phase of open aggression. It was one thing to assert German strength and revolutionize conditions at home, but it was quite another to risk war when, for many Germans, memories of the previous war remained painfully fresh. Such uneasiness, however, was not enough to derail Hitler's plans. Instead he was able to use 1938 and 1939 to construct a unified front for the cause of race and space. He did so by resorting to such old loyalties as nationalism, patriotism, and solidarity against common enemies. Even more important, he built support through success.

It is often said that nothing succeeds like success. Certainly Nazi Germany seems to confirm that saying. Every time Hitler took a risk and won, he decreased the anxiety among the German people and convinced more of them to trust him. Many feared war because they dreaded bloodshed, personal and financial loss, and defeat. The wounds of world war and especially its bitter outcome in 1918 were still raw for most adults, but what they perceived to be Hitler's foreign policy triumphs in 1938–1939 did a great deal to relieve their concerns.

Events in 1938–1939 demonstrate how domestic and foreign policies were intertwined in Hitler's Germany. Foreign policy successes helped ease concerns and buy support at home. Meanwhile Hitler's regime pursued the goals of race and space on both fronts: abroad it attacked Germany's supposed enemies and took steps toward a military offensive; at home it enforced "racial purity" and trained its people for war.

THE ANSCHLUSS—GERMAN
ANNEXATION OF AUSTRIA

The first of Hitler's string of foreign policy successes in 1938 and 1939 was the Anschluss, the German annexation of Austria in March 1938. The Treaty of Versailles had forbidden Austria and Germany from uniting. In 1936, in order to placate Mussolini's Italy, Hitler had issued assurances that Germany would not violate Austrian independence. Mussolini and some other Italians were worried about German designs on Austria and on territories long disputed between Austria and Italy: South Tyrol and Trieste. Like all of Hitler's promises, that pledge to respect Austrian independence was made to be broken.

In early March 1938, the Austrian chancellor Kurt von Schuschnigg announced a plebiscite to show Austria's determination to resist Nazi power. The next day, Hitler called together his military leaders to address the possibility of German occupation. It took only hours to prepare a plan; Hitler ordered German forces to cross the border into Austria on 12 March.

The plan was no work of genius. Supposedly, German tanks had to stop at commercial gas stations to refuel on the way. Rumors were that one commander relied on Baedeker's guide, a popular handbook for tourists, to plot his route. Nevertheless the Germans arrived, greeted by cheering crowds.

Contrary to the impression created by the Hollywood movie *The Sound of Music,* most Austrians did not oppose the German invasion. In fact the Anschluss sparked vicious displays of antisemitism within Austria. Austrian

A member of the Reich Department of Health, Racial Hygiene, and Population Biology visits a Roma family in Vienna sometime in 1938 or 1939 to gather data. Such information was used to monitor Gypsies; for scholars it also provided material for publications and career advancement.

gentiles, sometimes urged on by Germans but often acting on their own, seized the opportunity to assail their Jewish compatriots. They stole their property, harassed and beat them, and subjected many to public rituals of humiliation. For example, in Vienna, crowds took delight in forcing professors, artists, journalists, and other prominent Austrian Jews to scrub streets with toothbrushes. Decades after the war a small statue in Vienna commemorates the "Jew with a toothbrush" and reminds Austrians of the complicity of ordinary people from their country in the crimes of Nazism.

The other European and international powers did not try to stop the German annexation of Austria. Many foreign observers saw the event simply as Germans taking control of their own backyard. Meanwhile German authorities together with local supporters moved quickly to implement the Nazi revolution in Austria. Measures against Jews, Gypsies, the disabled, and others that had been implemented over five years in Germany were rushed through in the new Nazi lands within months. Members of target groups in Austria had even fewer options to help themselves than did their counterparts within the pre-1938 German borders.

Initially there were some popular misgivings about the Anschluss within Germany itself. Many Germans worried that this blatant defiance of the Versailles settlement could mean war. When the response instead was accolades within Austria and assent around Europe, they too welcomed this destruction of an independent nation as a legitimate expression of German strength. Once again Hitler had followed his familiar pattern, push forward hard and wait to see if anyone pushes back. If not, keep pushing.

Memoirs by Austrian Jews provide moving accounts of the impact of the Anschluss. In her memoir, *Still Alive,* Ruth Kluger, a young girl in Vienna in 1938, recalls the events of that year. She remembers lying in her bed hearing bands of men march by outside singing the song about "Jewish blood" spurting from German knives. One day her mother sent her to see the movie *Snow White and the Seven Dwarfs.* The girl was afraid to go; she knew Jews were not allowed in the cinema. Ridiculous, her mother insisted; no one would bother a child. They did bother, young Ruth learned. She ended up sitting next to the teenaged leader of the neighborhood Nazi girls' club, who threatened and shamed her. Sometimes children grasped more quickly than adults how things had changed.

THE SUDETENLAND CRISIS

Emboldened by success in Austria, Hitler made his next move against Czechoslovakia, a country he had identified in 1937 as the first target of his planned expansion. He was willing to risk war; in fact he sought it and was disappointed in 1938 when it did not happen. With regard to Czechoslovakia the issue used to generate a crisis was the ethnic German minority in the Sudetenland, near the border with Germany.

In the summer of 1938, members of the ethnic German minority became increasingly vocal with complaints of mistreatment at the hands of the Czech government. Nazi agents from Germany encouraged and provoked their discontent. In response to reports that Hitler planned military action to rescue the ethnic Germans of the Sudetenland, the Czechs began to mobilize their own forces. They also appealed to the French and the British for help.

Alarmed at the risk of war, representatives of the European powers agreed to meet with Czech and German negotiators to seek a resolution. At the Munich Conference in September 1938, French and British delegates decided Czechoslovakia should cede the Sudetenland to Germany. The area had a substantial ethnic German population, they reasoned, and if they made this concession to Hitler's demands, he and his supporters would be satisfied.

Decades after the Munich Conference, it and its most famous spokesman, British prime minister Neville Chamberlain, are still synonymous with the term "appeasement." The term is almost always invoked with contempt, and Chamberlain is mocked for his triumphant announcement that he and his col-

*ved peace in their time. Some critics even suggest that the
were somehow responsible for the Second World War, as if a harder
.ـe from them in 1938 would have melted Nazi aggression.

Chamberlain and the others may have shown weakness but they wanted
peace, whereas Hitler was set on war. Instead of rejoicing at his successful
maneuver, Hitler felt cheated when he returned to Berlin with a negotiated
settlement giving Germany control of territories that had belonged to Czechoslovakia. Hitler worried that the optimum moment for war might have passed
him by, because Germany's enemies would now have time to prepare for confrontation. A show of force at Munich from the British and the French would
not have prevented war. It would only have moved it to a timetable that Hitler
himself considered preferable.

This time too there were misgivings at home. At the peak of the war
scare, Protestant church leaders sponsored prayers for peace that landed a number of pastors in prison for their implied criticism of Hitler's actions. Within
the army, some of the top brass worried about what seemed a slide toward a
war they thought Germany could not win. There were even some tentative
plans for a coup against Hitler in case it came to hostilities. All came to nothing.
Instead Hitler's successful bid for the Sudetenland—although he regarded it as
a failure—gave his prestige within Germany another substantial boost.

In 1939, just months after the Munich Conference granted Sudetenland
to Germany, German troops entered the rest of Czechoslovakia. On Hitler's
orders the state was dismantled. Parts were incorporated into the German
Reich, and other parts were set up as a protectorate, a kind of colony. Slovakia
became a semi-independent client state under the government of the antisemitic Catholic priest Josef Tiso.

Those who blame the supposed harshness of the Treaty of Versailles for
the rise and expansion of Nazism would do well to note the considerable territories the Germans had gained even before war began in 1939. By the end of
1938 Germany had already recouped most of its World War I losses. With the
destruction of Czechoslovakia in 1939, Germany acquired lands it had never
controlled before, but Hitler was not satisfied. His ambitions went far beyond
merely revising the terms of Versailles.

THE KRISTALLNACHT POGROM

The year 1938 also signaled a heightened wave of aggression in racial policies.
The most dramatic expression of this new stage of Nazism was the attack on

Jews in Germany and Austria on the night of 9–10 November 1938. Nazi leaders called the pogrom the *Kristallnacht* (in English, the "night of broken glass"), and that name continues to be used.

In October 1938, the German government expelled fourteen thousand Jews who resided in Germany but were citizens of Poland. The order followed a Polish decree requiring citizens living outside the country to revalidate their passports or lose the right to return. Worried they would be stuck with these people, German authorities struck first, brutally rounding up Jews of Polish citizenship and dumping them at the border. But Polish authorities refused them entry. Only after weeks in limbo, when Jews inside Poland promised them shelter, were they allowed into the country.

Among those thrown out of Germany were the parents and sister of Herschel Grynszpan, a seventeen-year-old student in Paris. Grynszpan read about the situation in French newspapers and learned details in a postcard from his sister. Days later, he went to the German embassy and shot an official. His motive, he told French police, was outrage at the treatment of his family and all Jews. Rumors of a homosexual liaison between Grynszpan and the German official subsequently surfaced, perhaps invented by Grynszpan to undermine the show trial the Germans planned for him in 1942. It has also been suggested that Grynszpan was trying to blackmail the official in order to get papers he needed to stay in France. In any case, for the Nazi leadership, this incident provided the excuse for a violent assault against Jews. Hitler, Goebbels, and other believers in the stab-in-the-back notion considered forcing Jews out of Germany to be a necessary step in preparing a successful war.

Nazi propaganda described the pogrom that followed the announcement of Grynszpan's shooting of the German diplomat as a spontaneous expression of hatred of Jews by the majority German population. In fact the event was the carefully prepared culmination of a period of increasing pressure on Jews in Germany. Even the date was chosen with care: 9 November, the date of Hitler's attempted putsch in 1923, was a holy day in the Nazi calendar.

Permission—and instructions—from above unleashed the hatred of Stormtroopers and other Nazi activists. All over Germany they torched synagogues and destroyed ritual objects associated with Judaism, such as Torah scrolls. Others joined in the attack, some driven by antisemitic fervor, others lured by the possibility of loot, still others just eager for action. Crowds smashed the windows of businesses owned by Jews; they vandalized and stole Jewish property. The attackers did not spare Jewish homes. They forced their way in, robbing, beating, raping, and demolishing. Memoirs describe the clouds of feathers that surrounded Jewish residences as the aggressors slashed bedding in their quest for valuables and their lust for destruction. They burned

A Jewish woman, expelled from Germany in October 1938, washes clothes in the Zbaszyn refugee camp in Poland. Initially some of the homeless Jews found shelter in the stables of a military riding school and in a flour mill. Later Jewish relief workers organized the refugee camp, which operated until the summer of 1939.

scores of synagogues all over Germany and Austria and killed about a hundred Jews. Nazi authorities rounded up some twenty-six thousand Jewish men and sent them to concentration camps. Those men seized in the Kristallnacht pogrom were the first Jews in Germany arrested simply for being Jewish.

Responses to the violence varied widely. Alfons Heck recounts how he and another boy eagerly joined a crowd singing as it stormed a synagogue. For them the pogrom was a chance to throw rocks and "smash some stuff." An outraged uncle caught them and dragged them away by the ears. Foreign journalists watched the event with horror. Their accounts differ considerably in the degree of popular participation they describe. Some observed how onlookers joined the rampage and plunder, whereas others sensed disapproval from ordinary citizens. (You can read some of those reports for yourself on the front pages of such well-known newspapers as the *New York Times*.)

Certainly the German public as a whole was less enthusiastic about Kristallnacht than the pogrom's instigators had hoped. In this case it seemed that misgivings had less to do with fear of war or support of Jews than with a dislike of disorder. There was grumbling about the mess, the disruption, and the general impropriety of such open violence. Still such uneasiness did not produce a general outcry. At most it took the form of private aid to acquaintances. Peter Gay, a young boy in Berlin in 1938, recalls how a non-Jewish friend of the family hid his father from the police for weeks during and after the pogrom. Much more commonly, misgivings prompted non-Jews simply to turn their backs on the violence.

Nazi authorities, always alert to public opinion, noticed even that low level of disapproval. It is no coincidence that Kristallnacht marked the last open pogrom they organized in Germany and annexed Austria. In the future they would avoid having reluctant "Aryans" witness wide-scale violence at home. It would prove easy enough to move blatant attacks further from the public eye.

As in the cases of the Anschluss and the Sudetenland crisis, success made Kristallnacht more palatable for nervous Germans. Many Jews, terrified by the open attack and acutely aware of their vulnerability, became desperate to leave Germany. So-called Aryans benefited from that desperation as they scooped up Jewish property at bargain-basement prices. No doubt many who had shaken their heads at the unruly mobs on 9 November nevertheless were willing to share in the spoils. And once they had the goods those Germans had a stake in the continuation of Nazi anti-Jewish policies.

Afterward the German government added insult to injury by requiring the Jewish community to pay for the material damage of Kristallnacht. It extorted an estimated $400 million from Jews for the death of the German diplomat and another $100 million for damages to property. That cynical policy no doubt furthered the false notion within Germany that the Jews were a bottomless source of wealth they did not deserve. Even the name *Kristallnacht,* chosen by Goebbels, focused on the destruction of Jewish shop windows, as if the pogrom were somehow merely about correcting economic injustices within Germany. In fact it was the synagogues, sites of Jewish religious and communal life, that were the first targets of attack.

On 10 November 1938, the morning after Kristallnacht, local residents watch the synagogue in Ober Ramstadt, Hesse burn. The fire department prevented the blaze from spreading to a nearby home but did not try to limit damage to the synagogue. Georg Schmidt, a young man from an anti-Nazi family, took this photograph.

As for Jews themselves, how did they react? Between 1933 and the outbreak of war in September 1939, approximately half of the Jews in Germany—some three hundred thousand people—left. Much of this exodus took place in the wake of Kristallnacht, from what had been Austria and the Sudetenland as well as from all over Germany. For most European Jews it took enormous perseverance and ingenuity to get out, to find somewhere to go, and to figure out ways to start new lives.

Successful relocation also took luck. Many Austrian, Czech, and German Jews saw the threat of Nazism and tried to move beyond its reach. Some had the resources, connections, or relatives necessary to get to Palestine, the United States, Canada, Australia, or Britain. Others, often blocked from those most desirable destinations, took refuge in Cuba, the Dominican Republic, China, or Turkey. Many found their way to neighboring European countries: France, the Netherlands, and Poland. How could they know that within years, in some cases only months, they would end up in Nazi hands once again?

EXPANSION OF THE CONCENTRATION CAMP SYSTEM

Open aggression in 1938 and 1939 meant expanding the network of concentration camps begun in 1933 with the creation of Dachau. The history of the camps provides a kind of microcosm of the development of Nazi persecutions.

The German word for concentration camp is *Konzentrationslager,* often abbreviated as "KZ" or "Lager." Throughout the 1930s the SS set up new camps so as to provide regional coverage. For example, Buchenwald, built in 1937, was located near Weimar; Sachsenhausen was not far from Berlin. Camps for women inmates, such as Ravensbrück, started up as well. After 1935 many German municipalities set up Gypsy camps into which police forced thousands of the country's thirty-five thousand Roma and Sinti, ostensibly in order to prevent crime. Those camps, parallel structures within the concentration camp system, became sites of anthropological research and compulsory sterilization as well as sources of forced labor. The anthropologists Dr. Robert Ritter and Eva Justin found human subjects for their studies of Gypsies in Marzahn. One of them was Otto Rosenberg, who, as part of the project, slept overnight at Justin's home in Berlin and was served kohlrabi by her mother.

Concentration camps echoed the regime's ideological goals. Originally their founders described their purpose as reeducation. In the camps, political opponents—Communists, Social Democrats, liberals—and so-called antisocial elements—vagrants, Gypsies, homosexuals, Jehovah's Witnesses, and others—were to be turned into useful citizens. Authorities also spoke of the camps as a place to put troublemakers into "protective custody for the restoration of law and order." Under that guise, the Nazi government gave itself the legal right to imprison suspects without a trial. From their start the camps were brutal places with terrible conditions for inmates. Torture, beatings, and deprivation were the order of the day.

As we have seen elsewhere, the move from Nazism's revolutionary phase to the consolidation of power did not mitigate the suffering of its targets. Instead that transition gave violence new forms backed by the full weight of the state and its institutions. The camps were an example. Between 1933 and

In November 1938, police in Baden-Baden march Jewish men, including guests at the spa, through town to the synagogue. There SS men forced the Jews to read from Mein Kampf and sing the "Horst Wessel Song." Police later sent many of the men to Dachau.

1939 the number of inmates skyrocketed, as attacks on target groups proliferated and increased in intensity.

The Nazi revolution of 1933 and 1934 brought large numbers of Communists into the camps. Homosexuals and Jehovah's Witnesses followed. The Sterilization Law of July 1933 brought a wave of arrests of supposed degenerates. Despite the Concordat with the Vatican, Nazi suspicion of the Christian churches also brought people into the camps. In violation of the agreement reached with the pope, Nazi authorities placed restrictions on Catholic priests, in particular regarding youth work. Some German priests refused to comply, and more than one hundred served terms in the camps as a result.

The period of routinization also enlarged the camps. When German courts and police tightened the enforcement of antihomosexual laws, they caused a jump in camp populations. At the same time the authorities became more proactive, arresting men and then pressuring them to reveal the names of their sexual partners, so that they could be charged as well. The Nuremberg Laws created a whole new category of crime, *Rassenschande,* or crimes against the blood. The 1936 Berlin Olympics meant a "cleanup" of vagrants, prostitutes, pickpockets, and Gypsies. The result: more people dumped into camps.

In some cases police created new camps, such as Marzahn, outside of Berlin, which was set up especially for Gypsies. Meanwhile existing camps, among them Dachau, continued to expand.

Persecution of Jehovah's Witnesses

German Jehovah's Witnesses added to the population of the concentration camps as well. Arrests of group members peaked in 1937 and 1938. German authorities cooked up many reasons to be suspicious of them. Their organization had international connections, in particular to the United States, although the same was true of the Church of Jesus Christ of Latter-Day Saints, whose members were not generally persecuted in the Third Reich. Because Jehovah's Witnesses emphasized the Old Testament and believed Jews had to return to the "Holy Land" before the world would end, their critics accused them of being pro-Jewish and Zionist. Their door-to-door preaching made them an easily identifiable, unpopular, marginal minority whom other Christians ridiculed as a cult. Mockers dubbed them "Bible students," "Bible-worms," and "Bible-bees."

Perhaps most significant at a time when Germany was preparing for war, many Jehovah's Witnesses refused to serve in the military. Nor would they vote, give the Hitler salute, or do anything that would imply supremacy of the nation over God. Few in number, honest, and law abiding, Jehovah's Witnesses never posed a real threat to the stability of the Nazi German state. Evidence suggests that at least some of their leaders tried in 1933 to win the favor of Hitler's government by insisting that Witnesses were loyal Germans who did not look kindly on Jews. Nevertheless their insistence that their loyalty belonged to Jehovah alone and their firm refusal to abandon their beliefs made them dangerous in the eyes of a regime that tolerated no rivals for the allegiances of the German people.

Nazi authorities used their usual weapon—force—against the Jehovah's Witnesses, but with less success than they expected. Only about twenty thousand Jehovah's Witnesses lived in Germany in the 1930s; approximately ten thousand of them were arrested over the years and sent to concentration camps, where they were beaten and tormented like their fellow inmates. Some were executed for refusing military service. Some of those who managed to stay out of the camps had their children taken from them; many lost their jobs, their pensions, and their civil rights. Officials dragged them before special courts for refusing to enlist, to undertake air raid watches, or to stop their preaching.

The Jehovah's Witnesses proved remarkably strong against assault. Camp authorities gave most of them the option of release if they signed a statement repudiating their beliefs. Very few did so. Instead they concentrated on building a strong network within the camps. They sang hymns, preached to the guards, and continued to meet as best they could to provide psychological and emotional support to one another. They interpreted ridicule and persecution as a fulfillment of prophecy, proof that they were correct in their faith. Those who remained outside tried to keep the faith as well. When police arrested one local leader, another took his or her place. They persisted in meeting and distributing literature, even to Nazi Party headquarters. In all, between twenty-five hundred and five thousand Jehovah's Witnesses were killed in German camps and prisons between 1933 and 1945.

One such victim was Wolfgang Kusserow. In 1942, Kusserow, a twenty-year-old Witness, was executed for refusing to perform military service. One of eleven children in his family, he assured his parents, brothers, and sisters in a farewell letter, "Our faith will be victorious."

Helene Gotthold also paid for her faith with her life. The mother of two children, Gotthold was arrested many times for continuing her Jehovah's Witness activities despite the government's ban. Condemned to death, she was beheaded in Berlin in 1944.

German authorities viewed the Jehovah's Witnesses more as an annoyance than a major threat. Nevertheless members of the group suffered terribly during the Third Reich. Their strength and resolve earned them a kind of grudging respect, even from some top Nazis. Himmler, for example, considered using them to resettle parts of the territories to be conquered by Germany. They were docile, obedient, and productive, he said, perfect qualities for pioneers. Inside the camps Jehovah's Witnesses sometimes functioned as personal servants to the SS. Who else could be trusted as personal barbers wielding razors? Generally it seemed the Jehovah's Witnesses retained the respect of their fellow inmates and tried to do what they could within the camps to alleviate the sufferings of those even worse off than they were.

The third phase of Nazi development—open aggression in 1938–1939—added to the camp network in other ways too. The annexation of Austria meant building camps there; Mauthausen is the best known. The crisis around the Sudetenland brought some German Protestant clergy into the camps, mostly for short sentences. In November 1938 arrests of Jews during the Kristallnacht pogrom added about twenty-six thousand male inmates. Some died in the camps, many from being beaten; others were released in exchange for huge payments and often agreement to leave the country.

DIPLOMATIC INITIATIVES

Throughout this third phase of Nazi development—preparation for war—
Hitler's approach to foreign policy was to talk peace and plan for war. His diplomats had been active during the 1930s making pacts that, like the Concordat
with the Vatican and the Non-Aggression agreement with Poland, were
intended to be broken. In 1935, for example, Hitler signed the Anglo-German
Naval Agreement with Britain, which he then began spending enormous
amounts of money to contravene. The agreement was supposed to prevent a
naval arms race by limiting the German fleet to a certain percentage of the
British navy. Instead it got the British to approve a German violation of the
Treaty of Versailles. Meanwhile Hitler ordered construction of as many new
superbattleships and aircraft carriers as he pleased, all designed to be used
against Britain and the United States, on the assumption that the British would
not discover the violations until it was too late. Although only two of the
planned ships could be completed before the war was over, German intentions
were nevertheless clearly the exact opposite of the peaceful arrangement promised by the agreement.

In May 1939 Germany signed the Pact of Steel with Italy, promising
friendship and mutual aid. This arrangement would lay the foundation for
what would develop into the wartime alliance called the Rome-Berlin Axis.
The summer of 1939 also brought nonaggression treaties with Estonia, Latvia,
and Denmark. The crowning achievement of this phase of preparation for war,
however, came in August 1939 with the German-Soviet Non-Aggression Pact,
sometimes referred to as the Hitler-Stalin Pact or the Molotov-Ribbentrop
Pact, after the two foreign ministers involved.

The deal had two parts. The first included public proclamations of friendship and nonaggression between the two rival powers. To a world that had
seen six years of Nazi attacks on Communists and the proliferation of German
anti-Soviet propaganda, this part of the pact was shocking enough, but the
second part went much further. In a secret arrangement, Hitler's and Stalin's
negotiators agreed to divide eastern Europe between German and Soviet
spheres of interest. They settled on a line through the middle of Poland as their
secret boundary. Initially, the Baltic states were also divided, with Estonia and
Latvia going to the Soviets and Lithuania to Germany, but the Germans later
traded most of Lithuania for more of Poland.

For Hitler the pact with the Soviet Union required some fairly dramatic
reversals. In a sudden about-face he dropped his public anti-Communist stance

to proclaim friendship with his ideological foe Stalin. Given Hitler's goals, the gains were well worth the inconvenience. By cutting such a deal Hitler secured the eastern border of Poland in case of war. Instead of worrying that the Soviet Union might attack invading Germans, he could rest assured that the Soviets would be busy securing their own designated sphere of interest. Germany would have a free hand in Poland, at least in the half that the secret pact reserved for German control. Even more important, given Hitler's plans, he could wage war with the West with impunity. War with the Soviet Union, which Hitler believed was ultimately necessary to accomplish his mission, could wait.

In the meantime, Hitler and his henchmen spent the spring and summer of 1939 preparing for war. They conducted a massive propaganda campaign against Poland, accusing the Polish government and people of terrible viola-tions of the rights of ethnic German minorities.

Already on 30 January 1939, Hitler had proclaimed his vision of the war to come to the German representatives in the Reichstag. As his speech made clear, it would be a war for race and space. "Europe cannot find peace until the Jewish question has been solved," Hitler told his audience. By the end of his remarks he had become more explicit:

> In the course of my life I have very often been a prophet, and have usually been ridiculed for it. During the time of my struggle for power it was in the first instance only the Jewish race that received my prophecies with laughter when I said that I would one day take over the leadership of the State, and with it that of the whole nation, and that I would then among other things settle the Jewish problem. Their laughter was uproarious, but I think that for sometime now they have been laughing on the other side of their face. Today I will once more be a prophet: if the international Jewish financiers in and outside Europe should suc-ceed in plunging the nations once more into a world war, then the result will not be the Bolshevizing of the earth, and thus the victory of Jewry, but the annihilation of the Jewish race in Europe! (Noakes and Pridham 3:1049)

FLIGHT FROM NAZI GERMANY

Not everyone was deaf to Hitler's boastful warnings. Ever since 1933 large numbers of Germans had been leaving the country, fearful for their own safety. Finding a place of refuge could prove very difficult for all kinds of reasons. Thousands of German Communists fled to the Soviet Union after Hitler came to power. There some of them ran into troubles of their own with the paranoid

In February 1939, three months after Kristallnacht, a carnival parade in the south German town of Neustadt mocks Jews. The float features a burning synagogue; the man in front represents Moses with the Ten Commandments. Note the large false noses on some of the men.

and repressive regime of Josef Stalin. The purges of the 1930s did not spare these newcomers; Stalin and his associates had some evicted from the Communist Party, forced into labor camps in Siberia, imprisoned, and even killed. Still, to an important extent, German Communism would survive the Nazi era in the Soviet Union.

Other Germans also tried to get out or found themselves refused reentry by the Nazi government when they returned from trips abroad. Jews, liberals, pacifists, openly gay and lesbian activists, outspoken critics of National Socialism—all kinds of people went into exile. The writer Thomas Mann ended up in the United States as did the physicist Albert Einstein, the playwright Bertolt Brecht, the filmmaker Fritz Lang, and the actress Marlene Dietrich. In fact exiles from Nazi Germany played an enormous role in building the Hollywood film industry in the 1930s and 1940s.

The United States was not the only destination for exiles. International feminist activists and longtime companions Lida Gustava-Heymann and Anita

A float in the Shrove Tuesday parade in the German Catholic town of Singen am Hohentwiel in February 1939 features members of the local jesters club feeding "Jews"—men wearing paper noses—to the "Jew Devourer," a voracious monster.

Augspurg stayed in Switzerland after a trip rather than risk imprisonment back home. In the summer of 1939 some seventeen thousand Jews from Germany, Austria, and Poland made their way to Shanghai. Unable to get visas permitting them to enter places more culturally familiar to them, such as the United States and Great Britain, they seized the chance to get out of Europe even though it meant leaving behind almost everything they knew. Many of them would survive the war, including the Japanese occupation of China.

One family that left Germany for Shanghai in 1939 included seven-year-old Karin Zacharias. The Zachariases lived in a town in East Prussia not far from Königsberg (later the Russian city of Kaliningrad). Karin's father saw the writing on the wall early on with Hitler's government in Germany. Since the mid-1930s he wanted to get the family out of Europe, but his wife was not willing to go without her aging parents, who refused to leave their home.

Only in 1937, after the two older people both died, could the Zachariases begin to tackle the enormous project of getting out of Germany and finding a new home. Karin's father, educated as a lawyer, needed to learn a trade in order to get exit papers, so he became a welder. The family had to jump through endless bureaucratic hoops. To facilitate the process they relocated to Berlin.

Joseph Fiszman, a Yiddish writer from Warsaw, poses with Chinese children in Shanghai. In late 1939, Fiszman and his father fled to Vilna and then Japan, on visas obtained from the diplomat Sugihara. In Japan, they bought pearl necklaces for the women in their family, expecting to be reunited. Instead the men were deported to Shanghai, where they survived the war. The women, trapped in Warsaw, did not.

Finally in 1939 they left for China, where they would remain until 1948, when they were allowed to enter the United States. Karin, daughter of an assimilated German Jewish family, spent much of her childhood and her early teenage years in Shanghai. Karin Pardo, as she is now called, spent most of her life in Chicago and has many close friends who also grew up in China. Her experience is a reminder that the Holocaust was truly a worldwide event.

The Voyage of the St. Louis

Even for those who recognized the dangers of Nazi Germany it was very hard to escape. Money and occupational skills such as medical training helped but did not guarantee success. For some people, distant destinations in Africa, India, and the Caribbean proved the only possibility, and conditions upon arrival could be difficult. After war broke out, many Jews were interned as enemy aliens. In 1939, American immigration authorities decided to allow only about twenty thousand Germans and Austrians to immigrate to the United States. There was no separate quota for European Jews.

Of course a large proportion of the Germans and Austrians who applied for entry into the United States were Jewish. Only those who had relatives in the United States willing to sponsor them would be admitted. Sponsors had to demonstrate that they had enough money to support their European relatives once they arrived, if necessary. They also had to make their way through a mountain of red tape. Many Jews in Europe spent years trying to get visas to the United States, and most of them failed. It was no easier to get into Canada or Australia. In times of economic depression most people in those countries worried that immigrants would cost money and take away jobs.

In early 1939, the government of Cuba agreed to grant visas to a number of Jews desperate to get out of Europe. Between eight and nine hundred people set sail from Hamburg to Havana on board the steamship *St. Louis*. Before the ship came in, Cuban authorities changed their minds about the refugees; when the *St. Louis* arrived, they refused to allow the passengers to disembark. The ship remained offshore for days while representatives of the passengers tried to negotiate with the Cubans or find some alternative destination. Finally the *St. Louis* left Havana. Sailing slowly up the coast of Florida, its captain radioed to officials all along the way in the United States and Canada, but no one would permit the ship to dock.

The crew had no choice but to return to Europe. Negotiations by Jewish organizations managed to get refuge for many of the passengers from the *St.*

Louis in Great Britain, France, and the Netherlands. In the years ahead some of those people, like most of those forced to return to Germany, would end up dead at Nazi hands, but some also found ways to stay alive. Careful research at the U.S. Holocaust Memorial Museum has traced all but a handful of the passengers of the *St. Louis*. Their stories show that foresight alone could not save a Jew from the Nazi trap. Connections, money, and determination were all factors, but so, above all, was luck, or whatever one might call chance at a time when no Jews could be counted lucky.

THE PROGRAM TO KILL
HANDICAPPED CHILDREN

Like Jews in Germany, people deemed handicapped also experienced the open Nazi aggression of 1938–1939. Hitler and other proponents of so-called racial purification would have to wait for the cover provided by war to implement murder on a mass scale, but by 1939 they felt confident enough to take steps in that direction. They began with the most defenseless segment of an already vulnerable group: the children.

In the winter of 1938–1939, a man named Knauer wrote to Hitler. He and his wife had a deformed baby. They wanted to have "this creature," as he called the child, killed. Hitler seized on the request as a way to begin having children who were considered "unworthy of living" killed. He assigned his personal physician, Dr. Karl Brandt, and the head of his personal staff in the Nazi Party, Philipp Bouhler, to deal with the Knauer case. Hitler instructed Brandt and Bouhler to inform the doctors involved that they could kill the child. Brandt and Bouhler were to tell the doctors that if any legal action were taken against them, it would be thrown out of court.

Hitler authorized Brandt and Bouhler to deal with similar cases in the same way. They recruited a group of officials and doctors who were positively disposed toward such ideas. The group's official title was the Reich Committee for the Scientific Registration of Serious Hereditarily and Congenitally Based Illnesses. By August 1939 the Reich Committee required all midwives and doctors to report the existence of any children with deformities. It passed the forms on to three pediatricians. They marked each form with a plus or a minus sign to indicate whether the particular child was to die or be allowed to live. Those doctors never saw the children whose fates they decided.

Brandt, Bouhler, and their committee were not confident that most of the German people would support the killing of children with deformities, so they shrouded the process in secrecy. Still they had no trouble finding enough personnel to participate in these early stages of the program. The program to kill deformed children served Nazi planners as a kind of trial balloon, sent up to test reactions. The responses they perceived and the cooperation they received from the relevant professions indicated that it was possible to go even further in attacks on people considered handicapped.

5

EXPERIMENTS IN BRUTALITY, 1939–1940

WAR AGAINST POLAND AND THE SO-CALLED
EUTHANASIA PROGRAM

In 1939 Hitler got his war. It would not be against Czechoslovakia as he had hoped but against Poland. Still Poland was not a surprising target; along with many of Germany's leading military men, Hitler had always considered existence of an independent Polish state to be anathema, and of course for Germany, Poland was the gateway to the east, where Hitler intended to find Lebensraum—living space—for his superior "Aryan race."

With the German invasion and conquest in 1939, Poland would become a laboratory for experiments in spatial expansion and racial ideology. In Poland the Germans seized control of large numbers of Slavs, Jews, and Gypsies, those people Nazi teachings described as subhuman. In Poland, German planners began to implement schemes to recast the face of Europe. They forced millions of people to move, resettled those they deemed desirable, and robbed, evicted, enslaved, and eventually killed those they did not want. For two years, even before construction of the first killing centers in 1941, the German occupiers of Poland tried out various solutions to what they considered their population problems, above all their self-made "Jewish problem."

This first stage of the war also brought experiments of another kind—in the murder of people deemed handicapped. In 1939 and 1940 the so-called Euthanasia Program got into full swing within Germany. The word "euthanasia" comes from the Greek for "good death" or "good dying." In the Nazi case the label itself was a lie, suggesting as it did that the killings had something to do with concern for the patients' well-being. They did not. The program's initiators did not care about the suffering of their targets but asked only whether those people could contribute to the supremacy of the "Aryan race."

As in Poland, planners and functionaries in the Euthanasia Program tested methods and developed techniques to implement the teachings of race and space. The results involved learning how to kill large numbers of people and then dispose of their bodies most easily. In the years ahead the lessons of this early program against disabled people would be applied again and again.

This chapter traces Nazi German experiments in brutality in 1939 and 1940. From the outset we can identify two principles that seem to have guided German policy, both in defeated Poland and with regard to people deemed handicapped. First, Nazi leaders encouraged experimentation—even rivalry and organizational confusion—among the people who carried out their plans. Rather than easing the situation of those targeted for persecution, such chaotic conditions often increased the victims' vulnerability and exacerbated their suffering. Second, German decision makers endorsed the notion of divide and conquer. Whenever possible they stirred up dissension and hatred among those over whom they ruled in order to advance their own cause. That kind of cynical manipulation by Nazi overlords of their subject peoples added to the wartime misery too, first in Poland and later throughout Europe.

THE GERMANS IN POLAND

Blitzkrieg

On 1 September 1939 German forces invaded Poland. German planners tried to disguise this act of aggression as a defensive measure. They dressed 150 concentration camp inmates in Polish uniforms and used them to stage a mock attack on a German radio station near the border. The corpses of those men then served as "proof" of Polish belligerence and justification for attack.

Hitler and his inner circle were not confident that the German public was ready for war. They had already spent the summer of 1939 rousing anti-Polish sentiment in Germany, using the newspapers to publicize wild accusations of Polish crimes against the ethnic German minority in Poland. Still, within Germany the initial reaction to war was cautious. When Hitler appeared on his balcony in Berlin following announcements of the attack on Poland, he expected to be greeted by throngs of zealous supporters. Instead the crowd was so small that he went back inside to avoid embarrassment.

The assault of 1 September 1939 did not take the Poles completely by surprise, because they had had plenty of opportunities to observe German saber-rattling in the preceding months. They were, however, stunned by the rapidity of the German advance. The Germans' technological advantage enabled them to wage a blitzkrieg—a war at lightning speed. First their planes pounded the Poles from the sky. Then tanks rolled in to crush resistance and clear the way for occupying troops. With 11 cavalry brigades, a single tank division, and 750 armored vehicles, the Poles were no match for the Germans, who smashed into Poland with 15 tank divisions and some 3,600 armored vehicles. Jack Pomerantz, at the time a young Jewish man in the Polish town of Radzyn, recalls that he had never seen an airplane until the German attack on 1 September 1939. That day the sky was black with them.

The repercussions were enormous. France and Britain declared war on Germany, although for the time being they remained outside the fray. The Hitler-Stalin Pact of August 1939 assured the Germans of nonaggression from the Soviet Union. As the secret arrangements had anticipated, the German offensive was followed, beginning on 17 September, by a Soviet advance into Polish territory from the east, up to the line previously agreed upon. By early October, the Germans had forced the Poles on their side to surrender. Meanwhile eastern Poland would remain in Soviet control until mid-1941.

In the 1939 attack Germans killed at least seventy thousand Poles. German losses were much lower but still considerable, some eleven thousand men. At least 1 million Poles were taken prisoner—many by the Germans but also a substantial number by the Soviets. Anti-Polish prejudices and a military culture that called for absolute destruction of the enemy fueled German brutality against the Poles. The assumption that Poles were dangerous bandits, irregular combatants who attacked from concealed positions, served the Germans as justification for a massive assault on soldiers and civilians alike.

The Polish leadership fled to London to establish a government-in-exile. Members of the Polish army buried huge caches of arms rather than relinquish them to the Germans. Those weapons would provide the nucleus for the underground armies in the half decade of struggle that still lay ahead for the Poles.

Division of Poland

From the outset, "divide and conquer" was the German byword in Poland. The arrangement with the Soviet Union reflected that approach as did the German decision to divide its own part of conquered Poland into two parts. The western areas, known as the "incorporated territories," were annexed by the Greater German Reich. This area included such important cities as Danzig—now called Gdansk—and Lodz, which the German leadership would later rechristen Litzmannstadt. The incorporated territories were home to 10 million people, around 80 percent of them ethnic Poles. Also living there were ethnic Germans, Jews, and small numbers of other groups, including Gypsies, Czechs, and Ukrainians.

The Germans called the remaining part of their Polish territory the General Government and administered it like a colony. Warsaw, Krakow, and Lublin were its major cities. Under the leadership of Governor General Dr. Hans Frank, a longtime associate of Hitler, the General Government became a key site of Nazi brutality. Much of the mass killing of Jews after 1941 would be done there; plans to reduce Poles to slaves of Germany also found early implementation in the General Government.

Competing Authorities and German Plans for the Poles

Germans, in particular Nazi Germans, are often described as hyperefficient and organized. German rule in the territories of occupied Poland, however, contradicts that stereotype. Rather than orderly, it was chaotic, characterized by overlapping jurisdictions and competing authorities. The German military was involved as was the SS under Heinrich Himmler. Hans Frank and his administration in the General Government played an important role; so did Hermann Göring, Hitler's deputy and head of the Four-Year Plan for the German economy. Local Nazis got involved, especially in the incorporated territories, as did German police and representatives of the interior ministry.

Almost every ambitious German Nazi activist, military man, and bureaucrat wanted a piece of the action. So did many German women—social workers, teachers, nurses, and others—who sought adventure and new career opportunities. Germans who wanted to get ahead in defeated Poland found it expedient to further Nazi goals. Whether in the incorporated territories or in the General Government, they tried to distinguish themselves from their colleagues and rivals by being more effective—that is, harsher—and more ambitious—that is, more brutal—in their treatment of the local populations.

Hitler and his inner circle had grandiose plans for Polish territories. Initially they intended to force the ethnic Poles farther east, to confine Jews to some desolate reservation, and to establish an area of pure "Aryan"/German settlement. Although details remained vague, implementation began immediately.

On 7 September 1939, Reinhard Heydrich, head of the German Reich Security Main Office, issued an order to the special units of police and SS under his jurisdiction. It would be necessary, he instructed, to destroy the leadership class in Poland and expel all Jews from areas in German hands. In short, as he told a subordinate, the "nobility, clergy, and Jews must be killed."

Heydrich's position was in line with the views of his bosses Hitler and Himmler. They wanted to reduce the Poles to a people of slaves, to destroy their intellectuals and their sense of tradition—anything that might give them a way to organize against Germany. Accordingly they encouraged German forces to target Polish Catholic priests. In the opening months of the war, Germans shot fifteen hundred priests and imprisoned countless others. They also humiliated, arrested, and murdered many other prominent Poles, including journalists, professors, and artists.

German authorities prohibited any activities that advanced the education of Poles, fostered communal ties, or promoted national feelings. They imposed curfews and seized Polish businesses. They shut down Polish newspapers and

The execution of Piotr Sosnowski, a Roman Catholic priest, by Germans and local ethnic German militia in October 1939 near Bydgoszcz (Bromberg). Father Sosnowski was one of a group of forty-five Poles forced to dig a grave in the forest and then shot into it.

used forced labor and public hangings to make examples of Poles who defied them. Members of the SS, police, and regular military, along with local collaborators, also terrorized Poles in less organized ways that included theft, beating, castration, and rape.

The war in 1939 brought massive expansion of the network of concentration and labor camps. Some Poles were forced to build roads and dams in labor camps, where the terrible conditions were often deadly. Others were sent to Germany. The existing camps in Germany could not hold all of the new inmates, so German authorities also set up camps in their newly acquired territories—places such as Majdanek, near Lublin, or Plaschow, outside Krakow, depicted in Steven Spielberg's movie *Schindler's List*.

Officials also introduced a whole range of measures intended to differentiate Poles and Germans, two groups that in fact were not always easy to separate in a part of Europe that had traditionally been ethnically mixed. Poles were not permitted to say "Heil Hitler," nor could they serve Germans in shops. Laws forbade friendships between Germans and Poles and criminalized sexual relations. Nevertheless, sexual assault of Polish women by German men was common. Later in the war German military authorities would force some Polish gentile women into brothels to serve German men and non-Germans who fought for the Reich.

Most of these measures applied to Polish gentiles and Jews alike, but sometimes the Germans showed additional, often improvised brutality toward their numerous, new Jewish subjects. In the 1930s far more Jews lived in Poland than in Germany. Germany's half million Jews in 1933 made up less than 1 percent of the population; Poland's more than 3 million Jews in 1939 represented approximately 10 percent.

The first phase of the war became a kind of open season against Polish Jews for Stormtroopers, SS, Nazi Party members, and unruly soldiers. Undisciplined and often drunk, they roamed around Polish territories burning, looting, and raping. The distinctive appearance of Orthodox Jewish men made them favorite targets for ridicule and violence. Rowdy Germans pulled out their beards and forced them to crawl in the street. Thugs attacked synagogues, where they desecrated ritual objects and abused the observant.

Hostage takings and demands for ransom were common. On 18 October 1939, Germans murdered one hundred Jews in a café in Lodz and forced others to pay for their lives. Similar incidents occurred in many cities and towns.

Ethnic Germans and Resettlement Schemes

Nazi racial policy had two sides: attack on people deemed undesirable and advancement of those considered "Aryan." In 1939 and 1940 the second part

In late 1939, SS personnel lead Polish women from the Pawiak and Mokotow prisons in nearby Warsaw into the forest to be killed. Members of the Polish underground sent this photograph to the Polish government-in-exile in London to illustrate German terror in occupied Poland.

of that scheme included locating ethnic Germans, people living outside Germany who identified themselves culturally as Germans (but not as Jews). In 1939 German experts estimated there to be about seven hundred thousand ethnic Germans in Poland alone.

German forces used the ethnic Germans to increase the terror of the early months of the war. Some ethnic Germans were killed by their Polish neighbors for helping the invading Germans. The numbers are unclear; respectable estimates range from two to five thousand such casualties, but official German reports claimed that vengeful Poles had slaughtered fifty-eight thousand ethnic Germans in early September 1939. That charge served to whip up hatred against Poles within Germany and also helped the SS form ethnic Germans into vigilante groups that attacked Poles and stole their property.

Many German officials who flocked into the newly conquered Polish territories busied themselves drawing up lists of people who should count as ethnic Germans. They organized programs to relocate them to the most desirable areas and evict the Poles who had been living there.

Plans for resettlement went even further. In October and November 1939 German diplomats worked out deals with Estonia, Latvia, and the Soviet Union so that ethnic Germans in those parts of Europe would also be brought "home into the Reich." The idea was to move those ethnic Germans out of the Baltic states and eastern Poland into the newly incorporated territories. Of course moving ethnic Germans in meant moving other people out.

By 1940 some two hundred thousand ethnic Germans who had signed up for resettlement needed homes. That year German police forced 325,000 Poles to leave the incorporated territories for the General Government. Often they were given only hours to get out, with instructions to leave their houses swept and the keys in the cupboard for the new inhabitants. Meanwhile, in the General Government nothing awaited the deportees but misery.

In late 1939 and 1940 German police evicted tens of thousands of Polish Jews from their homes and squeezed them into ghettos in the cities. The most desirable residences and businesses went to ethnic Germans or Germans from the Reich. Poor properties were allotted to Polish gentiles.

Individual Initiatives—The Eichmann Example

Some German officials took their own initiatives against people whom Nazi ideology deemed inferior. By doing so they hoped to catch the attention of their bosses and advance their own careers. For example, in the fall of 1939, Adolf Eichmann (1906–1962), an ambitious bureaucrat in Heydrich's Reich Security Main Office, began to organize transports of Jews to the General Government—from Vienna, from Silesia in the incorporated territories, and from parts of the former Czechoslovakia.

After the war, when he was tried in Israel for his role in the Holocaust, Eichmann would insist that he had never been an antisemite. It does seem that in Eichmann's case, careerism was a more powerful motivation than antisemitism. In any case Eichmann played a central role organizing forced emigration of Austrian Jews in 1938 and of Czech Jews a year later. Throughout 1942 and 1943 he would be instrumental in arranging transportation of Jews from all over Europe to killing centers. He also coordinated deportation of Hungarian Jews to Auschwitz in 1944. In 1962 Adolf Eichmann was hanged in Israel.

Eichmann, trained as an expert in Jewish affairs, had no formal authorization for his 1939 project. Nor had he made any arrangements for the Jews when they arrived in the General Government. Instead his men simply dumped their prisoners off at a place called Nisko, near the city of Lublin, and told them to get lost. Most of the Jews fled into the woods, and the Germans shot those who returned.

As the Nisko incident illustrates, competition among German authorities often made the situation of the people they targeted worse. Sometimes, however, the resulting disorganization also undermined the Germans' ability to achieve their goals. By early 1941, top Nazis had to stop sending Poles to the General Government, because the situation had become too unstable. Hans Frank announced he could not take any more Poles in his area. Göring agreed that it was economically unwise to keep up the transports. Neither man was motivated by humanitarianism. Both were interested above all in expanding their own power, and during 1941 both would be instrumental in moving German policy from the confused resettlements and expulsions of 1939 and 1940 to the so-called Final Solution of the Jewish Question: annihilation.

Policies of Divide and Conquer and Protests against German Brutality

All of the German schemes in Poland relied on the notion of divide and conquer. Privileging ethnic Germans turned their neighbors against them. Dangling promises of Jewish property in front of gentile Poles gave them a stake in attacks on Jews and encouraged them to betray Jews to the Germans.

SS leader Himmler explicitly encouraged his men to do all they could to turn ethnic groups within Poland against one another. It was a good idea to recruit local policemen and mayors from minority groups, he suggested. That way the majority's anger would be diverted from the Germans onto those petty officials. Accordingly Germans in the General Government often used Ukrainians and Belorussians against ethnic Poles and Jews. In many cases German authorities relied on local Polish gentiles to point out who was Jewish.

Some people spoke out against German atrocities in Poland. Shocked by the slaughter of Polish Catholic priests, Roman Catholic leaders in Poland and even some Germans appealed to the Vatican. Perhaps Hitler would listen to the pope, they reasoned.

Many people begged the pope to take action, but Pope Pius XII remained silent. His reasons are unclear. He may have believed that a strict policy of neutrality was the most powerful position the Vatican could take. Perhaps he feared reprisals against Catholics within Germany, or against the Vatican itself. A staunch opponent of Communism, he may have thought that Nazi Germany—even given its excesses—was still preferable to Soviet domination of Europe. The anti-Communist argument, however, rings hollow for 1939, when Nazi Germany and the Soviet Union worked in tandem to dismember

Poland, and both powers singled out Polish Catholic clergy for abuse. In any case, the pope's silence in the fall of 1939—when the victims of German aggression were priests in his own church—would make it hard for him to speak out later in the face of crimes against Jews.

Some members of the German army also protested the brutality around them. The best known case involved General Johannes Blaskowitz, commander of a military region in occupied Poland. In early 1940 Blaskowitz sent a long memorandum directly to Hitler. It provided specific examples of German crimes against civilians. For example, Blaskowitz described how a drunk German policeman beat a Polish man to death and forced a woman who may have been his wife to bury the body while scores of Germans and Poles looked on. Blaskowitz also told about some German soldiers who raped a teenaged Jewish girl in a cemetery. His account included many other cases of viciousness on the part of German police and SS men.

Such behavior was counterproductive, Blaskowitz warned. It would lead to demoralization and a breakdown in discipline among the German forces. It would stir up bad press abroad, he wrote, and alienate even those elements of the population that might otherwise have been sympathetic to the Germans. According to Blaskowitz, German abuses would drive Polish Jews and gentiles together. Polish gentiles were particularly worried by German brutality toward the Jews, Blaskowitz reported, because they feared that anything done to Jews would eventually be done to them too.

Hitler dismissed Blaskowitz's memorandum as childish and naive. One could not "win a war with Salvation Army tactics," he allegedly responded. You might expect that Blaskowitz was shot or imprisoned for daring to send his report, but he was not. Instead he was merely transferred out of Poland. Others were happy to take over his powerful position there.

Over time such protests ceased. Other military men who felt as Blaskowitz did in the fall of 1939 probably got used to conditions or forgot their misgivings in the face of Germany's dramatic military triumphs. Meanwhile, those who showed they were willing or even eager to fight a war of atrocity found themselves favored for promotions. By consistently rewarding behavior that furthered the goals of race and space, the Nazi leadership made sure that it always had a supply of ambitious, loyal individuals at every level of the hierarchy.

As the case of Blaskowitz indicates, Nazi Germany did not need unanimity in order to function. The Third Reich was not merely the work of "true believers"—fanatics who blindly endorsed every detail of Hitler's ideology. It also built on the efforts of critical Nazis and even opponents of Nazism, people who grumbled about some of its excesses even while they applied their energies and abilities to ensuring its stability. Not mass brainwashing but the participation of ordinary people of all kinds enabled the Nazi system to operate as it did.

Ghettoization of Polish Jews

At first German decision makers were not sure what to do with the many Jews who fell into their hands in 1939. Not until 1941 would they cross the line to regarding total mass murder as the "solution" to the "Jewish problem." From the outset, however, they did all they could to isolate Polish Jews from the rest of the population. They targeted Jews in particular ways in order to make them so vulnerable and contemptible that non-Jews would lose any sympathy for them and would worry only about how to avoid being treated that badly themselves.

Ghettoization, the stopgap measure that German authorities developed in late 1939 and early 1940, was a logical extension of the approach of divide and conquer. All over Polish territories German officials forced Jews out of their homes, in villages, small towns, and cities, into designated urban areas called ghettos. There the Jews were to be concentrated and isolated. Meanwhile German authorities seized Jewish property to dispose of as they saw fit. In some cases eager non-Jewish neighbors rushed in before them to pick up the spoils. The Germans also forced many Jews in the ghettos to work for them producing supplies for the war.

German planners always considered ghettoization a temporary measure, a sort of holding pattern until subsequent steps could be taken. But what were those steps to be? In 1939 and 1940 some Nazi decision makers were still talking about a Jewish reservation in the east, near Lublin. Officials in the German Foreign Office would propose another scheme, the Madagascar Plan, to ship all of Europe's Jews to an island off the coast of Africa. Others floated different ideas such as using the Jews in the ghettos as enslaved labor or allowing them to die of starvation and disease there. The Nazi leadership encouraged every plan as long as it aimed to destroy Jewish life in Europe.

Between 1939 and 1941, during this phase of experimentation and uncertainty with regard to German policy toward the Jews, over half a million Polish Jews died in ghettos and labor camps. Many starved to death; many also died of diseases brought on by the crowding and terrible sanitary conditions. Police, guards, and overseers shot and beat others to death—for trying to escape; for stealing, as if the Germans themselves were not thieves on the largest conceivable scale; for failing to work to the level demanded; or simply for sport. The ghettos were not yet a formal program of annihilation, but they proved deadly enough for hundreds of thousands of Polish Jews of all ages.

In 1940 a visitor to the Warsaw ghetto offered the following description of living conditions there:

> On the streets children are crying in vain, children who are dying of hunger. They howl, beg, sing, moan, shiver with cold, without underwear, without clothing, without shoes, in rags, sacks, flannel which are bound in strips round the emaciated skeletons, children swollen with hunger, disfigured, half conscious, already completely grown-up at the age of five, gloomy and weary of life. They are like old people and are only conscious of one thing: "I'm cold." "I'm hungry." (Noakes and Pridham 3:1067)

Starvation and deprivation in the ghettos destroyed Jewish lives and at the same time undermined the possibilities for Jewish solidarity. Ghettoization broke up established communities and forced into close contact people who often had little in common. In the ghettos, wealthy, educated, and acculturated Jews competed for scraps of food with Jews who had grown up in poverty.

The German government-run leisure organization Strength Through Joy organized bus tours to the ghettos so that members of the supposed master race could see the degeneracy of their alleged inferiors. No matter that the Germans themselves had created the filth and desperation evident there. That squalor was offered as proof that Nazi theories of race and space held true.

THE EXAMPLE OF LODZ

One of the largest ghettos was established in Lodz in the incorporated territory in the winter of 1939. By April 1940 it had been sealed off completely from the rest of the city. The Lodz ghetto lasted in part at least until August 1944, when the Jews remaining there were shipped to Auschwitz. Although every ghetto was different, Lodz illustrates some general conditions.

In Lodz, as elsewhere, German authorities had varying opinions about the nature of the ghetto. Was it primarily for forced labor? Was it to be self-supporting? If so, how, when it was allocated no resources? To what extent was it to be self-administered? All of this uncertainty added to the misery of those imprisoned within the poorest parts of the city.

The ghetto was disastrously overcrowded. In Lodz, an average of seven people occupied a single room—that is, in 1940 an estimated 230,000 people were crammed into some 30,000 apartments, most of them one room only. Only about 725 of those lodgings had running water. Many had electricity, but

A postcard showing the entrance to the Lodz ghetto in 1940 or 1941. The small, round sign reads, "Closed to Pedestrians"; the larger sign reads, "Residential Area of the Jews: Entry Prohibited."

it did little good; police forbade those in the ghetto from using their lights most of the time.

Lodz was one of the most isolated of all of the ghettos. A kind of no-man's-land surrounded it, so smuggling anything in or out was almost impossible. Because it was in an industrialized region, there was no forest nearby to which the ghetto Jews could escape. The city of Lodz itself was slated to be "Germanized"—that is, German planners intended to remove ethnic Poles, Jews, and others from the area and replace them with Germans from the Reich and ethnic Germans from elsewhere in Europe. As a result, previous contacts in the city were of little help to Jews in the Lodz ghetto.

Food was extremely scarce—potato peels became a prized item. Lice and rats thrived; such diseases as typhus and tuberculosis ran rampant. Nevertheless hard work was required of everyone in the ghetto who wanted a chance to stay alive. By 1943 ghetto workshops were churning out uniforms, boots, underwear, and bed linen for the German military; ghetto workers produced goods of metal, wood, leather, fur, down, and paper, and even electrical and telecommunication devices. Children as young as eight slaved away for pathetically small rations of food.

Under these conditions it is no surprise that people died in terrible num-

The outdoor market in the Lodz ghetto. In desperate conditions where one in five ghetto inhabitants died of starvation and disease, people tried anything to get food: selling and trading remaining possessions, smuggling, performing, begging, stealing, and offering services of all kinds.

bers. In 1940, some six thousand Jews died in the Lodz ghetto. By the following year the number had almost doubled, to eleven thousand. In 1942 there would be eighteen thousand dead. Of course, by the end of 1941 the primary cause of Jewish death would no longer be starvation and illness in the ghettos but deportation to the new killing centers.

German racial experts came to think of the ghettos as repositories for people they considered human trash. Beginning in 1941 they dumped Jews from all over Europe—Luxembourg, Germany, Austria, Czechoslovakia—in Lodz. German officials also shipped some five thousand European Gypsies to the Lodz ghetto, where they inhabited a specially designated area and, like the Jews, suffered beatings, starvation, and disease. In December 1941 and January 1942 those Gypsies still in Lodz were gassed at Chelmno. It is said that no Roma survived the Lodz ghetto. Nazi authorities also sent Gypsies to Jewish ghettos in other cities, for example, Warsaw, Lublin, and Bialystok.

THE JEWISH COUNCILS

German officials saved themselves work by setting up Jewish Councils to administer aspects of the daily lives of the ghettos. They appointed recognized

Jewish leaders—prominent local people, businessmen, teachers, lawyers—to these boards and assigned them the task of carrying out German orders within the ghetto. In each ghetto the Jewish Council also distributed scarce resources, organized social life, set up charities, and tried to find ways to maintain some kind of human community.

The autonomy of the Jewish Council, often referred to by the German word *Judenrat,* was more apparent than real. It could not escape German goals and priorities. In cases when members of the councils refused to cooperate, German officials dismissed them or had them shot and then replaced them with more compliant men. In Lodz, for example, the Germans had some trouble recruiting twenty-four members because the first Council of Jewish Elders set up had been summoned to the Gestapo and never seen again.

The Jewish Councils have often been criticized, and some people have suggested that the Jewish leadership in eastern Europe formed part of the machinery of destruction. Hannah Arendt, a political philosopher and refugee from Nazi Germany, was accused of taking that stance in her famous study *Eichmann in Jerusalem.* Arendt drew attention to what she considered the com-

In this 1940 photograph, Rabbi David Lifszyc (left) and another man pose in front of a cabinet full of Torah scrolls they smuggled out of the Polish city of Suwalki. Rabbi Lifszyc and other community leaders feared the German occupiers would steal the Torah scrolls.

plicity, even collaboration, of the Jewish leadership with the Germans. Publication of her book in the early 1960s sparked a heated controversy.

Instead of viewing the Jewish leaders, especially those in the Jewish Councils, primarily as agents of Nazi destruction, it is more accurate to see them as caught between conflicting sets of demands. Above them loomed German orders; below them spread the ever more desperate needs of the Jewish communities of eastern Europe. Members of the Jewish Councils had to respond to German demands for funds, goods, information, a labor force. If they refused or failed to do so, German officials would come and take whatever they wanted anyway. On the other hand, the Jewish Councils tried to help their people, to maintain order, to save lives, and to feed, clothe, and doctor the Jews in the ghettos.

It was impossible to reconcile these two sets of goals in a situation where the German priority was destruction of the Jews. In the conditions that the victorious Germans created in Poland, however, the two tasks of the Jewish Councils could not be separated either. Attempts by Jewish leaders to accomplish both in some way led to hostility on the part of their own people; in many cases it also pushed them to behave in ways counter to their own principles. Once again we can see the familiar notion of divide and conquer at work.

The tasks the Germans set the Jewish Councils were straightforward. They were to make lists of the people and property in their ghettos and, as required, turn over the money, things, or people demanded. The tasks the Jewish Councils set themselves were more ambitious. They hoped to maintain order and sustain life in the ghettos. They intended to mediate with the Germans, to reason and plead on behalf of the Jews as a whole, and they tried to maintain productivity, to make the ghettos valuable to the German war effort so that Germans would want to keep Jews alive.

Critics of the Jewish Councils often imply an additional task—the councils should have warned their people. Is this charge justified? Could and should the Jewish Councils have done more to warn Jews in the ghettos of German intentions or to rouse resistance?

The case of the ghetto in Lublin illustrates the complexity of this issue. In 1939 there were thirty-eight thousand Jews in Lublin, 21 percent of the city's population. It was one of the oldest Jewish communities in Poland. After the German invasion in September, Jewish refugees flooded into the area. The Germans set up a ghetto and a Jewish Council, one of whose most prominent members was a lawyer named Mark Alten.

Alten believed that the terror of late 1939 was a temporary, local aberration. Things would get better once German power was centralized and control established, he assumed. Alten worked hard to cultivate contacts with Germans and used his influence to plead for exceptions, to urge a stop to arbitrary violence. More than once Alten was arrested for his efforts.

In the end everything Alten did was futile. In 1942 almost all the Jews of Lublin were murdered, just like their counterparts all over Poland.

Alten has been accused of ingratiating himself with the Nazis, the very people who would seek to kill every Jew alive. There is no doubt that Alten misread the situation, although his misjudgment came out of predictable, human tendencies. He looked to the past as people do when seeking guidance for the present. He saw persecutions of Jews, pogroms, and isolation. From that history he took the lesson that this attack too would pass, if the Jews could just hold on. Alten was wrong, but can he be faulted for failing to anticipate something that had never happened before? Can the Jewish Councils be blamed for not realizing in 1939 or 1940 what even top Nazis did not grasp until sometime in mid-1941, that this time the goal would be annihilation of every Jew in Europe? To decent people such a thing would long be unimaginable.

The Jewish Councils are sometimes charged with having handed Jews over to their deaths. There is no denying that German officials used the Jewish Councils to their own ends; they had been created for that purpose. Beginning in late 1941, the councils prepared lists for transports out of the ghettos—to killing centers. Often they used their own police forces to help round up those slated for destruction. Not surprisingly, they generally sent first those people in the ghetto they viewed as least useful: the sick, old, very young, and weak. Outsiders such as Gypsies could also expect to be on the early transports.

Nevertheless Jewish leaders varied considerably in their responses. Sometimes they even managed at least temporarily to thwart Nazi designs. Several brief examples give an idea of the kinds of activities possible among the councils.

By 1940 the Jewish Council in Lublin was dealing not only with the ghetto in that city but with about fifty work camps. Under the crowded and desperate conditions, food, medicine, and doctors were all woefully inadequate. Overwhelmed, the Jewish Council resorted in some cases to bringing in auxiliary police recruited from local ethnic Germans to keep order. Known for their viciousness toward Jews, those police contributed to the hatred that many Jews felt for the Jewish Council. Eventually the Lublin Council formed its own Jewish Order Police. To inhabitants of the ghetto, those enforcers, whether Jewish or not, were detested as the most visible representatives of German authority.

In Warsaw the head of the Jewish police, Jozef Szerynski, was a convert to Christianity who had been trained in the Polish police force. He was indifferent and even hostile to Jewish traditions. Most of the population of the ghetto regarded him and his seventeen hundred policemen as tyrannical. The requirement to pay a special police tax roused particular bitterness. In Riga, in contrast, the Jewish police were recruited from among the Zionist youth. They included some of the best of Jewish society. In the ghetto they were widely respected and viewed as helpers.

Some Jewish Councils were involved in resistance activities. For example, in the summer of 1941, during a search on a train, German police discovered copies of a Jewish underground newspaper. The courier was a Polish gentile woman who was carrying addresses, including some linked to the Jewish ghetto in Piotrków Trybunalski in the incorporated territories. The Gestapo found that the Jewish underground there was connected to the heads of the Jewish Council. They had the chairman and almost all of the community leaders arrested and tortured. In September they were sent to Auschwitz.

Critics of the Jewish Councils note that some of the Jewish leaders enriched themselves and relished the taste of power that their positions in the ghetto gave them. Here too the record is mixed. One can find cases of Jewish leaders who suffered from delusions of grandeur. Moishe Merin, the thirty-year-old head of the Central Council of Elders for Eastern Upper Silesia, fancied himself a kind of dictator of the European Jews. Chaim Rumkowski, head of the Jewish Council in Lodz, was even more blatant. He had money and stamps printed bearing his image; he encouraged a kind of cult of personality around himself. Still, both men tried to save the Jews in "their ghettos," not merely to expand their own power.

Jewish leaders came to recognize their powerlessness too. In 1943 Merin would address the remaining survivors of his jurisdiction with the following words: "I stand in a cage before a hungry and angry tiger. I stuff his mouth with meat, the flesh of my brothers and sisters, to keep him in his cage lest he break loose and tear us all to bits" (Hilberg, 197).

For most Jewish elders, leadership was a burden, not a reward. At first they were not paid but served in the tradition of volunteer community leadership. By 1940 they received some pay, and although it was meager, like that of the Jewish police, it still sparked resentment in a time of such terrible want.

Most Jewish leaders worked hard and suffered a great deal. Some, like Adam Czerniaków in Warsaw, saw no way out of their desperate situation but suicide. Few withstood the temptation to try to use their positions to save themselves and those close to them. Nevertheless in the end their thankless task guaranteed nothing. Jacob Gens spent years as head of the Jewish Council in Vilna, doing all he could to increase the productivity of the ghetto. He was shot anyway by the Germans in 1943 when they liquidated the ghetto. Rumkowski, for all his pomp, ended up in a transport from Lodz ghetto to a killing center. He too died with his people; rumor had it they killed him themselves.

Hell, according to the French philosopher Jean-Paul Sartre, is a self-service cafeteria—the worst suffering, in other words, is that which you inflict on yourself. Nazi planners seem to have understood that concept instinctively. By forcing Jewish leaders to involve themselves in decisions about the fate of people in the ghettos they both lightened their own sense of responsibility and increased the suffering within the Jewish community. Powerless as they were, the Jewish Councils had painfully few options. In a lose-lose situation where the options were destruction or destruction—death or death—there could be few, if any, right decisions. It should not be surprising that Jewish leaders based their strategies on the only two hopes available to them: that the Germans would be defeated sooner rather than later, and that somehow at least some Jews could be kept alive until that day.

Jewish-Christian Relations in Poland

Poland occupies a particular place in the history of the Holocaust. Half of the Jews murdered during the Nazi era were Polish, and much of the actual killing occurred in territories taken from Poland. The killing centers built after 1941 were concentrated there, although in the case of Auschwitz, the camp was in the part of Poland that was incorporated into the German Reich and most of the Polish locals were forcibly removed from the surrounding area. Of course there were also significant sites of slaughter elsewhere; for example, the killing fields in Transnistria, where many Romanian Jews were killed, and the shooting pits in Lithuania and Ukraine. There is also evidence that German planners intended to build a killing center near Minsk in Belorussia but decided against it. Nevertheless, the significance of Poland demands a special look at relations between Polish gentiles and Jews.

The topic remains very emotional. The most common interpretations can be categorized into three main groups. One idea might be called the "Poles as arch-antisemites" theory. Some observers argue that Polish gentiles in the early decades of the twentieth century were raised on the principles of antisemitism. According to this view, Polish Christians were even more hostile to Jews than were Nazi Germans, and Polish antisemitism was an essential factor in the Holocaust. The fact that many Polish gentiles benefited materially from Ger-

Wearing his tallis and tefillin (prayer shawl and phylacteries), Shmuel Grosman recites the morning prayer service in his bed in the Lodz ghetto. Grosman died in the ghetto at the age of sixty. His son, the photographer Mendel Grosman, took this picture in 1941 or 1942. The elderly were a particularly vulnerable segment of the ghetto population.

man attacks on Jews might seem to support this view. Although this interpretation may be emotionally satisfying in some ways, however, it oversimplifies the past and neglects in a cruel way the terrible situation of all Poles under Nazi rule.

At the other end of the scale is a position one might label "all Poles were victims of the Holocaust." Proponents of this view maintain that almost 6 million Poles died in the war—others put the number closer to 4.5 million—and they sometimes fail to mention that millions of the Polish dead were Jewish. They argue that Polish gentiles had no real choice in how they behaved under German rule. They did all they could for their Jewish neighbors under circumstances in which they too were victims. Scholars who take the stance that all Poles were victims may concede some uniqueness to the Jewish experience but consider it wrong for Jews to claim the Holocaust as their own. Some criticize the scholarship of Jewish historians as a kind of special pleading; some blame Jews themselves for the fact that Polish Christians did not do more to help them. Had the Jews not rejected assimilation into mainstream Polish society, they suggest? Were they not richer than their Christian compatriots? Did they not tend to be pro-Communist? Studies written from this perspective have done important work to draw attention to the suffering of Polish gentiles during World War II. They sometimes do so, however, by downplaying Jewish victimization or even reproducing antisemitic ideas.

A third alternative can be called the "unequal victims" theory. According to this view, Nazi Germany attacked Polish gentiles and Polish Jews, but in different ways and to different extents. Here too the numbers are instructive. For some time it was assumed that approximately equal numbers of Polish Christians and Jews were killed during the war. In the case of non-Jewish Poles, the estimate of 3 million included many people killed by the Soviets as well as by the Germans. That number computes to over 10 percent of Polish gentiles and, even if one accepts the lower estimate of 1.5 million, it is a terrible toll. The same number—3 million—amounts to close to 90 percent of Polish Jews, a total catastrophe. The "unequal victims" approach has validity, but as the label itself suggests, it all too easily disintegrates into a kind of competition in suffering or a numbers game in which human agony is quantified in ways that do not make moral sense.

These debates intensified with the publication of a book in 2000 called *Neighbors* by Jan Gross. In graphic detail, Gross recounts how on one day in July 1941, half of the residents of the Polish town of Jedwabne murdered most of the other half. In Jedwabne, according to Gross's account, Poles, not Germans, initiated and carried out the slaughter of hundreds of local Jews. Gross's study, however, is not simply one more accusation of some kind of intrinsic, uniquely Polish antisemitism. Instead he shows the complex interplay of forces in a region first terrorized by Soviet rule between 1939 and 1941, then overrun by the Germans. Poles accused Jews of collaborating with the Soviet oppressors, but in fact it was often precisely those Polish gentiles most deeply implicated in Soviet crimes who were quickest to take the lead in attacks on Jews—attacks that would serve both to deflect the anger of their neighbors and to curry favor with the new German occupiers.

Gross's analysis and the best of the controversy it has sparked caution against generalizing and emphasize instead the wide range of actions and experiences on the part of Poles during World War II. Some collaborated with the Soviets, some with the Germans; some helped their Jewish compatriots, often at great risk to themselves. The fates of Polish Christians and Polish Jews under Nazi occupation were linked in complicated ways that we cannot understand if we study those groups of people in isolation from each other.

A Polish gentile woman and two Polish Jewish men are forced to walk together, probably to an execution site, sometime in the 1940s. The sign around the woman's neck reads, "For selling merchandise to Jews."

Particular Features of the Polish Situation

As a whole Polish gentiles did not obstruct Nazi plans to isolate, expropriate, and eventually annihilate the Jews. What factors might help understand the Polish situation?

One important point involves chronology. Poland came under German domination very early—in 1939—and remained, at least in part, in German hands until early 1945. Unlike the Italians, who began to contend with German occupation only in 1943, the Poles were broken down by years of abuse and persecution.

A second factor was ideological. Nazi racial theory considered Poles, like all Slavic people, to be *Untermenschen,* "subhumans." Polish gentiles occupied a higher position on the ladder of Nazi racial theory than did Jews, but they nevertheless counted in German eyes as inferiors, worthy at most to serve their "Aryan" masters as slaves. Hitler's Germans considered the northern Europeans over whom they would come to rule—the Danes, Norwegians, and Dutch—to be racially related. Accordingly they tried to preserve what they considered their valuable "Nordic blood" and to co-opt them into their system of world domination, but they had no such intentions for the Poles, whose lives they regarded as worthless.

Demography—ethnic division within Poland—was a third factor that shaped the Polish situation. Many of the inhabitants of Poland in 1939 were not ethnic Poles. For example, the area seized by the Soviets in 1939 and held until 1941 was particularly mixed. Its 12 million inhabitants included only about 4.7 million ethnic Poles. The rest were Ukrainians, Belorussians, Russians, Jews, and others. Relations among these groups were not always harmonious, and as we have seen, the German invaders would prove adept at turning ethnic groups against one another to further their own ends.

The 1939 division of Poland between Germany and the Soviet Union seems to have deepened hostilities between Polish gentiles and Jews and exacerbated Polish antisemitism. It is unlikely that either Hitler or Stalin foresaw that outcome when the pact was signed in August 1939, but both stood to gain from anything that helped them divide and rule the Poles.

Both the Soviet Union and Germany were traditional enemies of Poland. Many Soviet leaders, like Hitler, opposed the existence of an independent Polish state. So when Soviet forces took over eastern Poland in 1939, they sent many prominent Poles to forced labor in Siberia. Moreover, in the decades since the Bolshevik Revolution, the Soviet Union had developed a reputation for attacking Christianity and the churches. No wonder then that many Poles, especially the wealthy, staunchly nationalist, or devoutly Catholic, considered Soviet rule the worst tragedy that could befall them. In the fall of 1939 some fled to the parts of Poland under German control.

Polish gentiles would find little to choose between regarding Soviet and German rule. As we have seen, policies of resettlement and Germanization meant that hundreds of thousands of ethnic Poles were forced out of the incorporated territories. Meanwhile life in the General Government became increasingly untenable as the Germans targeted Poles for impoverishment and forced labor. Still, at least initially, many Polish gentiles considered their chances better with the Germans than with the Soviets.

In 1939 Polish Jews, in contrast to their gentile neighbors, tended to regard Soviet rule as a lesser evil than Nazi German domination. At least in theory antisemitism did not exist under Communism. Even in practice, Jews had possibilities to make lives for themselves in the Soviet Union, including as officers in the military. Nazi Germany offered no such option. So while some Polish Christians fled west to the Germans, many Polish Jews, like the young Jack Pomerantz, took their chances by running east.

Suspicious Polish gentiles interpreted as a betrayal the tendency of some Polish Jews to cast their lot with the Soviets. Antisemites had long accused Jews of being Communists; here they could claim to have found proof. Some Christians had always charged Jews with trying to destroy Christianity; now they could say they had evidence of an atheist conspiracy. We tend to assume that shared hardships draw people together. Often, however, quite the opposite occurs. In the early stages of World War II, the tribulations faced by all Poles tended to drive wedges between Christians and Jews.

Polish Jews who welcomed the Soviets in 1939 would be disappointed. Their new rulers had no intention of protecting them. Instead they shut down Jewish community institutions, banned organized activities, and confiscated private assets from Jews as well as non-Jews. In some cases, they evacuated Jews to the interior of the Soviet Union and to distant regions as laborers. A higher percentage of Jews than non-Jews were subjected to such forced relocations.

Soviet authorities required all young men in the areas under their control to enlist in the Red Army. Some Poles—Jewish and gentile—chose that option. Others went west rather than risk being stranded in the Soviet Union and separated from Poland and their families forever. In 1939 they could not know that, within two years, for a Jew to be trapped anywhere in Poland would amount to a death sentence. At least in the Soviet Union Jews could keep moving east. From Poland there would be no place to go.

The Role of Property

Some scholars suggest that Polish antisemitism was not primarily religious or racial but economic—that is, Polish Christians' hatred of Jews was fueled by material resentments, often based on their own deprivation and fantasies of Jewish wealth. In this view it was not greed but pauperization that led to Polish gentiles taking advantage of German aggression to grab Jewish property.

Certainly the poverty of many Poles played into the hands of the Germans. In retrospect one is struck by the pathetically small stakes that induced some gentiles to betray Jews to the Germans or even kill them themselves. Life seems to have been worth very little. For example, in one Polish town during the war Germans promised a kilogram (2.2 pounds) of salt to anyone who brought in the head of a Jew. Local Ukrainians fanned out through the nearby forests and returned clasping severed heads. In other cases, bags of sugar served as a reward. Sometimes just the promise of whatever possessions the Jews carried with them sufficed.

Discussion of the role that greed played in the Holocaust draws our attention to the "banality of evil." Hannah Arendt first used that phrase in her book *Eichmann in Jerusalem*. Most of the people involved in mass killing—as perpetrators, onlookers, and beneficiaries—were not crazed maniacs but ordinary people with familiar motivations. There were Polish peasants who deplored German brutality but willingly took the property of Jews forced into ghettos. There were ethnic German families who moved into homes from which the Polish owners had been evicted and eagerly accepted the booty for themselves. Such people did not necessarily initiate destruction, but they profited from it and developed a stake in its continuation.

Nevertheless one can also find many accounts that show Poles who risked their lives for others, including Jews. Yad Vashem, the Holocaust memorial and archive in Israel, honors non-Jews who rescued Jews from the Holocaust as "the righteous among nations." One of the criteria for being recognized as one of the righteous is that the person received no monetary benefit for what she or he did. Of all the countries of Europe, Poland has the greatest number of gentiles recognized for heroism toward Jews—as well as the largest number of Jews killed in the Holocaust.

An important example of Polish rescue efforts is the organization known as Zegota. Its network of operatives provided aid, food, and medication to Jews all over Poland. Zegota also produced scores of forged documents. Its work is credited with saving the lives of forty to fifty thousand Jews.

The Polish Underground Army

War did not end in Poland with the German defeat of the Polish army in 1939. Instead many Poles fought on in the underground army. There were actually two variants of the Polish underground army, one nationalist, the other Communist.

The Polish nationalist army, know as the Home Army, or AK, maintained links to the Polish government-in-exile in London. Its leaders were prewar Polish officers, and it was quite well organized and equipped. For the most part the Home Army was not particularly sympathetic to the sufferings of Polish

A public execution with onlookers in occupied Poland. This photograph reveals the proximity and interaction of people we might categorize as "perpetrators, victims, and bystanders" of the Holocaust.

Jews. Some of its officers were themselves antisemitic, and in any case their priorities lay elsewhere. They generally refused to shelter Jews or to arm them, although there were exceptions, for example, in Warsaw where the Home Army passed some revolvers to the Jewish underground. In some cases members of the Home Army even participated in killing Jews themselves in the forests. Nevertheless the Home Army did devote considerable attention to learning about what was happening to the Jews in Poland. Its intelligence assumed that any methods applied to Jews would later be used against Polish gentiles.

Generally the Communist underground army was more open to Polish Jews, at least to those who wished to join its ranks. However, it was rather weak and disorganized in many places and had little time for people ill equipped to take part in fighting: children, elderly people, and the unarmed.

In some places Jews would form their own underground fighting organizations. At least one of those, the Bielski partisans in western Belorussia, did accept older people, women, and children. Led by the dynamic Tuvia Bielski, that forest community combined fighting and rescue activities. By 1944 it included more than twelve hundred Jews. Nechama Tec describes its efforts in her aptly titled book *Defiance*.

The Complexity of Polish-Jewish Issues: An Illustration

In his book *Anton the Dove Fancier,* Bernard Gotfryd recounts a story that shows how the lives of Polish Jews and gentiles were intertwined. When the war began Bernard was a young Jewish boy living in the Polish city of Radom. His neighbor Anton was a Polish Christian who raised and trained pigeons.

Anton was a rough man. He drank, threatened to cook his beloved birds, and neglected and scolded his wife. One day German officials requisitioned Anton's pigeons for the Reich. Instead of turning them over to the enemy, Anton killed every one of them. He was arrested for disobedience and sent to a camp.

Later during the war Bernard himself ended up in the concentration camp of Majdanek. There he saw Anton, now wearing the uniform of a kapo. A kapo was a prisoner whom the Germans had elevated to a position of authority over other prisoners. Many kapos were known for their extreme brutality.

Anton recognized Bernard and gave him some warm clothes and extra bread. Later he provided Bernard with water, cigarettes to barter, and advice. Somehow Bernard Gotfryd lived through the war. While he was still in a camp he learned that Anton had been killed by his fellow prisoners in revenge for his cruelty.

Gotfryd returned to Radom, where he saw Anton's wife. She told him that she too had been born Jewish. As a child she had been orphaned and taken in by Anton's mother. Anton had never known about her origins. Now she planned to leave for Palestine.

This case shows the danger of assuming clear-cut categories when studying a situation as complicated as that in Poland during the war. As Anton demonstrated, the same person could be a resistance figure, a perpetrator of brutality, a hero, and a victim of Nazi aggression. As his wife's experience suggests, even the line between "Christian" and "Jew" could be blurred. There is little that is simple about Polish-Jewish relations during the Nazi era.

MURDER OF THE DISABLED

Hitler's Germany first crossed the line from persecution to mass murder not with Jews but with people considered handicapped. The year 1939 would see initiation of a program to murder people defined as "lives unworthy of living." Here, too, experimentation would characterize the early stages of implementation, and the outbreak of war provided both cover and justification for the killers.

As we have seen, the idea of "purging" the population of elements considered undesirable predated Nazi rule and was not exclusive to Germany. Such notions, however, got a big boost with Nazi ideology and its idea that the "collective good"—at least the well-being of those judged superior—overrode the good of the individual. Nazi planners measured the value of a human life by its contribution to the national community, not by some inherent worth.

The T-4 Program

Even before the war began in 1939 Hitler had authorized Dr. Karl Brandt and Philipp Bouhler to organize a children's "euthanasia" program. Under this scheme children selected for killing were sent to special clinics where medical personnel starved them to death or gave them lethal injections. Doctors and research scientists also used some children for experiments that they hoped would advance their own careers.

In the summer of 1939, Hitler instructed another physician, Dr. Leonardo Conti, to organize a similar program for adults. Conti, the Reich Doctors' leader and state secretary in the interior ministry responsible for health matters, set up a huge administrative machinery that involved doctors, professors, social workers, nurses, and other health-care professionals. Their main target would be institutionalized adults with mental illnesses and disabilities. Code-named "T-4" for the address of its headquarters in Berlin, Tiergartenstrasse 4, the program was operating by October 1939.

Even before killings began, Conti's people developed a target number by using the following formula. Of every one thousand people in the German Reich, they estimated, ten needed psychiatric treatment. Five of those were institutionalized. One of those five was assumed to qualify for what was euphemistically called euthanasia. In fact, it was murder. That formula—1000:10:5:1—yielded between sixty-five and seventy-five thousand target cases in Germany. Conti's committee prepared forms to be sent to all mental institutions. The form was short and asked such questions as whether the patient received regular visitors or had any "non-Aryan" blood. Obviously the criteria for selection had little to do with the actual health of the person in question.

Teams of medical evaluators examined the forms. They marked with a red plus sign those people to be killed; they used a blue minus sign to specify who was to be left alive. Some doctors refused to participate. For example, the director of one asylum declined with the explanation that he was "too gentle" for such work. He and others like him did not suffer any consequences. It was no problem to find enough ambitious professionals to keep the program running smoothly.

The T-4 experts experimented with various methods of killing. They used injections and poison in the early months but soon sought quicker means. By January 1940 they had conducted the first successful gassing, at an asylum not far from Berlin.

Some of the earliest gassings were carried out at Grafeneck, a former palace in Württemberg that had been made into a hospital for physically handicapped people. State authorities moved the patients out and took over the building, which they revamped as a killing center.

An employee at the killing center of Hadamar, in Hesse, described viewing a gassing there. He "looked through the peephole in the side wall," he remembered:

Nuns walk along a road with patients in August 1940 at the Liebenau institution for mentally disabled people and others requiring long-term care. The Catholic and Protestant churches in Germany ran many hospitals and related institutions. Like a number of such places, Liebenau became a "euthanasia" facility.

Through it I saw 40–45 men who were pressed together in the next room and were now slowly dying. Some lay on the ground, others had slumped down, many had their mouths open as if they could not get any more air. The form of death was so painful that one cannot talk of a humane killing, especially since many of the dead men may have had moments of clarity. I watched the process for about 2–3 minutes and then left because I could no longer bear to look and felt sick. (Noakes and Pridham 3:1027)

Meanwhile, other initiatives began against the mentally ill in Poland. Already on 29 September 1939, Germans began shooting Polish mental patients in the district of Bromberg (the Polish name is Bydgoszcz). By 1 November they had murdered almost four thousand people this way.

Elsewhere in territories conquered from Poland, SS execution squads murdered residents of mental institutions in order to empty out buildings for their own purposes. Sometimes they responded to requests from bureaucrats in the resettlement offices who needed beds for ethnic Germans being brought into an area. One SS special commando used a van labeled "Kaiser's Coffee" as a mobile killing unit. Carbon monoxide gas was fed from a container in the cab into the back of the van to asphyxiate the passengers. During December 1939 and January 1940 the SS special commando murdered hundreds of patients from Polish asylums in that van.

Hitler's Backdated Authorization and Efforts to Maintain Secrecy

Worried about possible repercussions for their activity, the organizers of the T-4 program approached Hitler for formal authorization that would serve to cover them should objections be raised. Sometime in October 1939 T-4 officials persuaded Hitler to sign a short statement. He had it typed on his personal notepaper rather than issued as an official document. The statement read: "Reich leader Bouhler and Dr. Brandt are charged with responsibility to extend the powers of specific doctors in such a way that, after the most careful assessment of their condition, those suffering from illnesses deemed to be incurable may be granted a mercy death" (Noakes and Pridham, 3:1021).

It is significant that Hitler backdated this note to 1 September 1939, the day of the German invasion of Poland. Presumably he did so in order to link the decision to begin killing people deemed handicapped with the demands of war. In fact the murders were not a response to the exigencies of war; they were an expression of the ideology of race and space. The upheaval of wartime, however, provided the opportunity to carry out such plans with reduced public

View of a transport of disabled men from the Bruckberg care facility in 1941. Their destination is probably a "euthanasia" facility in Ansbach because the bus is marked "Reisedienst Ansbach" (travel agency Ansbach). In early 1941, there were three large transports of patients from Bruckberg to Ansbach for killing.

scrutiny. At the same time war increased Hitler's ability to appeal to the German nation to support his cause.

The program's organizers tried to keep the killings secret, but total concealment was impossible. There were simply too many people involved and too many ways for information to leak out. Staff at hospitals and asylums saw patients taken away for killing. Family members received letters that announced the deaths of their loved ones. In some cases officials made errors; for example, they wrote that someone had died of appendicitis when the person's appendix had been removed years earlier; they listed another cause of death as spinal disease, but the relatives had just seen the man and he had been in perfect health. The patients themselves in some cases figured out what was going on and pleaded for their lives.

News also circulated in the German communities near the killing centers and beyond. Employees of such places sometimes frequented local bars, where they spouted off about what they had seen. The stench of bodies burning in crematoria drifted beyond fences and walls that enclosed the sites of killing.

Even small children playing teased one another about being taken away in the buses with the darkened windows if they acted retarded.

Protest against the Killings

News of the killings of disabled people upset many Germans. Relatives of some of those murdered launched protests of various kinds. Some wrote directly to Hitler to express their disapproval. Some shared details with their pastors or priests. Probably the ease with which the program got started had convinced Hitler that the public would be indifferent. Perhaps most people were, but those opposed made their views known.

Leaders in both the Catholic and the Protestant churches in Germany learned about the killings in direct ways: many asylums were run by the churches. Most of those institutions and their personnel cooperated with the program, although there were exceptions. Nevertheless, it was from church circles that the most concerted protests to the killings would emerge.

Some local Protestant and Catholic clergy made public calls to respect the sanctity of human life. In December 1940, Pope Pius XII issued a statement that denounced "killing of an innocent person because of mental or physical defects." The most pointed protest did not come until the summer of 1941. By then between seventy and eighty thousand people had been killed in the program in Germany alone. The number of Polish disabled people murdered is unknown, but in all it is estimated that by 1945 the Germans murdered some 275,000 people they deemed handicapped from all over Europe.

In August 1941 the Catholic bishop of Münster, Cardinal August Count von Galen, decided to take a stand against the killings. He preached a sermon in which he made it clear that he knew exactly what was going on and considered it a crime against humanity. Galen quoted the German Penal Code's prohibition against murder and warned the government that its policies would backfire. He told of a German soldier whose father had been institutionalized for some mental disturbance. As the younger man went off to defend his nation, his father in Germany was being killed by his German national comrades. Whose life would be safe in such a society? Galen asked his parishioners.

Galen's sermon was duplicated and circulated all over Germany and even abroad by sympathetic elements within the Christian churches. Nazi leaders were furious, but they dared not take action against Galen. He was too well known and too popular. In wartime the government could not risk alienating its own population, so Galen kept his post.

Late in August 1941 Hitler gave an order to halt the "Euthanasia Program." That order was little more than a ploy. It is now known that the killings did not stop—nor did Hitler intend them to. The major gassing operations ended, the killing program was decentralized into hospitals, and the secrecy surrounding T-4 was increased. Meanwhile, the priorities of the German leadership had shifted to eastern Europe, after invasion of the Soviet Union in June 1941 and the accompanying massacres of Jews.

It is not clear to what extent Hitler's order to halt was a response to protests such as Bishop von Galen's sermon. Certainly the stepped-up efforts at concealment were intended to placate the public. German authorities also had an eye to morale in the military. During wartime the last thing soldiers needed was the worry that they would be killed by their own government if they were injured. Nevertheless, the killing of disabled people continued until the end of the war and even after. The last victim of the "euthanasia" program was a four-year-old boy murdered in a Bavarian hospital on 29 May 1945.

Map by Michael J. Fisher, cartographer

6

EXPANSION AND SYSTEMATIZATION

Exporting War and Terror, 1940–1941

The previous chapter described the first year of the war as a period of Nazi experiments in conquest, persecution, and mass killing. Just as Nazi revolution in 1933 had been followed by routinization, the experimental phase in 1939 gave way to what might be labeled a time of expansion and systematization. During 1940 and 1941 the size of Hitler's empire increased tremendously as German forces overwhelmed more and more of Europe. After Poland the Germans first turned their military attentions to the north and west, attacking Denmark, Norway, the Netherlands, Belgium, Luxembourg, France, and Britain in the spring and summer of 1940. Able to conquer all but the British, they moved south and east—against Yugoslavia and Greece in spring 1941, and then in June 1941 against the Soviet Union.

Terror and suffering grew along with Hitler's empire as programs of killing became both much larger and more efficient. By the end of 1941 German mobile killing units would have murdered close to a million Jews in eastern Europe—men, women, and children—many of them shot into mass graves. Preparation of killing centers to massacre even more stunning numbers of people would be under way. Millions of Soviet prisoners of war would be dead or dying in German captivity.

This chapter surveys the German campaigns of 1940 and 1941 that brought most of Europe under Nazi control. It explores the repercussions as Nazi Germans took their projects of supposed racial purification and territorial expansion ever farther from home.

135

WAR IN THE NORTH AND WEST

Within days of the German invasion of Poland on 1 September 1939, both Britain and France were officially at war with Germany. Bound by agreements to Poland, the British and French declared war on Germany on 3 September but initially remained fairly inactive. This early phase was known in Britain as the "phony war." The French referred to it as a *drôle de guerre*, a "funny war," and the Germans spoke of a *Sitzkrieg*, an immobile "war of sitting," in contrast to the rapid Blitzkrieg, "lightning war," in Poland.

There were a few skirmishes on the border between France and Germany in 1939 but nothing otherwise on land. Siegfried Knappe, a young German artillery officer, describes in his memoir *Soldat* how he spent much of the fall and winter of 1939–1940 in western Germany, mere miles from the border with Luxembourg. Days and then weeks passed as the Germans prepared for an attack from the French that never came. Rather than the dangers and strains of combat, Knappe and his men faced the challenge of readying their horses and themselves for action, tasks that left plenty of time to celebrate German victories in Poland by drinking beer and dancing with the locals. Knappe especially enjoyed an invitation to the Bismarck estate, where he and a group of fellow officers sipped cocktails and chatted with the vivacious, young granddaughter-in-law of Otto von Bismarck, the hero of German unification in 1871. From Knappe's vantage point, it must have been easy to view Hitler's early triumphs as confirmation of German superiority.

At sea there was more action as the Germans began their attack on Allied shipping. In return the British navy organized a convoy system and began actively breaking German codes. By mid-1940 this phase of the "phoney war" in the west would come to an abrupt halt.

In the spring of 1940, after a winter spent consolidating their hold on Poland and continuing preparations for further offensives, the Germans moved north and west. Hitler and his generals knew that their plan to dominate Europe remained impossible unless they crushed and subordinated the European powers of France and Britain. That goal could only be achieved through war.

For Hitler war in the west was a prerequisite for grabbing land in the east. It had been part of the plan all along. The western conflict, however, did not take quite the form Hitler had foreseen. Already in 1938 Hitler believed Germany was ready for war against France and Britain. He had expected that war to precede hostilities with Poland. The German air force—the Luftwaffe—had been built up under Hermann Göring with an eye to campaigns in the west. It was in the west that Hitler anticipated the most difficult fighting for the Germans. After all, in Nazi eyes, Europeans to Germany's east were racial inferiors, surely easy opponents for members of a master race.

In keeping with Nazi racial theories, German warfare in the west would be less excessive than in the east. Nazi ideology regarded western and northern Europeans as "racially valuable" people, suitable partners for German "Aryans." Still, Germans would do much stealing and plundering in these parts of Europe too. For leaders who believed that Germany had lost the previous war because of public discontent—the stab in the back from the home front—nothing was more important than placating the people back home. What easier way to do so than to let them enrich themselves at the expense of others?

In April 1940 German forces entered Denmark, and that small nation surrendered without a struggle. The Germans moved on to Norway, where they had to fight their way in, but by June 1940 they had defeated the Norwegians too. The British and French tried to help Norway, but without adequate air support and thorough coordination their landings failed.

The Norwegian government fled to London, where it established itself as a government-in-exile. Norwegian merchant ships also escaped to Britain, where they could be used in the war effort against Germany. A local fascist leader, Vidkun Quisling, took power—or more accurately, became the German puppet—at home. His name, "quisling," has become a synonym for "cowardly collaborator." The Norwegians would execute Quisling as a traitor in 1945.

What did German military planners want with Denmark and Norway? A look at a map gives some explanation. The Germans needed to secure the supply route of Swedish iron ore for their war machine. They also sought to broaden their base for a sea war with Britain and eventually the United States. Scandinavia would provide naval bases from which to attack the British with submarines and access to routes around Britain.

In May 1940, just a month after the offensive against Denmark and Norway began, German forces invaded and conquered the neutral nations of the Netherlands, Belgium, and Luxembourg. Here too victory was swift.

For example, in the Netherlands, German armored forces penetrated the borders, while airborne units took strategic airfields and bridges. The Dutch soon surrendered. First, however, there were some significant developments. The queen and her government left Holland for Britain, where they too formed a government-in-exile on the side of the Allies. The Dutch were important to the French and British cause because they controlled a large colonial empire and a substantial merchant fleet, both of which would prove valuable in the war effort.

On 14 May the Luftwaffe bombed the Dutch city of Rotterdam in an attempt to terrorize the Dutch into surrender. The Germans clearly aimed at civilian targets to intimidate and demoralize their opponents. They destroyed the center of the city and killed hundreds of civilians. At the time, the panicked British press reported the inflated figure of thirty thousand Dutch casualties. For the Allies, the bombing of Rotterdam provided an early manifestation of German brutality and introduced a new kind of warfare: unlimited war from the air. Within a few years the Germans would reap what they had sown with the destruction from the air of their own cities.

One of the eyewitnesses to the German conquest of the Netherlands was Anne Frank, a young girl living in Amsterdam. Her family were German Jews who had left Frankfurt for Holland after Hitler came to power. As it turned out, they had not fled far enough. Unable to get out of Europe in 1940, their only option would be to try to disappear within the city of Amsterdam.

Anne's father began to use his contacts to prepare a hiding place for his

The ruins of Rotterdam after bombing by the German air force on 14 May 1940. The attack destroyed the old city core and killed hundreds of civilians in a deliberate move intended to terrorize the Dutch into surrender.

family and some acquaintances. It was in their "secret annex" between July 1942 and August 1944 that Anne would write a diary, now one of the most famous documents of the Holocaust. Betrayed by an anonymous tip-off to police, the Franks and the people in hiding with them were sent first to the Dutch transit camp of Westerbork and then on to Auschwitz. A group of them were later moved to the Bergen-Belsen concentration camp in Germany, where Anne died in March 1945. Of the eight residents of the hiding place, only Anne Frank's father, Otto, survived the war.

German Victory over France

In May 1940 German troops entered France. They came through Belgium from two directions, the north and also the south. The French had concentrated their best forces in the north and were unprepared for a German attack through the Forest of Ardennes in southern Belgium. By 12 May, German soldiers were on French soil, and by 20 May, they had broken through to the sea, to the coast of the English Channel. In effect German forces cut the Anglo-French troops in two.

The Germans prepared to surround and annihilate the Allied forces converging on the French seaport of Dunkirk. Between the end of May and early June 1940, however, the Allies managed to evacuate some 338,000 of their own soldiers. Using merchant ships, motorboats, fishing boats, private yachts, destroyers, and any other craft they could muster, the British rescued their men from the beaches of Dunkirk while under continued attack from the Germans. They had no choice but to leave most of their equipment behind.

German actions in the French campaign revealed the priorities of racial warfare. Some one hundred thousand men from French West Africa served in the French military in 1939–1940. During May and June 1940, the Germans captured thousands of these soldiers, whom they separated from their white counterparts and targeted for special abuse. Sometimes on orders from their officers or on their own initiative, German soldiers shot them or blew them up with grenades. Supported by a massive propaganda campaign from Berlin, these slaughters of an estimated three thousand black French soldiers within two months echoed German behavior in Poland and anticipated the massacres of millions of Soviet POWs that began a year later.

By 14 June, German troops marched triumphantly into Paris. Hitler danced the jig that became famous from the newsreels when he visited Paris for the first time. Unlike the Dutch and Norwegian governments, the French government did not go into exile. Instead it remained and signed an Armistice

French colonial troops and their German captors in an unidentified prisoner of war camp. In May and June 1940, the Germans captured and killed thousands of black French soldiers, many of them from the units known as Tirailleurs Sénégalais.

Agreement on 22 June 1940. Under the terms of the armistice the Germans divided France into two parts: an occupied zone and an unoccupied zone known as Vichy France because its capital was located in the small, southern city of Vichy. Much of the French army entered prisoner of war camps, whereas the navy remained intact.

The head of the Vichy state was Marshal Henri Philippe Pétain (1856–1951), by 1940 an old man and a hero of World War I. His supporters would be known as Pétainists. For at least part of the war Pétain's prime minister was Pierre Laval (1883–1945). Together those two names would become symbols of French collaboration with Nazi Germany. Some of the French, however, refused to accept defeat. Among those, General Charles de Gaulle (1890–1970) emerged as leader of the Free French forces, and he too escaped to London.

In the years before 1940, France had been a haven for refugees from all over Europe. Many Communists and other supporters of the Spanish Republic had fled to France in 1939 when their side lost the civil war in Spain. Jews from other parts of Europe had taken refuge in France as their homelands fell prey to German aggression. Now all of these people came into the hands of the Germans and their new French partners.

Among the many foreigners residing in France in 1940 were a young boy named Saul Friedländer and his parents. Friedländer was born in Prague in 1932. He and his parents, middle-class, secular Jews, had left Czechoslovakia in 1939, even as German troops were moving in. France seemed a safe destination, and it was hard enough to move that far, leaving behind property, career, and relatives. It would prove difficult, and for Friedländer's parents eventually impossible, to remain safe in a society where one was a stranger, without money, friends, or adequate language skills. For the Friedländers the collapse of France in 1940 was not primarily a national humiliation; it was a personal catastrophe that eventually put the parents in the clutches of the Nazis and left the son an orphan.

A Gypsy woman with a group of children in the Rivesaltes internment camp in 1942. Located in the French Pyrenees Mountains, Rivesaltes was used in the late 1930s for refugees from . the Spanish Civil War. In 1941 and 1942, thousands of Roma and foreign-born Jews rounded up in France were interned there.

The Battle of Britain

With the fall of France, most textbooks will tell you that Great Britain stood alone against Germany. Indeed, Britain was the only European power both to declare war on Germany in 1939 and to stand firm until 1945. Neither the Soviet Union nor the United States would enter the war against Germany until 1941.

The British, however, were not entirely alone. The Dominions—Australia, New Zealand, Canada, and, after considerable internal debate, South Africa—joined in declarations of war against Germany. The British-controlled government of India also did so, although without consulting the Indian political parties or, for that matter, the Indian public. For its part, the Irish Free State proclaimed its neutrality.

Support of the Allied cause by countries all over the world was significant, both to the outcome of the war and after the fact, to the national pride of citizens of the nations concerned. People in the Dominions would bear a substantial burden in the war, and if the British Isles were to have fallen to the Germans, there would still have been the possibility of continuing the war effort. In fact, the British leadership planned to do so from Canada and moved large parts of Britain's gold reserves to Canada in case they would be needed to finance the war.

Within Europe Britain became the last refuge for many people fleeing Nazi Germany. The governments-in-exile—Polish, Norwegian, Dutch—were surrounded by communities of people forced to flee their homelands. Czech and French opponents of Germany also gathered in Britain, as did those Jews from the continent who could make it in. Among the people who had arrived before war began in 1939 were some ten thousand Jewish children from Germany, Austria, Czechoslovakia, and Poland. A special program organized by private citizens, known as the Kindertransport, brought them to Great Britain. Forced to leave their families behind on the continent, most of them never saw their parents again.

Two veterans of the Kindertransports were Ilona and Kurt Penner, children of a Polish Jewish father and a Hungarian Jewish mother. Born in Berlin in 1928, the twins were sent to England in March 1939, where they were placed separately. Their parents, owners of a dry goods store, managed to leave Germany in 1940, although they initially only got as far as France. Fortunately they were able to secure passage to the United States in 1941. Kurt joined them there that year; Ilona, two years later.

Now, more than sixty years later, the children of the Kindertransports are adults, many of them grandparents. One girl who came to England from Vienna became known as an adult as Ruth Morley, an Academy Award–nominated costume designer who worked on such well-known American movies as *Tootsie, The Miracle Worker,* and *Taxi Driver.* Morley's daughter, a filmmaker named Melissa Hacker, included some of her mother's experiences in a documentary film titled *My Knees Were Jumping: Remembering the Kindertransports.*

By May 1940, with the fall of France, Hitler saw the British as Germany's main enemy in Europe. He proceeded with plans for an invasion, while British prime minister Winston Churchill rallied the British population against the Germans. One of Churchill's most famous speeches included the following challenge: "The Battle of Britain is about to begin. Upon this battle depends the survival of Christian civilization. . . . If we fail then . . . all we have known and cared for will sink into the abyss of a new Dark Age." After the evacuation of Dunkirk, Churchill's rousing words helped strengthen and inspire British determination:

> Even though large tracts of Europe and many old and famous states have fallen or may fall into the grip of the Gestapo and all the odious apparatus of Nazi rule, we shall not flag or fail. We shall go on to the end. We shall fight in France, we shall fight on the seas and oceans, we shall fight with growing confidence and growing strength in the air, we shall defend our island, whatever the cost may be. We shall fight on the beaches, we shall fight on the landing grounds, we shall fight in the fields and in the streets, we shall fight in the hills; we shall never surrender; and even if, which I do not for a moment believe, this island or a large part of it were submerged and starving, then our Empire beyond the seas, armed and guarded by the British Fleet, would carry on the struggle, until, in God's good time, the new world, with all its power and might, steps forth to the rescue and the liberation of the old. (Sachse, 314–15)

The German plan for landings in Britain had the code name Operation Sea-Lion. German planners were convinced that successful crossing of the English Channel and establishment of beachheads on the English coast depended on control of the skies, and Göring assured Hitler that the Luftwaffe could destroy the Royal Air Force (RAF).

In July 1940 the Luftwaffe began massive attacks on British air and naval installations. Every day for the next two months hundreds of planes fought in the skies over Britain. The Germans, however, could not gain the mastery they expected. On 15 September 1940, the RAF shot down sixty aircraft, and two days later, Hitler postponed the invasion "until further notice." He hoped among other things that invasion and defeat of the Soviet Union—both of which were already planned—would isolate and weaken Britain so that the Germans could come back later for an easy victory. Those late-summer, early-autumn months of 1940 became known as the Battle of Britain. Throughout 1941, the Germans bombed British cities, industrial centers, and ports. Air raids became a nightly event, with the inhabitants of London, Coventry, Plymouth, and other cities seeking safety in subways, cellars, and homemade bomb shelters. German bombing took a heavy toll on civilian lives and property, but British morale remained firm. Meanwhile German air raids spurred the Allies to further develop radar technology that would play a crucial role in winning the war in the air.

Events on the Periphery of German Warfare

Some European countries remained neutral throughout World War II, most notably Spain, Portugal, Switzerland, Sweden, and Turkey. The neutrals would play different roles during the war. Some provided escape routes for victims of German persecution. For example, in October 1943 the small Jewish community of Denmark was smuggled out to safety in neutral Sweden. Others, such as Switzerland, turned many refugees away. Among those sent back at the border were the young Saul Friedländer's parents. In despair they ended up back in France, and eventually they were sent to Auschwitz and killed there.

Some of the neutrals profited considerably from the war. Swiss banks grew rich on stolen gold sent there by German authorities and on deposits from European Jews desperate to protect some assets from the German predators. The Swedes delivered massive amounts of iron ore to Germany. Turkey offered refuge to some European Jews but charged special taxes intended to transfer wealth from the refugees to native Turks. After the war Turkey also provided an escape route to the Middle East for many Nazi criminals. Neutral or not, no nation in Europe would be untouched by the war.

In 1940 Germany entered into the Three-Power Pact with Italy and Japan. Later that arrangement would be consolidated into a formal military alliance, although coordination among the three powers was minimal. For the time being the three states committed themselves to aid one another against their enemies.

Later in 1941, Hungary, Romania, Slovakia, Finland, Bulgaria, and Croatia would join the pact. Why were these less powerful nations interested in allying themselves with Germany and Italy? A look at a map suggests an answer.

All of these countries hoped to expand with German or Italian help at the expense of their neighbors. They operated on a common assumption: "the enemies of my enemies are my friends." By the end of World War II, that notion would prove disastrously false.

Soviet Assault on the Baltic States and Finland

As evident in the division of Poland in September 1939, Germany was not the only belligerent power in Europe. Under the leadership of Josef Stalin, the Soviet Union had its own expansionist program, linked to the goal of crushing all threats to internal security.

After seizing eastern Poland, Stalin turned his attention to the three tiny Baltic states, Estonia, Latvia, and Lithuania. By October 1939 massive Soviet threats had compelled all three to accept Soviet military bases with tens of thousands of Red Army troops. In June 1940, as the victorious Wehrmacht marched into defeated Paris, Stalin grabbed the opportunity to transform those "bases" into a full-scale invasion and occupation of the Baltic states.

Along with Red Army tanks came the Stalinist system of terror, presided over by the NKVD (People's Commissariat for Internal Affairs) and its political police, known after 1941 as the NKGB (People's Commissariat for State Security) or simply KGB. Soviet authorities organized a wave of purges and deportations of local nationalists of all ages. Hundreds of thousands of people simply vanished—into Soviet torture chambers, prisons, and labor camps in Siberia. In Latvia alone, 2 percent of the population "disappeared" as NKVD operatives sought to destroy the possibility of any national resistance. For the next year, Soviet interrogators and guards and local collaborators followed Stalin's injunction to "beat, beat, and again beat."

Likewise in June 1940, Stalin took advantage of the situation in western Europe to seize northern Bukovina and the province of Bessarabia in northern Romania. There too NKVD rule and ruthless state terror followed, with the same deadly consequences as in the Baltic states.

By the time the Germans launched their own invasion of these regions in mid-1941, the people of the Baltic states and northern Romania had been brutalized by deprivation, abuse, and violence. Small wonder that many of them in turn would seek revenge and scapegoats for their suffering by throwing their lot in with the Nazis. It can be tempting to set up competitions in evil between Hitler and Stalin. Who was worse? Who caused more murder and misery? This brief survey of the events of 1940, however, reminds us of an even more terrible reality; Nazism and Stalinism coexisted in time and place, and for many Europeans the horrors of one vicious system served to increase the destructive force of the other.

Already in November 1939 the Soviets had invaded Finland, another neighbor to the west. The gigantic attack was intended to overwhelm the 3.5 million Finns in rapid, blitzkrieg style. Instead the Finns mounted a resourceful, heroic resistance and held out until March 1940, when they were forced to sign a peace treaty and cede territories to the Soviet Union. In that conflict, known as the Winter War, Stalin again took advantage of British and French inability to aid the targets of his aggression and used the protective cover of German assaults elsewhere in Europe to pick up spoils of his own. At the same time, at least in the short run, Hitler and the Germans benefited from anything that further disrupted the stability of Europe and distracted attention from their own activities.

WAR AND ITS IMPACT
INSIDE NAZI GERMANY

War had many repercussions inside Germany too. For one thing, German military successes brought floods of luxury goods into the hands of Germans back home. Men sent furs and jewels to their wives; German museums and galleries acquired costly art treasures; the finest wines, chocolate, cheeses, pâtés, and other delicacies ended up on German tables. The wealthier the nation conquered, the richer the spoils of war.

In the words of the historian Robert Gellately, war also "revolutionized the revolution" in Nazi Germany. War allowed German authorities to step up the pace of change at home and crack down hard on dissenters. For example, restrictions on public meetings and control over the press tightened considerably after 1939. Numbers of arrests continued to climb: for spreading so-called malicious rumors critical of the government or the Nazi Party, for violating state monopolies on information, for maintaining illegal organizations, and for engaging in other activities considered subversive. The population of the ever-expanding network of concentration camps and their satellites grew accordingly.

War exported Nazi policies such as persecution of Jews and applied Nazi practices such as divide and conquer in new territories. Already between 1933 and 1939 Hitler's regime had built on the principle that nothing succeeds like success. In wartime that notion again proved extremely powerful.

The prewar triumphs of Hitler's rule—for example, the annexation of Austria and the seizure of the Sudetenland in 1938—had helped to bring some reluctant Germans in line. Germany's spectacular military successes in 1939 and 1940 turned out to be even more effective. German patriots of all kinds, including many who consistently had voted against Hitler, rejoiced with him at the destruction of Poland and the victory over France. To German nationalists these successes seemed to vindicate old desires for revenge and to legitimate German aggression.

The family of Alfons Heck, an eager member of the Hitler Youth, illustrates this particular effect of Germany's war. Before 1939 Heck's father, a committed Socialist, and his grandmother, a devout Catholic, had both opposed Adolf Hitler. They also disapproved openly of Heck's enthusiastic involvement in the Hitler Youth. Nevertheless both were thrilled with the German conquest of France in 1940. Living as they did near the border with France they were particularly aware of Germany's long enmity with its neighbor to the west. By mid-May 1940, Heck's father and grandmother had stopped complaining about Hitler's government and joined Alfons as supporters of the German war effort.

War brutalized life in ways that did not alter the goals of the German leaders but did transform what it was possible for them to achieve. War provided a cover for mass murder; remember Hitler's false dating of his order to murder the disabled to 1 September 1939 and his repeated claim that he had given his speech "predicting" annihilation of the European Jews not in January 1939 but in September of that year. War also made possible the training of large numbers of experienced killers, beginning in Poland in 1939.

War trapped the victims of Nazism inside Europe, making them ever more vulnerable. After September 1939 it became extremely difficult for Jews to leave Europe. By 1941 it was practically impossible. The German police regulation of September 1941 that required all people inside Germany who were defined as Jews to wear the identifying Star of David simply reinforced the obvious: Jews were now open targets.

War enabled Nazi propagandists to present attacks on innocent civilians of all ages as if they were defensive measures necessary to protect the German nation from its foes. For all these reasons, war was a necessary ingredient in what would develop into genocide—the deliberate effort at total annihilation of identifiable groups of people.

ASSAULT ON THE BALKANS—
YUGOSLAVIA AND GREECE

In 1941, the Germans again turned east, first to the Balkans in southeastern Europe. Mussolini had gotten in over his head when he sent his Italian forces in to conquer Greece in 1940. Now he needed the Germans to bail him out.

The German attack on the Balkans was also linked to preparation for an assault on the Soviet Union. Hitler and his generals considered it necessary to control the Balkan states in order to secure their southeastern flank and safeguard access to Romanian oil. With Romania, Bulgaria, and Hungary already bound to Germany through diplomatic arrangements, only Yugoslavia and Greece remained to be brought into the Nazi sphere.

On 6 April 1941 the Luftwaffe launched an air raid on Belgrade. German forces surrounded the Yugoslav army, which capitulated on 17 April. Italian, Hungarian, and Bulgarian troops invaded Yugoslavia in aid of the Germans, and the Yugoslavian king fled to Britain, where he too formed a government-in-exile.

Although the German offensive advanced rapidly, it faced tough resistance. Yugoslav partisans used the rugged terrain to their advantage and benefited from the effective, ruthless leadership of Tito (Josip Broz, 1892–1980). Aid from the British in the form of supplies and intelligence helped too.

In Yugoslavia the German forces stooped to new depths of organized brutality that may have surpassed even their behavior in Poland. Here too they relied on familiar techniques of divide and conquer. Part of the country (Croa-

Germans pose near the bodies of recently murdered Serbian civilians in 1941 in Yugoslavia. Many German soldiers took photographs like this one and sent them to their families. In Yugoslavia members of the regular military, not special SS units, were responsible for the massive death toll.

tia, Bosnia, and Herzegovina) became an independent Croatian state under Ante Pavelic (1889–1959) and his fascist Ustasha movement. The Germans used their ally Pavelic to carry out their will. At the same time they gave him and his henchmen license to do what they wanted against enemies of their own, which meant above all the Serbs.

Meanwhile the Germans annexed some northern parts of Yugoslavia to the German Reich and set up a military government in Serbia. Everywhere, they encouraged thugs to attack Jews, Gypsies, Communists, liberals, and anti-German nationalists of any kind.

The Germans' brutal occupation policies ensured a steady flow of people into the partisan groups. In particular the practice of reprisals roused hatred. For every one German whom Yugoslav partisans attacked or killed, German authorities ordered a certain number of Yugoslavs shot. Sometimes the ratio was fifty to one; sometimes it was one hundred or even two hundred to one. The victims seized included people of all ages, female as well as male. Germans used reprisals—often based only on fear or suspicion of partisan actions—as an excuse to massacre hundreds of thousands of Yugoslavs.

In Yugoslavia it was generally the regular German military, not some special SS units, who carried out mass shootings of civilians. Although soldiers were not forced to participate in these killings, there were always enough volunteers for such duties. Some of them even took photographs of their exploits to send home to their girlfriends and wives.

Often the Germans took their first victims from among the local Jewish and Gypsy populations, but they also took hostage and shot many Serbs. There were Croats, Bosnian Muslims, and people with mixed backgrounds among those shot in reprisals too. Some of the most damning evidence of atrocities committed by the Wehrmacht—the regular German military—during World War II comes out of Yugoslavia.

Already in 1940, Hitler's Italian ally, Mussolini, had launched his own military campaign against Greece, but the Italian offensive bogged down until the spring of 1941, when the Germans took over. In April and May 1941 German forces overran Greece. Here too the Germans brutally assaulted civilians as well as members of the military. In so-called special actions, often in retaliation for resistance or partisan activity, they wiped out entire villages and towns.

On Hitler's orders, German soldiers tried to spare Greece's artistic treasures. Hitler had always been fascinated by Greek and Roman art. He held the notion that the best artistic achievements had been made by "Aryans" who later migrated north and brought their superior creativity to Germany. According to Hitler, the Greeks of his own time were a lesser people unworthy of their country's glorious past. In Greece, as elsewhere, Hitler adjusted reality to fit his view of the world.

GERMAN ASSAULT ON THE SOVIET UNION

On 22 June 1941 German troops invaded the Soviet Union. The invasion was given the code name Operation Barbarossa. With this step Hitler's forces crossed the final line to what he called a "war of annihilation."

War in the Soviet Union was extremely bloody. An estimated 27 million Soviet citizens were killed, the majority of them civilians. Carnage on this scale was no mere replay of Napoleon's failed invasion of Russia 129 years earlier. The German assault on the Soviet Union was not a war of soldier against soldier or army against army. It was a war whose goal was total destruction of the Soviet Union, seizure of its land, colonization, enslavement, and murder of its people, in short, establishment of the Nazi new order in Europe.

By mid-1941 German forces were ready to wage a war of annihilation. Trained in conquest in Poland, proven capable of wholesale massacre of captured soldiers, flushed with successes in the west, and brutalized by war on partisans and civilians in the Balkans, they were no longer likely to protest atrocities as some had in 1939. From day one German operations in the Soviet Union would be characterized by a level of ruthlessness that has led the historian Omer Bartov to speak of the "barbarization of warfare."

You may have heard people say that Germany would have won the war if Hitler had not made the mistake of attacking the Soviet Union. Given Hitler's worldview this claim makes little sense. For Hitler the whole point of the war was to conquer land and resources to support his purportedly superior "Aryan race." The Lebensraum—living space—he sought could only be found in the east. He was interested not in some limited European empire but in world domination. Hitler had always planned on war with the Soviet Union; it was only a question of when. Recently some writers have contended that Hitler's assault on the Soviet Union was purely defensive. According to them, Stalin was poised to attack Germany, so Hitler ordered a preemptive strike. This theory simply does not hold. Neither the German nor the Russian archival records support such a notion. Hitler made his intentions against the Soviet Union very clear, not only in *Mein Kampf* and in his second, untitled book, written in 1928 and never published, but in numerous conversations and speeches. Most significantly, German military planners had worked out the details of an offensive against the Soviet Union long before June 1941. Operation Barbarossa was no defensive reaction.

Of course it is certainly possible that Stalin had his own violent plans for eastern and central Europe, but such schemes do not alter the fact of Hitler's aggression. Unfortunately there is no reason why two opponents cannot both be scoundrels.

What about the Hitler-Stalin nonaggression pact of 1939? Like all of Hitler's diplomatic agreements it was made to be broken. The deal had served Nazi goals well; it enabled rapid defeat of Poland in 1939, freed up German forces to concentrate in the west in 1940, and bought almost two years of time to prepare for war with the Soviet Union. It seems highly unlikely that Hitler or his generals even gave it a thought in June 1941.

The First Victims—Caught between Stalin and Hitler

It is important to note that the Germans invaded the Soviet Union, not just Russia. The Soviet Union was a multinational empire that included many republics in addition to Russia. In fact some of the worst devastation of World War II occurred not in Russia but in Ukraine, Belorussia, and the Baltic states of Latvia, Estonia, and Lithuania.

In June 1941, before the Germans reached Russia, they first entered territories that the Soviets had seized after the German attack on Poland in 1939. As a consequence, people in places such as Latvia and the eastern Polish city of Lvov—after the war part of western Ukraine and called L'viv—experienced two rounds of invasion in less than two years. In September 1939 Stalin's armies moved in; Hitler's troops arrived in 1941.

Some people in such areas had greeted the Soviets in 1939 as bearers of Communism and protectors from Nazism. By 1941 almost all had become disillusioned. That year some people in eastern Europe welcomed the German invasion, expecting Hitler's forces to crush Communism and grant them independence. For example, many Ukrainian nationalists hoped the Nazis would let them set up their own state. They too would be disappointed. Very quickly most eastern Europeans learned that they could expect only terror and destruction from a war fought not for them but on top of them.

An Account from Lvov

One person who experienced Soviet takeover in the fall of 1939 and then the German invasion in 1941 was Nelly Toll. Born in 1935, Nelly was just a little girl in 1939. Her family was among the 110,000 Jews in Lvov, home to Poland's third-largest Jewish community, after Warsaw and Lodz. About 1 million Jews lived in the surrounding region, called eastern Galicia.

Under Soviet rule more Jews streamed into the city to escape the Germans, but Soviet control brought its own hardships. Nelly Toll's father had to go into hiding to avoid being sent to a labor camp in Siberia. As the wealthy owner of a dry goods store he was considered an enemy of Communism. Soviet officials seized much of the Tolls' property and took over their spacious apartment. Nelly remembers her family's relationship with the Russian officers as a mixture of fear, friendliness, and contempt for people she and her relatives considered somewhat less civilized than themselves.

When the Germans came to Lvov in 1941 even some Jews there thought they might be an improvement over the Soviets. Nelly's grandfather, for example, at first regarded German takeover in 1941 as a good thing. In his view the Germans were more cultured and intelligent than the Russians. He was wrong. The Germans proved at least as barbaric.

In Lvov some of the local people saw arrival of the Germans as a chance to take revenge for all they had suffered under the Soviets. In particular Ukrainians in the region wanted to seize the chance to get back at the Russians as well as their Polish neighbors. Most of the Soviets had fled before the advancing Germans. So angry residents of Lvov attacked their Jewish neighbors as convenient scapegoats instead. They accused Jews of collaborating with the Soviets to oppress them. No doubt there had been Jews who supported the Soviet regime, but there had certainly also been gentile Poles and Ukrainians who had done the same.

As usual German authorities encouraged ethnic strife and rewarded pogroms. They urged local Ukrainians to take out their grievances against the Polish majority, in particular against those elements the Germans targeted too, intellectuals, Catholic priests, and other community leaders. They gave gentile Poles and Ukrainians license to terrorize Jews and steal their possessions.

In June 1941 Ukrainians in Lvov arrested some Jews on the charge that they had committed atrocities against Ukrainians during the Soviet occupation. Many of those Jews were executed in prisons and nearby forests. Others were taken to prison cells already stained with Jewish blood, forced to clean them, and then shot. Pogroms raged in the city throughout July 1941, and thousands of Jews were killed. On one occasion little Nelly Toll watched from the balcony with her cousins as German soldiers beat an old Jewish man. A crowd gathered to laugh and clap.

A local Jewish dignitary named Rabbi Levin appealed for help to Metropolitan Sheptytsky, the head of the local Ukrainian Catholic church. Sheptyt-sky called on Ukrainians to stop murdering Jews, but without effect. He then invited the rabbi to take refuge in his personal residence, but Rabbi Levin thought his place was with his people, so he left the metropolitan's residence to go home. He never made it. Instead rioters seized him and dragged him to prison, where he was murdered.

Nelly Toll was luckier than Rabbi Levin. She lived through 1941, although children threw stones at her in the street, her mother was beaten black and blue by a Ukrainian policeman, and the family was forced into a ghetto. Eventually Nelly's mother sent her to hide with a Christian family. When that place proved too risky she returned to the ghetto to learn that her brother, aunt, and little cousins had all been taken away by the Gestapo and put on a train. None of them returned.

In 1943, after more close calls and a failed attempt to escape to Hungary, Nelly and her mother went into hiding. They ended up with a Polish Catholic couple who sheltered them in exchange for money. The woman was kind and thoughtful but not her husband. He was violent, paranoid, and antisemitic, abusive to his wife yet overattentive to Nelly's mother. It was a very difficult situation. Somehow both Nelly and her mother survived the war, but they never saw Nelly's father again. Nelly Toll immigrated to the United States in 1951, where she became an artist and a counselor.

Hitler expected the campaign against the Soviet Union to be easy for the Germans. In this regard he and his military planners were caught in their own ethnic and racial stereotypes. They thought of Slavs as stupid and incompetent and believed that the Communist Soviet Union was in the grip of Jews, whom they viewed as cowardly and perfidious. Such attitudes caused the German leaders to make some severe miscalculations.

The German invasion did not turn out as planned. The Soviets were bet-ter equipped than German planners had thought; the Germans themselves were overextended and unprepared for winter. Contrary to what many Ger-man accounts claim, the winter of 1941 was neither unusually early nor extraordinarily harsh; it was more or less a typical Russian winter. Nor, as the historian Gerhard Weinberg has pointed out, did it snow only on the Germans; the Soviets faced the same winter conditions. Hitler and his generals, however, had anticipated quick victory, another "lightning war" that of course they would win. They had not thought it necessary to prepare for winter.

Crossing the Line to Annihilation

From the beginning of war with the Soviet Union, the German leader-ship advocated unprecedented, ruthless measures. In instructions to the military and the SS, Hitler, Himmler, and Heydrich made it clear that no mercy was to be shown Germany's enemies, whether they were Jews, Communists, or resistors. High-ranking officers passed the message down to their men.

With the invasion of the Soviet Union the Nazi leadership would move to full implementation of their ideas of race and space on a massive scale. Their warfare reached new depths of brutality, especially against civilians but also against Soviet prisoners of war. Most noticeably they crossed the line from persecution and killing of Jews to a systematic attempt at total destruction.

Yet in many ways 1941 was not a radical break with earlier Nazi practices. All of the pieces were already in place. Hitler had spelled out the quest for Lebensraum in *Mein Kampf*. The Germans had begun to grab territory in Europe even before the war. They had assaulted civilians on a wide scale in Poland since 1939; they had used their enemies as slave labor, forcibly relocated enormous numbers of people, and started to slaughter Jews, Gypsies, and people deemed handicapped even before June 1941. In 1940 in France they had massacred thousands of captured black soldiers. All of these terrible developments culminated in the Soviet Union in 1941 and the years to follow.

Perhaps the most glaring sign of Germany's brutal style of warfare in 1941 was the use of special murder squads. German authorities dispatched mobile killing units to follow the regular military into Soviet territory. The main units, known as the *Einsatzgruppen*, "special action groups," included between five hundred and one thousand men each, many of them well educated, lawyers, theologians, and other professionals. The Einsatzgruppen worked together with more numerous German units known as the Order Police. Both the Einsatzgruppen and the Order Police cooperated with the German military.

The task of the mobile killing units was straightforward. They had explicit instructions from Heydrich to kill Jews, prominent Communists, and anyone suspected of sabotage or anti-German activity. Officially their goal was to combat Bolshevism and prevent guerrilla warfare. In fact, during the summer of 1941, they began to interpret their primary job as slaughter of all Jews, including women, children, and old people. The Einsatzgruppen and Order Police also murdered Gypsies and inmates of mental hospitals, although they seem to have been less systematic against those target populations.

Members of the mobile killing units tried to involve local people in their work. Many non-German auxiliaries—Ukrainians, Latvians, ethnic Germans from eastern Europe, Belorussians, and others—helped in their grisly task. Threats, bribes, massive amounts of alcohol, and promises of privileges for recruits and their families all helped the Germans find willing henchmen.

The Einsatzgruppen and Order Police attempted to stir up pogroms wherever they went. In some cases locals did take spontaneous action against Jews, but the mobile killing groups were less successful in this regard than they had hoped. Local individuals sometimes launched spontaneous attacks on Jews and took the initiative to steal their property, but generally the impetus and organization for systematic killing came from the Germans.

Many of the actions of the mobile killing units more or less followed the same pattern. First they rounded up the Jews in a given area using various ruses to deceive them and relying on local collaborators for denunciations. The Germans ordered large pits dug in some convenient area—a local cemetery, nearby forest, or easily accessible field. Often they forced the prisoners themselves to dig what would be their own graves. At gunpoint they made the victims undress. Then they shot them by groups directly into the graves. In this manner the mobile killing units and their accomplices killed around a million people even before construction of killing centers for gassing had begun.

Of course, such mass killings in the open air could hardly be kept secret. Eyewitnesses of all kinds saw these shootings—German soldiers and workers, ethnic Germans who lived nearby, Russian, Polish, or Ukrainian families from the region, and others. Some of those observers gave detailed, chilling accounts of what they saw. For example, a German builder named Hermann Graebe watched while mobile killing squads shot scores of people of all ages near Dubno in Ukraine. He was surprised to be allowed to stay, but he noticed three uniformed postal workers looking on as well.

Elsewhere in Ukraine a fifteen-year-old Mennonite boy and his friends saw the slaughter of a group of Gypsies at a local cemetery. Later someone came around the village to distribute clothes taken from the murdered people. According to the eyewitness's account, no one in that particular Mennonite (and ethnic German) community wanted anything to do with booty won in such a way.

Most of our information about the mass shootings comes from the perpetrators themselves or from onlookers. Few victims lived to tell about their experiences. One of the exceptions is a man named Zvi Michalowsky, whose account appears in a book by Yaffa Eliach called *Hasidic Tales of the Holocaust*.

In 1941 on Rosh Hashanah, the Jewish new year, Germans and their local helpers murdered the Jews in a Lithuanian town called Eisysky. Michalowsky, a teenaged boy at the time, was among those forced to strip and wait at the edge of a grave for a bullet. A split second before the Germans fired, Zvi threw himself back into the pit. Miraculously he avoided serious injury.

For the rest of that day Zvi lay in the mass grave, feeling the bodies pile

Germans shoot a group of Poles in Lithuania in 1941 or 1942 as Lithuanian auxiliaries and others, including a young man taking a photograph, look on. Open-air killings were common throughout the war, and there was little attempt to conceal them from onlookers.

up on top of him. Only long after the shooting had stopped did he dare to climb out. He ran, naked and covered with blood, to the nearest house, but when he knocked, the terrified Polish Christians who lived there refused to let him in. Finally he approached an old woman. He told her he was Jesus Christ come down from the cross, and she opened the door to him. Zvi Michalowsky went on to found a Jewish resistance group in the woods of Lithuania. He survived the war.

Probably the biggest slaughter carried out by the Einsatzgruppen and their helpers was the massacre at Babi Yar. In just two days in September 1941, German mobile killing units and local collaborators shot more than thirty thousand Jews and an unknown number of other people at Babi Yar, a ravine on the outskirts of the Ukrainian city of Kiev. That act, just months after the invasion of the Soviet Union, destroyed the thriving Jewish community in Kiev and its surrounding area.

Germans continued to use Babi Yar as a killing field throughout the occupation of Ukraine. Some estimates of the total number of people killed there are as high as one hundred thousand. The majority were Jews, although others targeted by the German occupiers were murdered at Babi Yar as well. That massacre has become emblematic of the vicious brutality of Nazi Germans in the Soviet Union generally and particularly in Ukraine.

In Soviet times state authorities put up a monument to the victims of Babi Yar. The plaque dedicated the memorial to the more than one hundred thousand Soviet citizens killed there. Nowhere did it mention that most of those dead were murdered solely because they were Jews. Here the official act of remembering also became a way of forgetting.

The exact number of people killed by the mobile units cannot be known, although German records have allowed experts in the field to come to an estimate approaching 2 million total victims. Most were Jews—some 1.3 million— and there may have been as many as 250,000 Gypsies. The Einsatzgruppen and Order Police followed the regular military and in many cases even relied on them for provisions, security, and intelligence. They could not have carried out such an enormous number of killings without the knowledge and cooperation of the Wehrmacht. How did the military respond?

At first it seems there might have been some misgivings. One incident illustrates the forms such doubts might have taken. In mid-August 1941, German authorities in the Ukrainian town of Belaya Tserkov, more than two hundred miles east of Lvov, ordered local Jews to report for registration. Over the next few days, SS and German soldiers scoured the area for Jews, slaughtering hundreds of men and women.

In the summer of 1941 some of the killers still seemed unclear as to whether their task included murder of Jewish women and children as well as men. Perhaps for this reason, the shooters at Belaya Tserkov did not initially kill all the children. Instead they dumped about ninety of them and a handful of women in a school.

German soldiers in a field hospital nearby heard babies crying in the night. Uncertain how to respond, they appealed to their military chaplains. The two German clergy, a Protestant pastor and a Catholic priest, went to see for themselves. They were appalled. It was hot, but the children were crammed into a small space without water, food, or adult care. Some of the mothers were locked in an adjoining room, from which they could see the misery of their children without being able to get to them.

The chaplains appealed to the local military commander, an elderly Austrian, to take pity on the children. Their effort failed, one of them later reported, because the man was a convinced antisemite. Together the chaplains convinced another German officer to intervene. He got Army High Command to agree to postpone shooting of the children, but SS representatives and military officers on the spot prevailed, pointing to instructions from General Field Marshal Gerd von Runstedt, commander of Army Group South, that they were to show no mercy.

On 21 August 1941, the children were taken from the school and killed. It is unclear whether it was Germans or Ukrainian volunteers who did the job.

Killings of civilians did not end in the summer or fall of 1941 but continued throughout the war. Presumably German soldiers and the military chaplains who ministered to them got used to the routine. The comfort of knowing they were backed by orders from above must have helped too.

One of the most widely circulated of such orders came in October 1941 from German Field Marshal Walter von Reichenau. Reichenau admitted that there was "uncertainty" among the German troops as to the current situation in the east. However, he told his men, given the nature of this war and the need to destroy what he called the "Jewish-Bolshevist system" completely, it was necessary to break the conventional rules of war, to show no mercy to those defined as Germany's enemies, above all the people Reichenau labeled "Jewish subhumans."

It is certainly not common practice for military superiors to justify themselves and their decisions to their men. Reichenau, however, did just that. His order implies that there was some uneasiness in the ranks about military involvement in slaughter of civilians. We can assume that those reservations were overcome. After all, the killings continued with the necessary military support. Perhaps German soldiers accepted the official justifications offered to them, that such excesses were a necessary part of the German struggle against partisans, or later on, that they were some kind of revenge for Allied bombings of German cities.

Of course neither of those rationalizations actually makes sense. How could a baby be responsible for a partisan attack on German rail lines? What could an old Jewish woman more than a thousand miles away who spoke nothing but Yiddish possibly have to do with British planes dropping bombs on Hamburg or Cologne? Nevertheless these nonsensical explanations may have helped men live with themselves once they were already involved in killing. Many of their motivations for killing in the first place were undramatic. Their comrades were doing it, and they did not want to stand out; they considered it part of their job; they had gotten used to it.

What we do know is that Germans were not forced to be killers. Those who refused to participate were given other assignments or transferred. To this day no one has ever found a single example of a German who was executed for refusing to take part in the killing of Jews or other civilians. Defense attor-

German troops stand at the edge of a trench used as a mass grave for the bodies of Jews and Gypsies killed by the 750th Infantry Regiment in October 1941 in the Macva region of Yugoslavia. A German soldier sent this photograph to a woman friend in spring 1945.

neys of Germans accused of war crimes during World War II have looked hard for such a case because it would support the claim that their clients were forced to kill. The Nazi system, however, did not work that way. There were enough willing perpetrators. For the most part coercive violence could be reserved for those deemed enemies.

Romania and the Killing Fields in Transnistria

Brutalization, it seems, is contagious; violence tends to breed more of the same. This point is evident if we look briefly at Romania, one of Germany's

World War II allies, in 1941. The Romanian army took an active part in the German offensive against the southern Soviet Union. In the areas conquered, German and Romanian armies cooperated with the Einsatzgruppen in massacring Jews and Gypsies.

The case of the Jews in the Ukrainian city of Odessa provides an example. In the fall of 1941, several days after German and Romanian forces occupied Odessa, an explosion rocked Romanian army headquarters there. In retaliation, Romanian leader Ion Antonescu ordered the execution of two hundred "Communists" for every Romanian officer killed and one hundred for each soldier. Most of the victims selected were Jews. Einsatzgruppen killers worked together with German and Romanian military, Ukrainian auxiliary police, and recruits from the local ethnic German population to slaughter some thirty-five thousand Jews. In February 1942, Odessa was proclaimed "Judenrein," or "cleansed of Jews."

Beginning in 1941, persecution of Jews also exploded within Romania. The Romanian government introduced laws restricting Jews in all kinds of ways, and pogroms resulted in the death of well over a thousand Romanian Jews. Antisemitism was not new to Romania, but the war and German leadership gave antisemites license to act on their hatreds in dramatic, large-scale ways.

In the fall of 1941, Romanian authorities began moving Jews out of Romania and forcing them east across the Dniester River and then the Bug River into an area of intense Einsatzgruppen operations. First 50,000 and then another 120,000 Romanian Jews were driven into the hands of the Germans and their accomplices in Transnistria in the occupied Ukraine.

Among those deported in this way was a young boy named Aharon Appelfeld. Separated from his father, he ended up in a makeshift Transnistrian camp. Somehow he escaped, dodged the killing fields of the Einsatzgruppen, and evaded the reach of local collaborators. Just nine years old in 1941, he survived for four years working as a shepherd, hiding in the woods, stealing, begging, and taking refuge with people who helped him. After the war Appelfeld moved to Israel. He is the author of many acclaimed works of fiction dealing with themes from the Holocaust.

Many Romanian Gypsies shared the fate of their Jewish compatriots. A woman named Drina Radu survived deportation to Transnistria as a girl of about ten. She remembers crossing the Dniester River into the part of Ukraine occupied by Romania. Everyone rushed to get on the first boatloads, she told the journalist Isabel Fonseca, not because they were eager to reach the other side but because, in her words, "the boats were made of paper." Hastily constructed from cheap, porous material, they became waterlogged and sank after three or four trips. That detail reveals the deadly cynicism of the Romanians in charge. Why go to any effort or expense to protect the lives of people they knew were slated for death anyway? Between 1941 and 1944, approximately thirty-six thousand Roma were killed in Transnistria.

For the Romanian Jews and Gypsies murdered in the killing fields of Transnistria, there was nothing ambiguous about their government's plan for them. It was deadly, but there were ways in which the Romanian situation was complex too. For one thing, German authorities did not welcome Romanian initiatives, such as the expulsion of almost two hundred thousand Jews into territories the Germans held. The German masterminds of mass killing preferred to retain control themselves. Accordingly Antonescu was told to stop striking out on his own and to wait for Germans to take the lead.

Romanian gentiles continued to have their own ideas about how to solve what they considered their "Jewish problem." The Romanian government set up an office to look after Jewish affairs. It tolerated the existence of Jewish mutual-aid activities and allowed them to try to help the Jewish expellees. Leaders of the Jewish community maintained relations with some heads of state and in some incidents even managed to mitigate anti-Jewish measures. There were prominent Romanians—including the queen—who approached the Germans on behalf of Romanian Jews. Those efforts were rejected.

In wartime Romania, traditional antisemitism and widespread persecution of Jews were the norm. Nevertheless the Romanian leadership, for all its viciousness, did not show the same single-minded and systematic dedication to eradication of the Jews that the Nazi Germans introduced in the countries they controlled. Traditional Jewish means of self-preservation—mutual aid, intercession with rulers, evasion, and bribery—continued to have some effect in Romania. For all the horrors of 1941 and the years to follow, a higher percentage of Jews in Romania would survive the war than would be the case in Poland or the Netherlands.

German Treatment of Soviet POWs

Hitler's war of annihilation against the Soviet Union included killing of prisoners of war on a massive scale. Of the millions of non-Jews killed in German camps, by far the largest group of dead was Soviet POWs. Their brutal treatment violated every standard of warfare.

Statistics only begin to tell the story. Initial German successes in the summer and fall of 1941 brought an enormous number of POWs into German hands. In total, between 22 June 1941 and the end of the war, Germans took approximately 5.7 million Red Army soldiers prisoner. As of January 1945, about 930,000 Soviet POWs remained in Wehrmacht prison camps. About 1 million had been released as helpers of the German military. Another estimated half million had escaped or been liberated by the Red Army. That still leaves 3.3 million—57 percent—unaccounted for. They were dead.

Such a staggering death rate was neither an accident nor an automatic result of war. It was deliberate policy. German treatment of Soviet POWs differed wildly from German handling of POWs from Britain and the United States. Of the 231,000 British and American prisoners held by the Germans, only about 8,300—3.6 percent—died before the end of the war.

Death came in various ways to the more than 3 million Soviet POWs who died in German hands. In the early stages of the conflict the Germans shot many of the prisoners they took. They had made few provisions to accommodate their captives; they simply disposed of them. Eventually they erected some makeshift camps, but the lack of proper food, clothing, and shelter took a terri-

In September 1941, a column of Soviet POWs heads toward the rear and internment. Most Soviet POWs were held in facilities administered by the German military, not the SS. Such sites of detention hardly merited the label "camp" because in many cases they provided neither shelter nor food.

ble toll. By the end of 1941, epidemics—especially typhoid and dysentery—emerged as the big killers. In October 1941 alone, as many as 4,600 Soviet POWs died per day. Death rates fell off somewhat in 1942 as German authorities decided POWs could be a useful source of wartime labor. In 1943 and 1944, however, they soared again, due above all to hunger.

Starvation of Soviet POWs was directly tied to the Nazi policy of making sure there was plenty of food for the German home front. No doubt Hitler and others remembered the food riots of World War I, a war they believed Germany had lost because of its weak home front. This time they intended to keep food supplies—and morale—up, even if it meant starvation of what one bureaucrat called "umpteen million people."

German authorities viewed Soviet POWs as a particular threat, regarding them not only as Slavic subhumans but as part of the "Bolshevik menace," linked in their minds to some imaginary Jewish conspiracy. They spared no violence against the Soviet prisoners. In the camp of Gross-Rosen, in Germany, the commandant had sixty-five thousand Soviet inmates killed within six months by feeding them a soup made only of grass, water, and salt. In Flossenbürg, SS men burned Soviet POWs alive. In Majdanek, they shot them into trenches. In Mauthausen, in Austria, so many POWs were killed that people living near the camp complained about pollution of their water supply; for days the rivers and streams of the area ran red with blood.

The notorious German camps of Auschwitz, near Krakow, and Majdanek, by Lublin, were originally built to shelter Soviet POWs and to exploit their labor for the industrial complexes Himmler planned there. In 1941 some fifteen thousand Soviet POWs were taken to those camps; by January 1942, only a few hundred remained alive. In early 1942, Himmler filled those sites with 150,000 German Jews and transformed the camps into killing centers. In this way camps constructed for Soviet POWs became part of the machinery for destruction of Jews.

It was when dealing with Soviet POWs at Auschwitz that camp commandant Rudolf Hoess and his assistants experimented with the means of killing that have become the symbol of Nazi genocide: Zyklon B. In early September 1941, six hundred Soviet prisoners selected for execution by the SS arrived at Auschwitz. In order to avoid the cumbersome task of shooting so many people, Hoess and his men decided to gas them with the pesticide Zyklon B, also known as hydrogen cyanide. While they were at it they included another 250 inmates who had been designated unfit for work.

The T-4 killers had already experimented with gassing as a way to murder people considered handicapped. Those lessons were subsequently applied first to Soviet POWs and then to Jews.

THE WANNSEE CONFERENCE— STREAMLINING THE KILLING OPERATIONS

By the end of 1941, the German leadership concluded that mass shootings were not the most efficient way to carry out their so-called Final Solution. Their concerns were not about the victims but rather about the perpetrators, who found it physically and psychologically difficult to shoot people all day long at close range.

Led by Heydrich, top German officials met in early 1942 to coordinate and streamline their efforts to annihilate the Jews. This meeting was called the Wannsee Conference because it took place in a villa in Wannsee, a suburb of Berlin.

At the conference were representatives from the offices and agencies in the German government and Nazi Party who had a direct hand in the killing process. High officials from the Foreign Office were on hand as were representatives of the SS, Einsatzgruppen, Nazi Party headquarters, Justice Ministry, Hans Frank in the General Government in Poland, and others. Heydrich himself chaired the meeting. Eichmann, who would later be in charge of transporting Jews to the killing centers, produced the official report.

Wannsee focused on Jews as the top priority of Nazi destruction. Eichmann's report makes it clear that all 11 million Jews in Europe were targeted for murder. The list even included Jews in Sweden, Ireland, and England, places not in German hands in 1942. Also specified were Jews in the "European part" of Turkey, an indication that Jews living outside Europe would be slated for destruction in a subsequent phase of operations.

The Wannsee Conference marked another step in the killing process. Mass murder was already under way when the conference met, but at Wannsee the global scope of annihilation was indicated. Meanwhile the SS asserted its leadership in the murder of Jews. Heydrich needed the cooperation of the other agencies and offices represented, but he made it clear who called the shots. Of course, by their very presence those other bureaucrats, party functionaries, and occupation authorities demonstrated that they understood what was going on and endorsed it. The line to genocide was not one Hitler would cross alone.

Participants at the Wannsee Conference also addressed methods of killing.

Killing centers with gas chambers emerged as their means of choice. Instead of bringing the killers to their victims, it was decided that the victims should be transported to their killers. Accordingly, construction of new killing centers began within months. Meanwhile, existing camps such as Auschwitz were ordered expanded and equipped with gassing facilities. At the same time, the methods of killing already introduced continued, that is, shootings, starvation, death by overwork, abuse, and disease. It was remarkable how quickly things could move forward once the line to annihilation had been crossed.

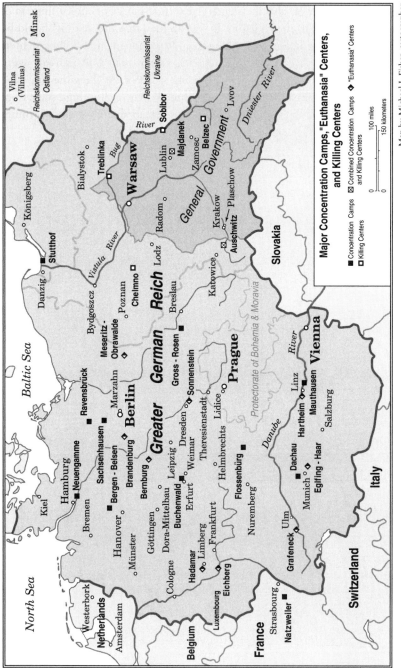

Major Concentration Camps, "Euthanasia" Centers, and Killing Centers

■ Concentration Camps   ⊠ Combined Concentration Camps and Killing Centers   ◆ "Euthanasia" Centers
□ Killing Centers

0 ___ 100 miles
0 ___ 150 kilometers

North Sea

Baltic Sea

Netherlands
Amsterdam
Westerbork
Belgium
Luxembourg
Eichberg
France
Strasbourg
Natzweiler

Kiel
Hamburg
Neuengamme
Bremen
Hanover
Münster
Cologne
Hadamar
Limberg
Frankfurt
Göttingen
Dora-Mittelbau
Buchenwald
Erfurt
Weimar
Leipzig
Dresden
Bernburg
Brandenburg
Berlin
Marzahn
Ravensbrück
Sachsenhausen

Greater German Reich

Bergen - Belsen
Sonnenstein
Gross - Rosen
Theresienstadt
Lidice
Helmbrechts
Flossenburg
Nuremberg
Ulm
Grafeneck
Munich
Dachau
Eglfing - Haar

Prague
Protectorate of Bohemia & Moravia

Linz
Hartheim
Mauthausen
Salzburg
Vienna

Danube River
Italy
Switzerland

Stutthof
Danzig
Königsberg
Bydgoszcz
Meseritz - Obrawalde
Poznan
Chelmno
Lodz
Breslau
Katowice
Auschwitz
Krakow
Plaschow
Radom

Vistula River

Bialystok
Treblinka
Warsaw
Bug River
Sobibor
Lublin
Majdanek
Zamosc
Belzec
Lvov
Dniester River

General Government

Slovakia

Vilna (Vilnius)
Reichskommissariat Ostland
Minsk
Reichskommissariat Ukraine

Map by Michael J. Fisher, cartographer

7

THE PEAK YEARS OF KILLING

1942 AND 1943

W hen it comes to human suffering, each year of a war tends to be worse than the year before. The passage of time adds further material deprivation, more wounded, and more dead to the accumulated misery of the people involved.

This depressing observation certainly holds true for the Second World War. By the end of 1942 the Germans were heading into their fourth year of war. At least in the short term their victories insulated them from much of the bereavement and hardship that war brings. The same was not true for the people they conquered. The devastation of Poland—economically, politically, socially—became ever more terrible as the Poles endured year after year of defeat and occupation. The Nazi German hand may have been less heavy on western Europe, but there too—in occupied Denmark, Norway, the Netherlands, Belgium, France, and elsewhere—adversity and demoralization continued to build. Meanwhile, in the Balkans and the Soviet territories overrun in 1941, German occupation practices produced an ever-escalating reign of terror.

It was not just the normal dynamic of war that served to multiply human suffering as World War II continued. The Nazi principles of spatial expansion and "racial purification" meant that more and more killing was itself a direct goal of the German war effort. The more Hitler's empire extended its reach and consolidated its hold on subject lands and peoples, the more its forces sought to destroy those it deemed enemies—Jews above all, but also Slavs and others defined as unwanted inferiors. For this reason, 1942 and 1943—the years when German power in Europe reached its height—were also the peak years of killing.

This chapter examines both sides of the space and race equation during those two years. What did German military conquest mean for the people of Europe? How did Nazi Germans and their accomplices carry out this most deadly stage of their program to annihilate Jews? Who resisted them?

GERMAN MILITARY POWER AT ITS HEIGHT

One point is so obvious it is often not stated: Hitler and the Nazis planned to win the war. War, Hitler believed, would not merely defeat the enemy militarily; it would create a "new order."

General Plan East, Germanization, and the Nazi "New Order"

German planners developed in detail the implications of their notion of Lebensraum—living space—in an important memorandum called "General Plan East." Drafted in 1941, that document presented the Nazi vision for eastern Europe. One of its primary authors was a young historian named Theodor Schieder. After the war Schieder pursued a successful academic career in West Germany. Only after his death, half a century after the war had ended, would his students and many people who admired his scholarship realize the use to which he had put his training and skills during the war.

General Plan East called for Germans and ethnic Germans to settle vast areas of eastern Europe, where they would produce food and babies for the "Aryan master race." To make such settlements possible, the plan demanded expulsion of those currently living there. Those tens of millions of people, most of them Slavs, were to be forced into less desirable areas, allowed to die of starvation and disease, or turned into slaves for the German empire. According to General Plan East, Jews were to disappear altogether.

Like so much Nazi writing, General Plan East was full of euphemisms. Instead of spelling out the goal as to kill people or make sure they died of starvation, overwork, or disease, the document talked about "reducing" or "removing" certain populations. Nevertheless its intentions were obvious. It also made clear that German policies toward different population groups were closely connected. Settlement of Germans and ethnic Germans in the east;

expulsion, enslavement, and decimation of Slavs; and murder of Jews were all parts of the same plan.

General Plan East envisioned "Germanization" of an enormous territory that stretched eastward from the old German Reich all the way to the Ural Mountains. Someday, according to the plan, 500 to 600 million people would live there: "Aryan" Germans and their slaves.

German population planners realized that even a massively increased birthrate could not produce enough children to achieve the rate of population growth they wanted. As a result, they proposed taking "racially valuable" children away from supposedly inferior parents in order to "Germanize" them. In other words, they intended to transform some of the children of non-Germans into members of the "Aryan race." So-called racial experts estimated that about 50 percent of Czech children were suitable for "Germanization." They thought as many as 75 percent of the children in some parts of western Belorussia might be acceptable, but under no conditions were Jewish children to be "Germanized."

Concrete steps were taken to increase numbers of Germans while weakening the peoples of the territories they occupied. Under a program code-named Operation *Heuaktion*, the "hay action," German agencies kidnapped thousands of children and adolescents from eastern Europe and sent them to the Reich, in some cases to be raised by German families, in other cases to work in factories or handicrafts. Meanwhile, German doctors, many of them working in concentration camps and using inmates as subjects, experimented with methods of mass sterilization. Those medical scientists working in Auschwitz must have known full well that Jews would not be the people intended for the new techniques of sterilization: the Jews were in the process of being annihilated. Sterilization was to be the fate of the non-Jewish population of eastern Europe.

Schemes of Germanization remind us just how artificial Nazi notions of blood and race were. The case of two Polish women provides an illustration. Although the parents of Johanna and Danuta W. were "pure Polish," the sisters both applied for Germanization. No doubt they hoped to get the benefits that being classified as German rather than Polish would bring.

In 1944 SS racial authorities in one city approved Johanna's application, and she became officially recognized as an ethnic German. A similar office elsewhere rejected Danuta. Meanwhile both women went to Germany to work as housemaids.

Danuta became pregnant by an SS man. When her baby was born he received ethnic German status, but his mother was still classified as a Pole. The only reason German authorities gave for rejecting Danuta was that "she did not look so good."

Danuta's status caused practical problems because the sisters lived together. Under the terms of Nazi racial law, ethnic Germans such as Johanna were to have no social contact with Poles like Danuta. Nor was Danuta's own child permitted to interact with his mother. The postwar fates of Johanna, Danuta, and her son are unknown.

Slave Labor

During 1942 and 1943 Germans enslaved millions of people, women as well as men, from the Soviet Union and elsewhere in eastern Europe. Some were forced to labor in the occupied areas; millions of others were sent to Germany to work in factories, on farms, and in private homes.

Hitler and other planners considered slave labor a way to keep the German home front happy. They did not want to introduce measures that might have been unpopular with many Germans: for example, recruiting large numbers of German women into factory work or curtailing supplies of food and consumer goods. After all, Hitler and others like him still believed that discontent at home had led to German defeat in the last war. So they brought in millions of people they considered disposable and used them to make waging a war of annihilation as comfortable as possible for the German people.

The German occupiers also seized agricultural produce in the areas they controlled, causing famine and starvation among the people left behind. They took over whatever industrial production had not been evacuated by the Soviet Army as it had fled in 1941. In the name of fighting partisans, German forces burned entire villages, often along with many of the people who lived in them. Public hangings, torture, rape, and sexual slavery were all common occurrences in the occupied east.

German Reactions

Some German authorities worried that such brutality was counterproductive because it sparked opposition that could have been avoided. As one high-ranking German official observed, many of the Soviet people had suffered terribly under Stalin. It would not have taken much to persuade them that their lives under German rule would be better than they could expect with the return of Communism. The extreme viciousness of German occupation, however, convinced the vast majority of Soviets that even Stalin was preferable to Hitler.

Hitler and propaganda minister Goebbels paid lip service to the need to soften up in order to prevent an explosion of opposition in the east, but German policies did not change. To the contrary, reprisals against guerrilla activity kept increasing in their ferocity. Meanwhile the Germans defined partisan activity, or "banditry," as they preferred to call it, more and more broadly.

SS leader Himmler summed up dominant German views in a speech to top SS men in October 1943:

> We must be honest, decent, loyal, and comradely to members of our own blood and to nobody else. What happens to a Russian or to a Czech does not interest me in the slightest. What the nations can offer in the way of good blood of our type we will take, if necessary by kidnapping their children and raising them here with us. . . . Whether 10,000 Russian females fall down from exhaustion while digging an anti-tank ditch interests me only in so far as the anti-tank ditch for Germany is finished. We shall never be rough and heartless when it is not necessary, that is clear. We Germans, who are the only people in the world who have a decent attitude towards animals, will also assume a decent attitude towards these human animals. But it is a crime against our own blood to worry about them and give them ideals, thus causing our sons and grandsons to have a more difficult time with them. (Noakes and Pridham 3:919–20)

In Himmler's mind Russians and Czechs merited nothing more than the self-interested care one would show a beast of burden.

Hitler and many top Nazis rejected Christianity. They considered it an offshoot of Judaism that encouraged weakness and humility instead of aggression. In wartime, however, they realized that it was counterproductive to deprive Germans of the comfort of the traditional religion. Accordingly they allowed Christian military chaplains—Roman Catholic as well as Protestant—to minister to the men of the Wehrmacht. Accounts from these German clergy give another perspective on conditions in the east.

One Catholic chaplain buried 120 German soldiers in the first five months of 1942. In a report to superiors he admitted that the "long duration of the war and the many dead have brought a certain indifference to death." If the Germans had become numb toward their own casualties, how much less must they have cared about anyone else?

Christian clergy also heard confessions of terrible crimes. For example, a German Catholic priest stationed in Ukraine met a wounded soldier who confided to him about his past. The man had taken part in a mass shooting of Jews near Sevastopol in the Crimea. According to the priest, the soldier was ruined by his experience. He described the Jews, lined up, naked—women, children, and men. Although he had manned one of the machine guns he insisted he had only shot in the air. What should he have done, he asked the priest?

We do not know what the priest answered, but it seems evident that at least some Germans could not tolerate conditions in the east. Desertions and self-mutilations were not uncommon, although military authorities punished them severely, often with death. Nervous breakdowns generally led to transfers to less trying duties.

Not only military men but German civilians too were drawn into the war of annihilation. In Poland, for example, German employees of a bank found themselves assigned to guard the street between a Jewish ghetto and the train station as SS and Gestapo cleared out Jews and sent them on trains to be killed. Some people accepted such tasks, eager to win promotions or prove their hardness. Others sought transfers to places where it was easier to shut out the realities of the war, back home in Germany, perhaps, or in western Europe.

When it came to his top military leaders, Hitler used bribery to make sure that their consciences did not protest too loudly. Every month, on orders from the Führer, German generals received special tax-free supplements of between 2,000 and 4,000 Reich Marks. They had their pick of the finest estates in Poland and elsewhere, stolen, of course, from the original owners. On special birthdays—when a general turned fifty, for example—he received a bonus of as much as 250,000 Reich Marks. Of course cooperation and good behavior increased the amount.

Such sums made the German generals fabulously wealthy. In contrast, German infantry who cleared mines during the war—an extremely dangerous job—received supplements to their regular incomes of only one mark per day.

Military Developments and Nonmilitary Repercussions

Discussions of the Holocaust often pay little attention to the war itself, but without war and German victories there would have been no genocide of the European Jews. The vast majority of Jews murdered by Nazi Germans—about 95 percent—came from outside Germany. Without military conquests the perpetrators would never have got those victims in their hands.

Yet even during the war itself many people on the Allied side did not see the links between the German war effort and mass murder. Soviet, British, and American military planners tended to take a fairly narrow view of events. Their goal was to win the war, whatever that meant; their objectives were military ones. It is probably fair to say that they devoted little thought to what seemed bizarre, nonmilitary "sideshows" on the part of the Germans, such as attacks on handicapped people, Gypsies, and Jews.

Nevertheless military decisions and developments in 1942 and 1943 had repercussions far beyond the military sphere. We will look at just three examples: the events surrounding Stalingrad, North Africa, and Italy.

THE BATTLE OF STALINGRAD

From 1941 to 1943 most of the combat in Europe occurred between German and Soviet forces on Germany's eastern front. In 1941 the Red Army had checked the Germans and their Axis partners, but by mid-1942 the Germans took the offensive again.

The new German offensive had two prongs. One entered the Caucasus region with an eye to the oil fields there. The other moved toward the city of Stalingrad—modern Volgograd—on the lower Volga River. What is now known as the Battle of Stalingrad began in the late summer and fall of 1942 as the advancing Germans were blocked by the defending Red Army.

Hitler instructed the German 6th Army under General (later Field Marshal) Friedrich Paulus to take Stalingrad. In September the 6th Army and the 4th Panzer Army advanced into the outskirts; by mid-November they had captured much of the city.

Fighting was extraordinarily fierce. The Soviets, ordered by Stalin to defend the city with everything they had, contested every inch. Losses on both sides were staggering. Between 21 August and 16 October 1942, the German 6th Army alone suffered some forty thousand casualties. In late November, a Soviet offensive cut off the 6th Army, parts of another German army, and two Romanian armies in the Stalingrad area. The Red Army surrounded them. German attempts to relieve their forces in December failed, and the Soviets demanded capitulation.

Already earlier, some of Hitler's generals had advised a withdrawal, but he and others were determined to hold on. The territory had been won at such a high cost, and Stalingrad was an important hub of Soviet transport. Hitler did agree to retrenchment in the Caucasus, so it is not the case that he never authorized retreats. With Stalingrad, however, Hitler did not give in.

On 31 January 1943, the German southern contingent under Paulus capitulated. A few days later the northern contingent followed. The Soviets took ninety thousand German prisoners of war; there were hundreds of thousands dead on both sides.

Even after the Battle of Stalingrad, the outcome of the war was far from a foregone conclusion. Just a month later, in late February 1943, the Germans mounted a successful counteroffensive at the southern part of their eastern front. Still, at least in hindsight, Stalingrad appeared to have been an important military and symbolic turning point.

Back home Goebbels's propaganda machine presented Stalingrad as a strategic retreat, but few were fooled. The Red Army victory at Stalingrad marked a visible departure from the way the war had gone so far for Germany. At least some Germans were scared. SS reports indicate that the Nazi Party began to lose support. Many Germans had lost family members at Stalingrad; they wanted the war to end as soon as possible.

Discontent for the most part did not translate into open opposition to the regime. Instead the German public became more cynical and withdrawn. Distracted by increasing Allied air raids on their cities, Germans at home busied themselves with the practical matters of staying alive and keeping their families together. The regime did make some concessions to try to boost public spirits; it eased restrictions on the churches and slackened its campaign against cigarette smoking.

Reports prepared by the Nazi Security Service, the SD, indicate that many Germans knew quite a lot about the atrocities their country was committing in the east. In 1943, when mass graves of Polish officers shot by the Soviets were found at Katyn, there was little reaction within Germany. The Soviets would soon find plenty of mass graves of murdered Jews, some muttered, so it was better not to draw too much attention to similar crimes on the other side.

In the meantime, the German leadership cracked down tighter on its critics at home. Beginning in early 1943, offenses such as "defeatism" were often punished by death. For example, the sister of Erich Maria Remarque, author of the World War I classic *All Quiet on the Western Front,* was condemned to death for remarking that Hitler should resign. German authorities also introduced draconian measures against accused deserters and traitors in the military, at least twenty-five thousand of whom they had shot over the course of the war, mostly in its later stages.

Still, being defined as "Aryan" continued to offer considerable protection for Germans throughout the war. An important illustration involves a group of German gentile women in Berlin who were married to German Jewish men. In early 1943, in preparation for Hitler's upcoming birthday, Goebbels planned to remove the last Jews from the city and send them east to be killed. Most of Germany's Jews had already been deported and killed, beginning in late 1941. Many of those who remained were married to non-Jews.

German officials had long been uncertain as to how to proceed against German Jews married to "Aryans." Participants at the Wannsee Conference in early 1942 had debated the issue without reaching a decision. On the one hand, Nazi principles of racial purity left no room for exceptions. According to that logic, any Jew left alive represented the possible pollution of generations of "Aryan blood."

On the other hand, however, practical considerations made it dangerous to strike against Jews married to "Aryan" Germans or to attack the "half-Jewish" offspring of such unions. Obviously any "mixed" families had a "pure Aryan" side, which meant lots of relatives who would be antagonized by the deportation and murder of their husband, uncle, son-in-law, niece, granddaughter, or so forth. During wartime the Nazi regime was reluctant to risk stirring up discontent among its own public and its fighting men.

Outside Germany of course the matter was easy. German officials hardly cared if they alienated Polish or Ukrainian gentiles or mistakenly included some of them among the people they defined as Jews. Inside Germany the situation demanded much more delicacy.

By early 1943 Nazi planners decided the remaining Berlin Jews had to go. Police arrested most of the men at the factories where they worked and locked them in a building on the Rosenstrasse—German for "Street of Roses." From there they were to be deported and killed.

In a spontaneous show of disobedience, the gentile wives of those German Jewish men gathered in the Rosenstrasse to protest the arrest of their husbands and demand their release. Sympathizers joined them until there were several thousand people milling about. Hitler and Goebbels were furious, but they did not dare order police or military to open fire on a crowd of Germans. Instead they allowed the men to be released. Many of the internees of the Rosenstrasse survived the war. The historian Nathan Stoltzfus recounts these events in his book *Resistance of the Heart.*

Meanwhile the Nazi regime's air of invincibility was challenged from outside Germany too. In 1942, at German insistence, Romanian and Hungarian troops had also been included in the advance on Stalingrad. Improperly armed and trained, those satellite forces were crushed in the Red Army offensives. Small wonder that by 1943 the leadership of those countries began looking for ways to get out of the war. Suddenly partnership with Germany seemed more a liability than an advantage.

After Stalingrad, Romanian and Hungarian leaders also became less willing to turn over the Jews among their populations to the Germans to be killed. It was not that those authorities suddenly became humanitarian. Rather they recognized that, should they need to negotiate with the Allies, Jews might be useful bargaining chips. Perhaps, they reasoned, they could barter Jewish lives for things they needed. Thus the German setback at Stalingrad might have had the unanticipated effect of prolonging and maybe even saving the lives of some Romanian and Hungarian Jews. On the whole, however, Stalingrad left the situation of Jews in Europe even more catastrophic than it had been before.

The Battle of Stalingrad is often described as the beginning of the end for Nazi Germany, but it signaled no change in the assault on the Jews. To the contrary, Stalingrad occurred right in the peak of the killing process, and genocide continued unabated.

Meanwhile, the guards, SS men, and German bureaucrats who were attached to the program for killing Jews found a new reason to step up their efforts. For them it was clearly preferable to be in the camps and offices overseeing mass murder of unarmed people than to face the Red Army on the eastern front. The chances of living through the war seemed quite good for Germans engaged in the slaughter of defenseless civilians. The odds were much lower for those assigned to fight armed opponents.

Even after Stalingrad the Germans had substantial military resources and a solid eastern front. Germany still held Poland and the killing centers built there—places such as Treblinka, Majdanek, and Auschwitz. Forced to begin to pull back from the east, the Germans concentrated their destructive energies on the territories they still controlled. From that base of power the Nazi leadership would launch the effort in late 1943 to destroy the last remnants of the Jewish communities in Poland.

People often wonder why Nazi Germans wasted manpower and other resources slaughtering Jewish civilians when there was a war to be won. According to Nazi logic, however, murder of the Jews was just as much part of the war effort as were offensives against the Soviet Union. To the proponents of race and space, it was as urgent to use trains to transport Jews to killing centers as it was to move German troops from place to place. As Hitler had proclaimed in January 1939, and as Nazi propaganda insisted, Jews purportedly pulled the strings behind the Allied war effort. Military setbacks in 1943 did not slow down the killing operations; if anything, they speeded them up.

In the fall of 1943, the Germans launched a new offensive against the remaining Jews of Poland. Its code name was Harvest Festival. Within just a few days in November 1943, Germans and their accomplices massacred forty-two thousand Jews in the Lublin area. The Harvest Festival relied heavily on mass shootings. In special "Jew Hunts," the German Order Police and Einsatz-

A German poster (from December 1941 or later) with the slogan: "Behind the enemy powers: the Jew." By depicting the Allied war effort as a cover for an international Jewish conspiracy, Nazi propaganda presented mass murder of Jews as defense of Germany.

gruppen worked with local collaborators to locate and kill as many Jews as they could.

By the end of 1943, only a few thousand Jews remained alive in German-occupied eastern Europe. Many of those were in hiding or fighting in partisan units. German officials kept some alive in the Lodz ghetto for economic reasons, and a few survived in work camps.

In the case of Stalingrad, a military setback for the Germans did not improve the immediate situation of European Jews or, for that matter, of other civilians under the German yoke. However, it may have helped to break down the myth of the invincible Germans and to encourage resistance.

NORTH AFRICA

The years 1942 and 1943 also brought German setbacks in North Africa. In this case too, military developments had enormous nonmilitary results.

Africa had been the focus of Fascist Italian ambitions ever since the 1920s when Mussolini's forces invaded Ethiopia. By 1940, the Italians requested German help against the British and their Allies in Africa. The following year saw formation of the German Africa Corps under the popular General Erwin Rommel (1891–1944), the "Desert Fox."

In late October and early November 1942, the British 8th Army under Bernard L. Montgomery (1887–1976) defeated Rommel's German-Italian forces at El Alamein. At the same time, the American and British "Operation Torch" landed 106,000 Allied forces in Morocco and Algeria under the command of General Dwight D. Eisenhower. Soon Allied troops had pushed the Axis back into Tunisia and a small part of Libya.

The Germans managed to halt the initial Anglo-American advance and reinforce their position. By March 1943, however, Rommel was unable to supply his troops. He flew to Hitler's headquarters to request an evacuation, but Hitler refused. In May 1943 Tunis, the last Axis outpost in Africa, fell to the Allies, who took more than 230,000 soldiers prisoner. About half of them were German.

The reverberations of military action in North Africa were felt all over the world. Already in 1942 Hitler had blamed his Vichy French collaborators in North Africa for capitulating to the Allies, and in November of that year, he ordered German occupation of Vichy France. From then on Germans would administer the territory directly, as they did the rest of France. There would be no more concessions to French independence.

Developments in North Africa also generated a chain reaction that affected the Soviet Union. Thanks to massive reinforcements in November 1942, the Germans held their bridgehead in Tunisia until May 1943. As a result, the Allies had to mount a campaign to crush those remaining Axis forces in North Africa. In turn it became impossible for the Allies to undertake the long-awaited invasion of northwestern Europe in 1943.

Stalin nonetheless continued to call for the western Allies to invade northwestern Europe as soon as possible. Since 1941 the Soviet Union had borne the brunt of German power, and Stalin and the Red Army were desperate for relief.

The western Allies could not liberate Tunisia and make the switch to operations in northwestern Europe during the same year. Instead British and American planners decided for landings in Sicily, then on the Italian mainland for 1943, and postponed invasion of France until 1944.

In the meantime, during 1943 and 1944, Germans in Soviet territories and other parts of Europe slaughtered millions of people: Red Army soldiers, Soviet civilians, and Jews from all over Europe. Military developments in North Africa, worked out by both sides with little regard to the impact on Soviet civilians, Jews, or Italians, had enormous—and unforeseen—consequences for all those groups of people.

In 1942 and 1943, the territory that today is the State of Israel was still part of the British mandate of Palestine. Arabs as well as some Jews lived in the area. During meetings with Arab leaders, most notably the Grand Mufti of Jerusalem, Hitler had promised that German forces would drive the British out of Palestine, occupy the territory, and slaughter the Jews there. Thanks to Allied victories in North Africa, the Germans never occupied the British mandate of Palestine, so the Jews there remained alive. Allied military planners probably gave no thought to the fate of the world's Jews as they made their moves in North Africa. Nevertheless their triumphs there in 1942 and 1943 made possible the eventual establishment of a Jewish state in Israel by saving the lives of those Jews already in the area.

ITALY

Military developments in North Africa also affected Italy, Germany's longest-standing alliance partner. The loss of North Africa completed Italy's disillusionment with the Axis. German demands, German arrogance, and German contempt for Italian officials and the Italian armed forces had also led to growing discontent.

In July 1943, Allied forces landed on Sicily. Soon they were advancing northward through the Italian peninsula. Committed Italian Fascists and their German backers retreated to the north of Naples, around the top of the ankle on the Italian boot.

After more than twenty-one years, Benito Mussolini's regime collapsed. In July 1943 the Italian king assumed supreme command, dismissed Mussolini from office, and had him arrested. A new Italian government under Marshal

Badoglio dissolved the Fascist Party and surrendered to the Allies. Badoglio's government then fled to southern Italy and abandoned most of the country, as well as the Italian-occupied portions of France, Yugoslavia, Albania, and Greece, to the Germans.

The Germans took severe countermeasures. German troops occupied Rome and disarmed Italian soldiers, discharged them from service, or placed them in POW camps. By December 1943, the Germans had interned 725,000 Italian soldiers and had sent 615,000 Italian men to Germany as forced laborers.

Badoglio's government declared war on Germany. Meanwhile the Germans managed to free Mussolini by using a special paratroop unit and install him in a puppet state in northern Italy. Not until the end of April 1945 did the German forces in Italy capitulate. That month Italian partisans shot Mussolini and his mistress as they tried to flee to Switzerland.

Events in Italy had devastating effects for civilians in Yugoslavia, Albania, Greece, and France. In those countries the Germans had divided occupation duties with their Italian allies. The Italians tended to be less brutal than the Germans as occupiers, especially when it came to genocide of Jews. Neither the Italian military nor diplomatic officials would cooperate with the Germans in what they considered a barbaric procedure unworthy of any civilized society.

As a result, many Jews from German-occupied areas had fled into the Italian zones. When the Germans took over in 1943, those refuges disappeared. Already in the spring, Nazi Germans had begun to destroy the ancient Sephardic Jewish communities in Greece and Yugoslavia, deporting their members to Auschwitz to be killed. Now, with the Italians out of the way, the job could be completed. They even sent boats to take the last old Jewish men from remote Greek islands.

In Italy itself, Jews had been fairly safe until 1943. In the late 1930s, under German pressure and for reasons of his own, Mussolini had introduced legislation limiting Jews' activities. In contrast to the leadership in Slovakia and Vichy France—partners who cooperated eagerly with German plans for the Jews—Italians had been reluctant to turn over their Jews for killing.

Beginning in 1943, Germans came in to Italy and took the Jews out themselves. Most of the Italian Jews murdered in the Holocaust died in 1944 or early 1945.

Primo Levi, an Italian survivor of the Holocaust, produced some of the most insightful reflections on that event ever written. Born in Turin in 1919, Levi was arrested with his Italian partisan group in December 1943. When his German captors discovered he was Jewish, they sent him to Auschwitz.

A group of Jewish women and children see their fathers, husbands, and sons as they are driven away from the deportation assembly point in Ioannina, Greece. Of the ten people who have been identified in this March 1944 photograph, only one, Elda Levi, survived.

Levi survived, but almost all of the inmates he knew in the camp did not. His closest friend in Auschwitz was another Italian named Alberto. Levi and Alberto shared what little food they received or "organized" for themselves. They encouraged each other to muster the energy and will to try to stay alive, both physically and in some deeper, moral way that meant retaining an awareness of themselves as human beings.

Thanks to Levi's prewar training as a chemist, he got a job in the camp that protected him from some of the harshest conditions there. Somehow he lived through the war. Alberto, however, did not. He too was a resourceful, intelligent young man full of the desire to survive. In early 1945, as the Red Army advanced from the east, the Germans evacuated the camp at Auschwitz. Guards marched Alberto, along with most other inmates, out of the camp to the west. Levi, sick in the infirmary at the time, was left behind with others too weak to walk. Who could have known that what seemed the chance for life—leaving the camp at last—would be Alberto's death, whereas Levi, abandoned by the guards as almost dead, would survive?

In his writings about the Holocaust, Levi described the camp as above all a place of dehumanization. The English translation of Levi's memoir is called *Survival in Auschwitz*, but he originally titled the book *Se questo è un uomo*, "If this is a man." For Levi, to be human meant more than merely to eat and breathe. It meant having an identity, relationships with others, ties to a past and a future, and a sense of decency and dignity.

The camp took all that away. Physical abuses heaped on the prisoners—starvation, beatings, exposure—together with the many humiliations and indignities they suffered attacked their sense of humanity. In the camp, prisoners lost their names and became numbers. Emaciated, sick, shorn, and forced to wear rags, they looked nothing like their former selves. Brutality and deprivation turned them against one another; pain and despair made them forget the values and ideals they had cherished. It was this destruction of people's humanity that Levi considered the most terrible crime of the Holocaust.

After the war Levi did everything he could to share his insights and to warn against dehumanization and brutality in the postwar world. Already in Auschwitz he had nightmares that people "outside" would not listen to his story. Toward the end of his life he expressed frustration that the world refused to learn from the past. Primo Levi died in 1987 when he fell down the stairs in his home. Many people believe he committed suicide.

THE HOLOCAUST AT ITS PEAK

The Killing Centers

By the time of the Wannsee Conference in January 1942, Nazi Germans and their helpers were already engaged in mass killing of Jews from all over Europe. Since late 1939 they had been starving Jews to death in the ghettos of Poland. Mobile murder squads followed the regular military into Soviet territory in June 1941 and began immediately to concentrate their slaughter on Jewish civilians. In September 1941 German police introduced a regulation forcing all Jews in Germany to wear an identifying Star of David. A month later they began deporting Jews from Germany and elsewhere in central and western Europe to the east for killing. One killing center, at Chelmno, near Lodz, started operations in December 1941.

Although it may have seemed impossible, for European Jews 1942 and 1943 went even beyond the horrors of the years before. At the beginning of 1942, even after three years of war, ghettoization, torture, and forced labor, 75 percent of the Jews who would be murdered in the Holocaust were still alive.

By the beginning of 1943, 75 percent of the approximately 6 million who would be killed were already dead.

In December 1941 the SS opened its first killing center at Chelmno, called Kulmhof by the Germans. Located just forty miles from Lodz, the Chelmno facility used specially equipped gas vans to kill Jews and also Gypsies. Guards loaded their victims into the cargo compartment and sealed the doors. As the van was driven, pipes brought the diesel exhaust directly into the back so that the people there were asphyxiated. T-4 killers had developed this technique, which they used first against people deemed handicapped. Within months of the Wannsee Conference of January 1942, five more killing centers were in operation, all of them, like Chelmno, in territories that had once been part of Poland. Contrary to popular notions, German mass killing of Jews was not some perfectly coordinated, "clean" enterprise. Like the entire Nazi regime it was characterized by confusion and rivalry, which only served to exacerbate the horror.

CHELMNO

The killing center at Chelmno was located in the incorporated territory, that is, the part of Poland annexed to the Reich and earmarked for Germanization. Chelmno was a small village on a railway branch line. An unoccupied castle proved useful as headquarters for the killing process.

Trains brought Jews, mostly from the surrounding area, to Chelmno, and then trucks drove them to the courtyard of the castle. There an SS man addressed them. They were to be sent to Germany, he told them, but first they had to take a shower. Ordered to strip, they were handed towels and soap and pushed through a corridor labeled "washroom" into the vans.

About ninety people were forced into a van at once. The vans drove slowly for a few miles into the forest. There personnel opened the doors and dumped the bodies. Guards shot anyone who was still alive.

The Germans kept a few Jews around to unload the corpses and bury the bodies. Known as the *Sonderkommando*, "special unit," this small group of men handled twelve to thirteen vans—about one thousand bodies—each day. Jews were also assigned to sort the clothing left behind and clean out the vans. The more lucrative task of extracting any gold teeth went to the Nazis' Ukrainian helpers.

Most members of the Jewish Sonderkommando did not hold that position for long. As additional shipments of Jews arrived the German guards selected new workers and killed the old ones. Some of the Jewish workers tried to escape, and a few succeeded. The Germans responded to those attempts by chaining the legs of Sonderkommando members.

By the spring and summer of 1942, the area around Chelmno was filled with the stench of rotting bodies. German officials ordered ovens brought in so that the mass graves could be opened and the bodies exhumed and burned. Of course they delegated this gruesome job to members of the Jewish Sonderkommando.

Mordechai Podchlebnik, a Jewish man assigned to the task, found the bodies of his wife and two children in a mass grave. He begged the SS guards to shoot him. When they refused, he tried to commit suicide. This time his comrades stopped him. Eventually he escaped. One of very few survivors of the killing center at Chelmno, Podchlebnik later served as a central witness at the postwar Chelmno trial.

Rumors about the killing center at Chelmno soon spread. Jews in the region struggled to know how to react, but their options were extremely lim-

A Jewish woman in the Lodz ghetto writes a last letter before being transported to the killing center at Chelmno. Such letters, written on scraps of paper, cloth, wood, or anything else available, were thrown out windows, stuffed through cracks in freight cars, or scattered along roadsides in an attempt to make contact with the world of the still-living.

ited. In December 1941, German authorities demanded that Rumkowski, head of the Jewish Council at Lodz, hand over twenty thousand members of his community for "special treatment." Aware that selection most likely meant death, Rumkowski and his committee tried to fill their list with outsiders and people considered asocial. Among those early victims were the remainder of some five thousand Gypsies who had been sent to Lodz from the Reich. Located in a separate part of the ghetto, many had already died from hunger and disease. Now those left would be murdered in Chelmno.

By mid-1942, the German district commander reported to Himmler that in the next two to three months, the "special treatment" of some one hundred thousand Jews from the area would be complete. Given the "success" of the project, he suggested a similar program for Poles with tuberculosis.

From December 1941 to the end of 1942, Germans and their henchmen killed about 145,000 people, most of them Jews, in Chelmno. About five thousand Gypsies from the ghetto in Lodz were murdered in the gas vans at Chelmno as well. In late 1942 the SS closed the killing center until 1944, when it was reactivated briefly. Its job in the area had been completed.

BELZEC

Only one inmate of the killing center at Belzec survived the war. Located near the Polish city of Lublin, Belzec began operations in March 1942. German governor Hans Frank of the General Government in Poland had boasted that Jews in his territory would be the first victims of the so-called Final Solution. To that end, after the Wannsee Conference, the labor camp at Belzec was outfitted as a killing center.

Belzec had a fixed installation for gassing that used diesel fumes. On 1 April 1942, the first night of the Jewish holiday of Passover, the SS brought more than fifteen thousand Jews from the city of Lvov to Belzec to be killed. By the time the camp was dismantled in the spring of 1943, some six hundred thousand Jews had been murdered there, along with perhaps several thousand Gypsies.

We have an early account of a gassing at Belzec from an unusual source: an SS man named Kurt Gerstein. Gerstein was a Nazi Party member and devout Protestant. He had served a brief term in a concentration camp himself for criticizing the anti-Christian attitudes of the SS. Nevertheless, thanks to family connections, he was able to have his name cleared and join the SS.

Gerstein was an engineer with some training in sanitation and medical matters. Accordingly he received a post as SS chief disinfection officer. Early in 1942, a deputy of Eichmann's assigned Gerstein to transport Zyklon B to a secret place. The destination was Belzec.

At Belzec the commandant, Dr. Christian Wirth, an old T-4 expert, invited Gerstein to witness the killing of Jews using diesel fumes. That day the diesel motor broke down. About eight hundred Jews were forced to wait naked for nearly three hours until the gassing began. The killing itself took thirty-two minutes; Gerstein timed it with his stopwatch.

Horrified by what he had seen, Gerstein decided to try to use his position to stop the killings. He destroyed some of the Zyklon B he was supposed to deliver to Auschwitz, and he tried to get the word out about German mass murder of Jews in Poland. When he met a Swedish diplomat on a train, Gerstein blurted out the whole story. He went to the papal nuncio—the Vatican's representative—in Berlin to pass the news to the pope. Gerstein's efforts met with little response.

At the end of the war, Gerstein was captured by the French. Arrested and charged with war crimes, he died in prison, either by his own hand or as a

Drawing by an unidentified artist of camp guards watching prisoners die in a gas chamber. In 1942, SS-man Kurt Gerstein watched through a peephole at Belzec as Jews were murdered with diesel fumes.

victim of foul play. Only half a century later, due to efforts by his family, did he gain a reputation as a hero.

Gerstein's story is instructive. A lone individual who tried to sabotage a murderous process from within, he ended up caught in the system himself and destroyed. Gerstein did not have the public backing within Germany that allowed someone like Bishop von Galen to protest the killing of the disabled with some effect. Nor would or could the foreigners he told about what he knew grasp what must have seemed to them the ravings of a madman.

SOBIBOR

The camp at Sobibor was constructed solely for the purpose of killing. Its first commandant was an Austrian named Franz Stangl, a policeman trained in the T-4 program.

Sobibor was one of the Operation Reinhard camps, named after Reinhard Heydrich, Himmler's deputy and the driving force at the Wannsee Conference. Mass slaughter of Jews began there in April 1942. Sobibor functioned as a killing center until October 1943.

At Sobibor, Germans and their accomplices murdered 250,000 Jews from eastern Poland, the occupied Soviet Union, and other European countries. Many Dutch Jews, for example, were killed in Sobibor. Trains brought the victims right into the camp. Guards selected some Jews as workers in the killing process, and the rest they gassed immediately.

In October 1943 Sobibor was the site of an uprising by its Jewish workers, who staged a mass escape. Most were recaptured, but some survived the war. The Germans closed the camp shortly after the revolt. It is not clear whether the revolt hastened the camp's closure, but by the time Sobibor stopped operations, most of the Jews in the territories from which it had drawn its victims were already dead.

TREBLINKA

Another Operation Reinhard camp built solely as a killing center, Treblinka began operations in July 1942. Just eighty miles from Warsaw, it became the grave of a staggering number of Polish Jews. Its first victims were some three hundred thousand Jews from Warsaw, but Gypsies from the Warsaw ghetto and Jews from all over central Poland, Germany, Austria, Czechoslovakia, and

Greece were killed there. In all close to a million Jews were murdered at Treblinka.

Treblinka too had its Sonderkommando, more than eight hundred Jews who worked in the camp. They included craftspeople employed by the SS as well as men assigned to work in the gas chambers, cutting hair and burying and burning bodies. In August 1943 Jewish workers at Treblinka revolted, after which German authorities gradually shut the camp down.

A number of Nazi high-ranking officials visited Treblinka. Eichmann, for example, paid a call. He described the fake railway station that greeted arrivals to Treblinka as looking "just like Germany." Camp organizers intended the facade to create a semblance of normalcy so that people would not suspect they were about to be killed. Eichmann also saw guards chase Jews into the gas chambers through a path between barbed wire fences that the Germans in charge of the camp called the "hose," the "funnel," or the "way to heaven."

Treblinka was far from perfectly organized. Often corpses littered the train tracks both inside and outside the compound. Eventually the commandant of Sobibor, Franz Stangl, was transferred to Treblinka to clean the place up. Even Stangl's "improvements"—increased efficiency and a beautification scheme that included planting flower beds—could not conceal the unbearable smell that surrounded the place. Fields came right up to the security fence, so that Polish farmers who lived nearby could see much of what happened inside. No one in the area could be unaware of the massive killing operations at Treblinka.

MAJDANEK

Majdanek combined a labor camp with a killing center. Just a mile from the city of Lublin, the camp, modeled after Dachau in Germany, was built in the winter of 1940–1941 for prisoners of war. In fact, the Jewish POWs from the Polish army who were its first inmates did much of the construction.

In July 1941 the Germans brought Soviet POWs to Majdanek. Over time they added many Polish gentiles, especially political prisoners. They built gas chambers in 1942, but death vans and shooting were also widely used at Majdanek. All of Majdanek's inmates were subjected to terrible abuses, and many were worked to death. Most of the Soviet POWs died from torture and starvation. The SS men in Majdanek were known as sadists who enjoyed killing children in front of their mothers and forcing the prisoners to engage in deadly "sports."

At Majdanek, gassing, for the most part, was reserved for Jews. Guards brought most transports of Jews straight to the gas chambers. Those kept alive to work had a precarious existence.

In late 1942 Eichmann visited Majdanek. Guards forced the inmates to spend the entire day on parade. Eichmann looked at them and said, "Get rid of the whole lot." In Nazi eyes, the lives of the inmates at Majdanek were worth less than nothing. In just one day, 3 November 1943, guards at Majdanek mowed down some seventeen thousand prisoners with machine gun fire and forced the few left alive to conceal the evidence. In all, two hundred thousand people were killed in the camp. About 75,000 were gentiles; the other 125,000 were Jews.

AUSCHWITZ-BIRKENAU

Auschwitz-Birkenau was the last camp established as a killing center, but it functioned the longest in that capacity. Like Belzec and Majdanek, Auschwitz started as a labor camp. Many of the early inmates were political prisoners from Poland. Facilities for mass killing were added later as were a number of factories using slave labor drawn from the camp; the chemical company IG Farben had a plant at Auschwitz III (Buna-Monowitz) to produce artificial rubber.

In the summer of 1941—before the Wannsee Conference—Himmler decided to transform the camp at Auschwitz into a killing center. He assigned a man named Rudolf Hoess, trained at Dachau, to the task. Auschwitz seemed an ideal location to Himmler. It was near the small Polish town of Oswiecim and convenient to rail lines yet securely distant from the front. The prisoners already on hand provided a ready source of manpower.

Germans conducted some early trial gassings at Auschwitz. In September 1941 they killed nine hundred Soviet POWs using Zyklon B. By March 1942 Jews were being sent there from the surrounding area to be gassed. The killing center was known as Auschwitz II or Birkenau. Eventually Birkenau would be the destination of Jews rounded up for killing from Slovakia, France, and then all over Europe. An estimated 6,400 Gypsies would be gassed at Birkenau too.

The killing procedure at Auschwitz-Birkenau was similar to that elsewhere. Often German officials met the transports of Jews right at the ramp as they came off the trains. There they made their "selections"—the decision as to who would go immediately to the gas and who would be kept alive in the camp for a time as laborers.

Many survivors remember selections conducted by Dr. Josef Mengele. Mengele was a scientist and SS doctor who had his own special projects that involved experiments with dwarfs, twins, and others. Mengele's abusive experiments killed the vast majority of his subjects. With a wave of the hand, Mengele and his counterparts sorted those deemed useful for work from those considered fit only for killing. Children, women with children, pregnant women, older men and women, the sick, and the weak were sent to one side and then on to the gas. Others were admitted into the camp.

The officials who presided over the killing process developed a series of tricks and deceits to keep their victims calm. Often SS men addressed those selected for gassing in polite, helpful tones as they entered the gas chambers. "You have been on a journey, and you are dirty," the SS informed their victims. "You will take a shower." Sometimes they even handed out soap and towels before cramming the people in the "Shower Room." Hoess was proud of arrangements at his camp; he had a sense that he had perfected procedures.

Auschwitz-Birkenau represented another refinement to the Nazi system of killing. From early in the process German officials had worried about conflicts between German economic interests and the goal of annihilating Jews. In Auschwitz, those two aims were combined. The SS found they could make money by essentially renting out slave laborers to manufacturers and industrialists. Employers need not worry about keeping their workers alive; there were always more where they came from. In addition to the concentration camp and the killing center known as Birkenau, the Auschwitz system included a massive industrial complex and labor camp called Monowitz. There was also a model town where thousands of employees and their families, Germans and ethnic Germans, enjoyed the fruits of state-of-the-art urban planning.

Bizarre as it may seem, some Germans made a rather pleasant life for themselves at the killing centers. Ambitious Nazi doctors had an endless supply of disposable human subjects on whom to conduct experiments. Commandants and other high-ranking administrators often brought their wives and children to be near them. They had access to every luxury and of course to free labor. Hoess's wife supposedly said about Auschwitz, "Here I want to live until the end of my days." Himmler authorized fish farms, gardens, brothels, and even zoos on the sites for the employees' enjoyment. As for the guards, assignment to a killing center was certainly preferable to being sent to the front.

The killing centers marked the culmination of the killing process. They were not separate from the Nazi German war for race and space but were an integral part of it. In all, an estimated 3 million Jews were murdered in the six killing centers outlined here. The number of Gypsies killed with them is even harder to pin down, but it was certainly in the tens of thousands. Approximately twenty thousand Roma died in Auschwitz-Birkenau alone—two thirds of them from starvation, disease, experimentation, beatings, and shootings; the rest in the gas chambers.

GENDER AND GENOCIDE

Women's and men's experiences in the Holocaust converged and diverged in significant ways, summed up in the scholar Myrna Goldenberg's phrase "different horrors, same hell." Jewish men were more likely to be killed in labor camps in Poland in 1939 and 1940, but more women were among the groups "selected" from the ghettos in 1941 and 1942 for transport to killing centers. In places like Auschwitz, men had a better chance of being chosen for work; SS authorities regularly consigned women, particularly if pregnant or with small children, directly to the gas.

Accounts by Jewish women in Auschwitz and other Nazi camps often emphasize the physical transformation that their bodies underwent. Isabella Leitner, a survivor from Hungary, described her feelings in Auschwitz in May 1944:

> Our heads are shaved. We look like neither boys nor girls. We haven't menstruated for a long time. We have diarrhea. No, not diarrhea—typhus. Summer and winter we have but one type of clothing. Its name is "rag." Not an inch of it without a hole. Our shoulders are exposed. The rain is pouring on our skeletal bodies. The lice are having an orgy in our armpits, their favorite spots. Their bloodsucking, the irritation, their busy scurrying give the illusion of warmth. We're hot at least under our armpits, while our bodies are shivering. (Rittner and Roth, 67)

Secrecy, Denial, Disbelief

German authorities tried to keep the operation of the killing centers secret, just as they had attempted to conceal the murder of people deemed handicapped and the mass shootings of Jews and others in 1941, but in no case was secrecy really possible. The killing operations were simply too big and involved far too many people to keep them quiet.

Local populations watched full trains pull in and saw them depart empty. The air for miles around was thick with the ashes of burning bodies and heavy with the stench of death. Civilians of all kinds came from Germany and elsewhere for jobs in the camps. There were guards, of course, but also architects and engineers, suppliers, telephone operators, and secretaries. What did the

Painting by Halina Olomucki, Le camp des litières dans le bloc (The camp of litters in the block). Olomucki, born Halina Olszewski, arrived at Auschwitz-Birkenau from Warsaw via Majdanek in July 1943. She received prisoner number 48652.

German and Polish women think whose job it was to type up lists of the dead and prepare statistics of the numbers of people killed?

Presumably perpetrators, bystanders, and onlookers found ways to live with their knowledge of the killing centers. One individual's account illustrates some of the forms denial and rationalization could take. Teresa Stangl was married to Franz Stangl, commandant first of Sobibor and then of Treblinka. A devout Catholic, she had initially opposed her husband's involvement with the Nazi Party. According to Mrs. Stangl, she had never really understood his position in the T-4 program; she claimed she did not know the nature of the programs he administered.

Later Teresa Stangl moved to Sobibor to be near her husband. From their house near the camp she could not see the activities inside. One day a drunken coworker of her husband's called on her. He told her the details of Franz's job.

Horrified Mrs. Stangl confronted her husband. He denied any direct connection with killing and assured his wife that he was just responsible for routine administration. Nevertheless she found herself unable to have sexual relations with him for some time. Eventually she moved away, and they continued their marriage from a distance.

Despite her misgivings Mrs. Stangl stood by her husband. He loved her and would have done anything for her, she said. Once, she admitted in an interview that he would have chosen her over his work if she had given him an ultimatum, but later she insisted that she could have done nothing.

What of the Jews? What could Jews in Europe know in 1942 and 1943 of the killing centers? The answer is complicated by geography. Clearly Jews farther away—in Greece, for example—might have access to very little reliable information, but even Polish Jews, at least in the early stages of the killing centers' operation, could have problems grasping the reality of genocide. The word "genocide" did not even exist until after World War II.

Perhaps one account can illustrate. Piotrków Trybunalski, in the incorporated territories, was home to about 11,400 Jews, some 22 percent of the overall population. Since October 1939 the Jews of Piotrków had been confined to a ghetto.

In the spring of 1942, two young Jewish men escaped from Chelmno. They arrived in Piotrków and revealed the truth about German gassings of Jews. Most people refused to believe their ears. Why, during wartime, when it was well known that Germany had a serious shortage of labor, would the Germans try to slaughter every Polish Jew?

The leaders of the community met. Desperate to reassure themselves, they decided that the excesses the two young men had witnessed must be regional aberrations. Everyone knew that the SS commander Odilo Globocnik in Lublin was exceptionally vicious. Surely nothing so terrible could happen in their district.

Were the Jewish leaders of Piotrków naive? Maybe, but perhaps that innocence is to their credit. Who could imagine mass gassings as part of systematic annihilation of Jews? Such a thing had never happened. Nazi planners in turn manipulated and exploited that inability to believe the worst.

Hope, even false hope, had some advantages over despair. One of the chroniclers of the Warsaw ghetto wrote, "It is good that we console ourselves, for even if these are false hopes, they keep us from collapsing." For the most part those Jews who grasped German intentions toward them could do nothing anyway. In the summer of 1942, Adam Czerniaków was head of the Jewish Council in Warsaw. When the Germans ordered him to hand over the children of the ghetto, he knew that they would be killed. Powerless to stop the slaughter, Czerniaków took the only way out still left to him: he committed suicide.

Jews in Hiding

Not all of the Jews targeted in the Holocaust ended up in killing centers. Many Jews fled, taking refuge where they could. Others hid, and still others "passed" as gentiles. An estimated 80,000 to 120,000 Jews were hidden in Poland; maybe half of those survived the war.

Many of the Jews in hiding were children. It was easier to persuade non-Jews to have pity on children than on adults, who took up more space, ate more, and were harder to explain. It tended to be more difficult to find hiding places for Jewish boys than for girls. In Europe very few Christian parents had their sons circumcised. So Jewish boys had their religion marked on their bodies in a visible way. It was not uncommon for police or local collaborators hunting for Jews to demand that men or boys pull down their pants so that they could see if they had been circumcised.

The decision to put a child into hiding was agonizing for parents. Whom could one trust? When was hiding the best option? Was it not better to stay together no matter what? How could one leave a child one might never see again?

Only as adults have many of the people hidden as Jewish children during the war recounted their experiences publicly. Here are two of their stories.

Henia Wisgardisky (now Henia Lewin) was the daughter of Lithuanian Jews from Kovno. When she was just a year and a half old she and her parents were forced to move into the ghetto. For more than two years Henny's parents hid her in a small room that had been a walk-in pantry, but when she developed whooping cough it became too risky to keep her there. So they arranged for a Lithuanian Christian family outside the ghetto to take her in.

Henny's mother also arranged a hiding place for her two-year-old niece, Shoshana Bluma Berk (now Sarid), after Germans shot the little girl's father. She made contact with a Lithuanian priest who got false papers for Shoshana and placed her in a convent. Later the nuns passed her on to a family of pig farmers. Miraculously, Shoshana, Henny, and Henny's parents all survived the war.

Rudy was a little boy in the Netherlands. He survived the war in about twenty different hiding places, most of them in rural Holland. He remembers

Cousins Henia Wisgardisky (right) and Bluma Berk, wearing wooden stars carved by their uncle. This photograph was taken in July 1943, a few months before Henia's mother smuggled the girls out of the Kovno ghetto. Hidden by Lithuanian families, both of them survived the war.

spending three days with a Jewish family in the woods while Germans searched the area. He heard German vehicles and dogs at night, but he stayed hidden under branches and leaves, and they did not find him. Later two young women hid him with a group of ten other children. Several times a local Dutch policeman warned them of an impending raid. Once, they stayed in a cave for two days until it was safe to return. Eventually the group had to be split up. Only after the war, as adults, did some of them find one another again. Rudy, who returned to his original name, Yehudi Lindeman, had little contact with other former hidden children or with study of the Holocaust until the 1980s, when he cofounded "Living Testimonies," a video archive of survivor accounts in Montreal.

Concentration Camps: Microcosms of the Third Reich

Killing centers were just one part of the vast network of German camps that had been expanding since 1933. Those who passed through the killing centers were overwhelmingly Jewish, although Gypsies were murdered there as well. Other kinds of camps included a much wider range of inmates. The years 1942 and 1943 were also a time when the Germans incarcerated huge numbers of people from all over Europe. A closer look at the concentration camps belongs in this discussion of the peak years of killing.

The total number of Nazi German camps of various kinds is not known, but it must be in the thousands. An estimated 18 million people passed through the camps; some 11 million died there. Many of those who survived bore deep scars, physical and psychological.

In crucial ways Nazi concentration camps were microcosms of the Third Reich. The camps reflected the nature of Nazism, and the Nazi system would have been impossible without the camps. German practices inside the camps echoed methods used elsewhere. The principle of divide and conquer was evident, for example, as was promotion of rivalry among German authorities with the end result of increasing brutality toward the victims.

NATURE OF THE CONCENTRATION CAMPS

Political prisoners, such as Communists, Jehovah's Witnesses, homosexual men, common criminals, so-called asocials, and critics of the regime, all served terms that in some cases proved fatal. Representatives of all those groups were still found in large numbers in the German camps during the war.

German conquests brought influxes of new kinds of prisoners too. German police arrested Polish and French Communists and Socialists as well as members of resistance groups from all over Europe. These inmates were not gassed, but they were beaten, starved, used for experiments, and forced to do backbreaking labor. Some of them survived only a few weeks. Others lived for months, and a few made it longer, often because they managed to wrangle some kind of privileged position in the camp.

Camps often used for political prisoners included Gross-Rosen, Stutthof, Bergen-Belsen, Flossenbürg, and Ravensbrück for women, but there were many others. Even these names often encompassed a vast network of satellite facilities; Buchenwald, for example, included some 134 satellite camps.

Another type of mass-detention facility was the labor camps. Most of their inmates were non-Jewish women and men from conquered nations. German authorities used them for work connected to military requirements, in factor-

Bogumila Babinska (Jasiuk), a prisoner in Ravensbrück, shows wounds inflicted by German doctors who used her as "rabbit" (guinea pig) for medical experimentation. A member of the Polish underground, Babinska and her friends documented the experiments through invisible messages written in urine and photographs taken clandestinely with a camera they "bought" from another prisoner for bread.

ies, mines, quarries, and production of armaments. One example was Dora-Mittelbau, a camp in north-central Germany not far from the city of Göttingen. In its extensive underground facility slave laborers built V-2 rockets.

The German state viewed slave workers as a renewable resource; their lives had no value. Death tolls in such camps were astronomical. Toward the end of the war, as more Jews were kept alive for labor, they died in even greater numbers than the rest of the prisoners. Camp organizers quartered the Jews separately, gave them less food, and treated them even more harshly than they did the gentile inmates.

Like the killing centers, concentration camps specialized in brutality, with an eye to comfort and ease for the staff. Buchenwald had a zoo; many had gardens and, beginning in 1943, brothels staffed by sex slaves from the occupied territories. Sometimes camp authorities also assigned German "asocial" women—lesbians, Communists, and criminals—to brothels. Clients included staff and especially privileged male prisoners.

All of the big camps, even places such as Dora-Mittelbau, had orchestras. Often they included Gypsies, popular as musicians in Europe, or trained classical musicians. There was no shortage of candidates; Europe in the 1940s was a very musical place. Orchestras performed to entertain the guards, to send the prisoners off to work, and sometimes during executions in the camps. They played well-known marches, arias, folk songs, and even Christmas carols.

The cynicism of those behind the camp system is evident in other ways too. A sign over the gate of Auschwitz read *Arbeit macht frei*, "work liberates." Buchenwald, built in 1937, had its own slogan: *Jedem das Seine*, "to each his own."

German authorities recruited for high-ranking positions at the camps from within the German police. They hired unskilled or semiskilled workers to be guards at the lower levels. At Ravensbrück, for example, women guards were recruited through ads that promised job security, a responsible position, and wages higher than many nonskilled positions. Successful candidates underwent only a very short training course.

Outside of Germany, SS men took the top positions in the camps. Often they had been trained at German camps such as Dachau. Lowlier guards commonly came from subject populations; for example, ethnic Germans from eastern Europe, Ukrainians, Latvians, Croatians.

Jobs in the camps gave individuals a chance to enrich themselves at the expense of the inmates. They also provided an opportunity to lord it over one's local enemies. For example, the Germans hired Croatians to guard Serbs,

Yugoslavian Gypsies, and Jews; they often used Ukrainians against Poles. Working conditions that tolerated and even encouraged drunkenness, rape, and brutality appealed especially to sadists and thugs.

Women occupied almost all of the same positions that men did, at least at the lower levels. Generally women prisoners had women guards. There were also female SS units, usually assigned to communication duties and housekeeping for SS men at the front. It was no secret that these women, chosen on the basis of their supposedly valuable "blood," were expected to help German SS men resist the temptation of sexual liaisons with "non-Aryans" by making themselves available.

About two thousand female guards assisted the SS at the Ravensbrück camp for women. Some women, like some men, were notorious for cruelty. Most infamous were Irma Grese, a guard at Auschwitz, and the "Bitch of Buchenwald," Ilse Koch, wife of Commander Karl Koch. Koch, though not herself a guard, was active and visible in the camp. After the war, wild rumors circulated about her sexual deviancy and fondness for lampshades and other household decorations made of tattooed human flesh. Some of the most horrific stories about Ilse Koch were never proven, but what seems clear is that to prisoners and outside observers alike, the involvement of women in Nazi brutality seemed even more shocking than the behavior of men.

German authorities in the camps also appointed some prisoners to supervise and control other inmates. Such prisoner functionaries became known as kapos. Often the leaders of labor gangs, kapos had access to some power and privilege. At the same time they remained answerable to camp authorities.

The use of kapos encouraged development of elaborate hierarchies of power within the camps. Such divisions, of course, benefited the Nazis, who needed to invest less time and energy to control prisoners who were at odds with one another. By rewarding kapos for brutality against fellow prisoners, German officials continued to undermine solidarity. Every kapo realized that he or she could be replaced at a moment's notice. There were plenty of prisoners eager to increase their chances to survive by accepting positions of privilege within the camp.

To reinforce divisions among prisoners, camp officials introduced a system of colored badges to identify the various groups. Criminals wore a green triangle; Communists received red. Gypsies and "asocials" were marked with a black badge, and Jehovah's Witnesses with purple. A pink triangle designated homosexual men. A yellow triangle—or more often two triangles together to form a six-pointed star—identified Jews.

Camp authorities recruited most kapos from the green and red triangles, the two groups at the top of the hierarchy. Kapos from the other groups were not unknown, but it was hard for people to assert authority over those considered above them. Jews, marked as they were for death, invariably occupied the bottom of the hierarchy. Often the other prisoners ostracized and tormented homosexual men in particularly vicious ways. Nevertheless, in a few cases Jews and homosexuals too served as kapos or in similar positions.

The perpetrators devised special humiliations for members of each of their victim groups, and even the same treatment was experienced in different ways by people whose own values and taboos set them apart from one another. German aggressors often launched attacks on Jews on the Jewish holidays. Camp officials frequently put tough, homophobic kapos in charge of gay prisoners. Nakedness of adults in front of their own children was particularly taboo among Roma, so orders to strip carried extra humiliation for members of that group.

Many accounts from the camps stress the importance of support from other prisoners. German officials tried to divide and conquer their prey. They set people against one another by forcing competition for absurdly small prizes—an extra crust of bread, a button, a piece of string.

Some of the most powerful stories of the camps explain how inmates countered such efforts to isolate them. Primo Levi, an Italian Jew, tells how he reminded himself and a coworker of their humanity by reciting lines from Dante's *Divine Comedy*: "Think of your breed; for brutish ignorance / Your mettle was not made; you were made men, / To follow after knowledge and excellence." Sara Nomberg-Przytyk, a Jewish Communist woman from Poland, attributes her survival to an anonymous woman in the next train car who sacrificed her own blanket so that Sara would not freeze to death.

THE ROMA/GYPSIES

Almost every memoir of the concentration camps mentions Gypsies. For Gypsies, like Jews, 1942 and 1943 were the peak years of killing. As German forces consolidated their hold on subject territories, they located more and more groups of Roma. In all, German perpetrators and their accomplices killed an estimated one-quarter to half a million Roma, including many children. Thousands of others were sterilized.

Nazi ideology considered Gypsies impure and unworthy to live. One of the absurdities of the situation was that according to Nazi terminology, Gypsies were in fact more "Aryan" than the Nordic Germans. Gypsies originated in

A group of Roma, awaiting instructions from their German captors, sits in an open area near the fence at Belzec in late 1941 or 1942. Gypsies were murdered in all of the killing centers used for annihilating Jews.

India, home of the original Aryan tribe, whose name was appropriated by European racists for their own purposes. The Romani language even bears some similarity to Indian languages.

SS leader Himmler was fascinated by Gypsies. He set up an office within the German Ministry of Health called the Racial Hygiene and Population Research Center. Its main task was to study the approximately thirty thousand German Gypsies, draw up genealogies of them, and identify those considered "pure." Information it gathered made it possible to locate Gypsies and kill them.

Initially Himmler wanted to preserve some "pure Gypsies" in a kind of reservation or zoo, where they could be examined by future German scientists. "Experts" estimated that between 3 and 4 percent of the Gypsies would fall into that category. Later Himmler abandoned that idea. The German government provided generous funding for research on the Roma, and many scientists got involved in the project, especially social scientists such as anthropologists.

As we have seen earlier, Gypsies shared many of the experiences of Jews in the Holocaust. Classified, dispossessed, deported, forced into ghettos, shot into mass graves, and gassed, they too were marked for annihilation, but Nazi authorities never devoted the same fanatical energy to killing Gypsies as they did to eradication of Jews. They seemed to regard Gypsies as a nuisance rather than part of some diabolical, international conspiracy. Either way, however, Sinti and Roma were targeted for murder.

The experience of Nazi persecution highlighted just how isolated Gypsies were within Europe. Church leaders in Germany protested the killing of people deemed handicapped in 1941. In the 1943 Rosenstrasse protest, the gentile wives of German Jewish men forced cancellation of plans to transport their husbands to the east to be killed. In Poland, the Netherlands, Ukraine, Yugoslavia, and elsewhere, non-Jews risked their lives to hide Jewish children and adults, sometimes for years. Who protested on behalf of the Roma? Who beyond their own circles sheltered Gypsy children from death? There may have been some people who did so, but their stories are not well known.

HOMOSEXUALS—THE "MEN WITH THE PINK TRIANGLE"

Hitler's regime had harassed and persecuted homosexuals since its early years in power. Between 1933 and 1945 German courts convicted fifty thousand men on charges related to homosexuality. The year 1942 brought a record number of arrests, mostly of Germans. Nazi ideology regarded homosexuals, particularly men, as a threat to "Aryan racial health" because they refused to take part in producing children for the fatherland. In wartime, especially in 1942 and 1943, as German casualties began to climb, the German leadership took that offense very seriously. German police arrested thousands of men accused of homosexual activity. Between five and seven thousand of these men perished in World War II, perhaps half of them in concentration camps.

Like every group targeted by Nazi Germany, homosexuals had experiences unique to them. For one thing, Nazi theorists and practitioners were confused as to whether homosexuality was biological or acquired. So German officials vacillated between treating gay men as if they were racial enemies or handling them as candidates for reeducation. In 1933 Himmler had estimated there were between 1 and 4 million homosexually inclined men in Germany, but even the homophobic Himmler never mounted a systematic effort to wipe out homosexuality as such. Instead police made arrests on the basis of denunciations and raids.

By 1942 many concentration camps had homosexual inmates. Sachsenhausen and Buchenwald housed the largest numbers, at times in separate "queer blocks." Gay men, like Jews and Gypsies, fell near the bottom of the camp hierarchy. Viewed even by many fellow prisoners as the scum of humanity, they suffered severely from torture, beating, and medical experimentation. Perhaps their isolation from other prisoners explains the extremely high death rate among gay inmates in Nazi camps; it was about 60 percent as compared to 41 percent for political prisoners and 35 percent for Jehovah's Witnesses.

As the war went on and German demands for labor increased, officials allowed some of the homosexuals in Sachsenhausen to be released as civilian laborers, but there were strings attached. In order to be pronounced "cured," a candidate for rehabilitation had to perform "properly" with a prostitute from the camp brothel. If he failed but agreed to castration, he might still be released for heavy labor. Some gay men also won release by volunteering for special penal units sent to the very worst areas of the front. Few of those individuals survived.

Harry Pauli, an actor from Berlin, was one of the rare exceptions. Sentenced on grounds of homosexual activity to twenty months' imprisonment, he served eight months before being drafted into the Wehrmacht. Ridiculed and abused by the other men, he tried to desert but was caught. His punishment was a year with the penal battalion Dirlewanger. Thanks to a nonfatal wound, he witnessed the end of the war from a military hospital in Prague.

In significant ways persecution of homosexual men in Nazi camps continued what went on outside. After liberation of the camps in 1945, occupation authorities arrested again some gay men, reconvicted them, and sent them back to prison. Homosexual activity remained a criminal act in West Germany until the 1960s. Illegality and social stigma account for the silence that shrouded the treatment of gay men in Nazi Germany until the 1970s and 1980s.

RESISTANCE

All over Europe people resisted Nazism in many ways. There were individual acts of defiance and heroism; there was sabotage and rescue of people targeted for killing. The Communist Party organized resistance groups, often with backing from the Soviet Union. The British Special Operations Executive supported nationalist guerrilla movements from France to Yugoslavia and Greece.

Any discussion of resistance has to define the term. Does opposition have to be effective to count as resistance? Does it need to be organized? Armed? Unmixed with collaboration or opportunism? I define "resistance" as any actions taken with the intent of thwarting Nazi German goals in the war, actions that carried with them risk of punishment. Under this definition, resistance could be individual or group, armed or unarmed. Whether we talk about intelligence as resistance, Jewish resistance, or resistance within Germany, all discussion of resistance serves to counter some popular misconceptions about World War II.

The Spread of Information as Resistance

Resistance can take many forms. Many anti-Nazi organizations took enormous risks to collect and transmit information that would undermine the German war effort. One of the most remarkable examples of intelligence as resistance involved a member of the Polish underground named Jan Karski.

Born in 1914 Karski made a career before the war in the Polish Foreign Service. He joined the Polish army in 1939 and was taken prisoner of war by the Soviets. Karski escaped and became part of the Polish underground. In the fall of 1942, Karski was charged with a mission to London. He was to carry a report to the Polish government-in-exile that described the situation in German-occupied Poland.

Leaders of two Jewish organizations learned of Karski's impending trip to London and asked if he would also carry a report for them. Karski agreed. The Jews of Poland were being exterminated, the Jewish leaders told Karski. Eventually Hitler would lose the war, they said, but he would win his war against Polish Jewry. The Jewish leaders asked Karski to tell the highest circles of the Allied governments that Hitler planned to kill every Jew regardless of the outcome of the war. Polish Jews and even Polish gentiles were helpless to stop the destruction. Only the Allied governments could save the Jews.

Before they sent him off with their message, the Jewish leaders wanted Karski to see for himself what they meant. They smuggled him into the Jewish ghetto in Warsaw and then into the killing center at Belzec. Karski was devastated by what he saw. After an hour in Belzec disguised as a guard he broke down and had to be taken out, vomiting blood. Karski became one of the first eyewitnesses to present to the West the whole truth about the fate of the Jews in occupied Poland.

Karski delivered his reports as promised. He met with British, American, and Polish representatives; he spoke directly with Prime Minister Churchill in Britain and President Roosevelt in the United States and sought out journalists and other opinion leaders.

All of Karski's perseverance and heroism did not get the results he so des-

Stjepan Filipovic, commander of a partisan detachment, calls on the people of Serbia to fight, just before his execution in May 1942. Such shows of defiance often had a profound impact on those who saw them.

perately wanted. People simply did not comprehend. After U.S. Supreme Court justice Felix Frankfurter listened to Karski's report, he responded that he could not believe it. Frankfurter did not mean he thought Karski was lying; he simply could not grasp the enormity of what he had heard. Karski found no effective help for the Jews of Poland from any nation, government, or church. Only a few courageous individuals like himself were willing to act. Karski survived the war and moved to Washington, D.C., where he taught political science for many years. He died in 2000.

Jan Karski's experience highlights the issue of Allied knowledge of Nazi

Willem Arondeus (left) and friends dancing at a garden party. During the war, Arondeus led a Dutch gay resistance group that bombed the Amsterdam Population Registry offices in an effort to destroy government records on Jews and others hunted by the Germans. Arondeus was executed in 1943.

crimes. What did the British or the Americans know and when? By late 1942, when Karski prepared his report, at least some people within the Allied leadership had access to a great deal of information about German atrocities. Already in 1941 British code breakers were reading German dispatches, including those from the Soviet Union describing murders of Jews and other civilians by the Order Police. Reports from eyewitnesses and individuals who had managed to escape from Nazi prisons and camps reached world leaders through all kinds of channels, and every government had its own sources of intelligence. The press offered considerable detail for the reading public—in the United States, Canada, Switzerland, and elsewhere—so that it is not possible to speak of mass murder as if it were a Nazi secret.

Nevertheless a number of factors prevented the Allies from broadcasting their knowledge of slaughter of European Jews and other people. Most important, there was a war to be won, a war whose outcome was by no means clear in 1942 or even 1943. In particular military leaders in the United States and Britain emphasized the need to stay focused and avoid being distracted by "sideshows." No doubt some individuals were indifferent to the fate of Europe's Jews or even had antisemitic notions of their own. Nevertheless it is probably fair to assume that many people simply could not grasp the unprecedented nature of this war of annihilation, and even those who could tended to be preoccupied with their own issues and struggles.

Jewish Resistance

Jewish resistance of various kinds was much more widespread than many people used to assume. All across German-occupied Europe, Jews and other opponents of Nazism took to the woods, often forming partisan units to combat the Germans.

The existence of Jewish partisans was precarious at best. They lived from hand to mouth, stealing when necessary, arranging secretly for deliveries of food, and spending hours and even days in holes in the ground when danger threatened. Afraid that the presence of Jews nearby would jeopardize their own security, gentiles often denounced or killed their Jewish counterparts. Nevertheless, as German police records for 1943 indicate, Jews in the woods of eastern Europe managed to acquire explosives and weapons and to perform acts of sabotage against the Nazi system. In some cases, young Jewish men and women even married in the woods and gave birth to children there.

In Lithuania in early 1942, about ten thousand Jewish men and women were fighting as partisans. At least thirty different Jewish partisan groups existed in the General Government alone. Jews also revolted in such major ghettos as Warsaw and Bialystok. In general, the groups that banded together were desperate, pitifully small, and barely armed. Their chances of success were minimal, but still they defied Nazi power.

Even in the camps, under the most adverse conditions, resistance in many forms occurred. Numerous survivors' memoirs tell the story of the beautiful dancer in Auschwitz who seized a gun from an SS man and shot him. Both Sobibor and Treblinka had revolts in 1943. In October 1944, Jewish prisoners at Auschwitz-Birkenau blew up the camp's fourth crematorium. Starved, abandoned by the world, and robbed of their property, the Jews were in a weak position to offer resistance to the Germans. Nevertheless, like others they did

Sara Ginaite, a Jewish partisan fighter from Kovno, at the liberation of Vilna in August 1944. A Red Army major took the photograph and published it in the Soviet Union. Sara Ginaite remained in Lithuania after the war, where she made a successful career as an economist. She moved to Canada in the 1980s.

resist—violently, passively, spiritually, physically, and emotionally—throughout the entire process of the "Final Solution."

The Jewish ghetto in Warsaw must have been one of the last places the Germans expected an uprising in the spring of 1943. By then 80 percent of the population of the Warsaw ghetto was already gone, most of them murdered at Treblinka in the summer of 1942.

Initially the Warsaw Jewish rebels had little support even within their own community. The Jewish Fighting Organization had fewer than five hundred fighters. Armed only with gasoline bombs, hand grenades, pistols, one or two submachine guns, and about ten rifles, they must have seemed unlikely to accomplish anything other than rapid mass suicide. Yet this ragtag band managed to mount the largest armed resistance organized by any targets of Nazi mass murder during the Second World War. What happened?

In January 1943 German SS planned to liquidate what was left of the Warsaw ghetto. To their surprise they met with organized resistance from ghetto Jews. Unwilling to risk casualties in the wake of the defeat at Stalingrad, they gave up the attempt a few days later.

Four months later, on 19 April 1943, the Germans returned much better prepared. More than two thousand men came with armored vehicles, artillery, flame throwers, heavy-caliber machine guns, and aircraft. For their part Warsaw Jews had prepared an elaborate system of bunkers and underground passages. Determined to make a stand they held off the Germans for four weeks.

The SS burned down buildings, dynamited, and smoked out the Jews' bunkers until they won the upper hand. The Jewish fighters' tenacity was astounding, especially because the ghetto was sealed off and it was almost impossible to get weapons or supplies. The Nazis crushed the uprising at a huge cost in human lives, almost all of them Jewish. The SS commander reported sixteen German dead; the actual number may have been slightly higher.

Small pockets of Jewish resistance continued for weeks, but in the end, more than fifty-six thousand Jews surrendered. The Germans shot many on the spot and transported the others to killing centers and labor camps. Thousands of Jewish dead remained buried in the rubble.

The Warsaw ghetto uprising marked the first large-scale urban revolt against German occupation. It did not save Jewish lives. To the contrary, it may have led the Germans to use more force more quickly in the future when they set out to liquidate ghettos. Given their intention to kill the Jews anyway, however, it could hardly have worsened the Jews' situation. Certainly its moral and symbolic importance as an assertion of life cannot be underestimated.

Resistance within Germany

Examples of resistance within Germany are few although so-called Aryan Germans were certainly in the strongest position to oppose the Nazi regime. The early years of Hitler's rule had paralyzed organizations that might have been the focal point for resistance activities. Members of the Communist Party, for example, had been dispersed, although they managed to retain some links

Jews in the Westerbork camp light Hanukkah candles inside a barracks. This photograph, taken in December 1944, came from the personal album of the camp commander. According to one survivor, many of the people shown here were sent to Auschwitz the following day.

to one another and preserve some pockets of resistance. The time to oppose Nazism had been in the first phases of its rule in Germany. By 1942 and 1943 the stakes were much higher. Only in 1944, once Germany was clearly losing the war, would more opponents of the regime be emboldened to acts of resistance.

Still there were some important incidents earlier on. In the winter of 1942 a professor and a handful of students at the University of Munich formed an organization they called the White Rose. The key figures were Kurt Huber, a professor of philosophy; Willi Graf, a devout Catholic; Alexander Schmorell, son of a Russian woman; Christoph Probst and Hans Leipelt, both of whom had Jewish family members; and a brother and sister, Hans and Sophie Scholl. Both Scholls had been enthusiastic Nazis as children, but as students they broke from those ideas. Hans's tour of duty as a medical orderly on the eastern front gave him firsthand exposure to the horrors of Nazi German warfare.

Under the name "the White Rose," the group printed a series of leaflets decrying the crimes of Nazism. The last issue, in February 1943, was called "The Spirit Lives!" In it the students protested the moral destruction of German youth. Nazism, they wrote, had turned German young people into godless, shameless, unscrupulous murderers.

Police caught Hans and Sophie Scholl along with three of their friends, including Professor Huber. They were interrogated and tried for spreading malicious and defeatist rumors against the state. Sophie, a twenty-two-year-old philosophy student at the time, addressed the court as guards led her away: "What we have written is in all your minds, but you lack the courage to say it aloud."

Hans and Sophie Scholl and Christoph Probst were executed in February 1943. Schmorell, Huber, Graf, and Leipelt were tried and executed later. Their university remained silent; there was neither protest nor any show of solidarity from administrators, faculty, or students on behalf of the members of their community. After the war the University of Munich named its main quadrangle after the Scholl siblings.

Obstacles to Resistance

There were enormous barriers to resistance, especially for members of groups targeted for persecution and death, in German-controlled Europe. One of the most significant was the Nazi policy of exacting reprisals. As we have seen, the Germans made entire communities suffer for acts of resistance on a scale massively out of proportion to the supposed offense.

In June 1942 members of the Czech underground, with support from the British Special Operations Executive, assassinated Reinhard Heydrich. The Germans responded with total destruction of the town of Lidice, near Prague. They murdered all 199 men there as well as many of the women and children. Those remaining were removed for Germanization.

In 1943 a group of Jewish fighters from Vilna escaped from the ghetto to join partisans in the forest. Somehow they got their hands on a few weapons and attacked some Germans outside the city. In retaliation, the Gestapo seized the entire family of each Jewish fugitive or everyone who lived with him or her. They also arrested the leaders of all of the Jewish work parties in the vicinity, together with their families. All of those people were shot.

The policy of reprisals was a major deterrent. It probably explains why revolts in the Jewish ghettos often occurred only after the rebels were certain that death was planned for them and those close to them anyway.

Divisions within communities could present another obstacle to resistance. What would be the prospects? What were the best tactics? Were some would-be heroes risking increased horror for other people?

After years of war and occupation few people had the prerequisites for resistance. Overwhelmed by events, isolated, exhausted, and hungry, they could not hope for much success when it came to stopping Nazi Germany. Given those conditions we should perhaps be surprised at how much rather than how little resistance there was in German-occupied Europe.

The topic of resistance easily lends itself to manipulation and stereotypes. For decades the insistence of the postwar French governments that they were the heirs of the heroic French resistance made it impossible to face the realities of French collaboration. The fact that Jews were enormously overrepresented among French resisters was rarely acknowledged. Old stereotypes of Jewish passivity in turn blinded many scholars and other observers to the abundant evidence of Jewish resistance.

It is tempting to offer resistance as a sort of antidote to the depressing subject of World War II and the Holocaust, but some caution is in order. For one thing, a focus on heroism—those "lights in the darkness" who dared to defy the Nazi juggernaut—can serve both to encourage us with the possibilities for resistance and to remind us of just how many people participated in the crimes of the Third Reich or stood by silently.

It is also important to keep in mind that resistance arguably did not change the course of the war. It was military might that defeated Nazi Germany; with very few exceptions it was the Red Army and the western Allies that liberated occupied territories from German control.

Nevertheless resistance had a crucial impact. To other conquered peoples it sent a message that they were not alone and that the Germans were not invincible. Resistance also left a positive legacy for a postwar world in which so many people had been compromised by collaboration and opportunism or paralyzed by death and misery.

A CASE STUDY: THADDEUS STABHOLZ

Thaddeus Stabholz experienced many of the events that have been addressed in this chapter. "Teddy" Stabholz grew up in a middle-class, assimilated Jewish family in Poland. He was a young medical student in Warsaw when World War II began. Months after the Germans defeated Poland, they forced Teddy, his father, his grandmother, and the rest of his relatives to move into the Warsaw ghetto. Teddy's mother had died in 1938 of cancer; in 1941 his father was killed by the Germans.

Teddy was left alone "like a homeless dog," he wrote later. With his fiancée, Fredzia, he survived as best he could on the food they could scrounge. Teddy cared for his grandmother too, until January 1943, when Germans beat her to death in the street. By that time, many of the Jews—especially the old, very young, and sick—had already been taken out of the ghetto and sent to the gas chambers at the killing center of Treblinka.

In early 1943 some of the young Jews left in the Warsaw ghetto organized an uprising against the Germans. Teddy and Fredzia were among them. They fought desperately with whatever weapons they had, but they were no match for the SS firepower. The Germans burned the ghetto, killed most of the people in it, and sent the remaining few to Treblinka. There Fredzia was murdered, but Teddy, for some reason, was sent on to Majdanek, a labor camp as well as a killing center. He remained a prisoner of the Germans in various camps for two more years.

Through extraordinary luck—if one can speak of good fortune in the

Dr. Bigula Vajs, a Jewish member of the resistance, attending to a sick child in Yugoslavia during the war.

context of genocide—Teddy Stabholz survived. Guards selected him to be killed at Majdanek but at the last minute pulled him out of the group and made him a medic. At Auschwitz-Birkenau he was starved, beaten, and forced to carry enormous loads of water and cement for miles. He almost died of pneumonia. For a time he even had a "job" delousing the body hair of fellow prisoners with Zyklon B, the same insecticide used in the gas chambers. Stabholz managed to win the favor of some senior prisoners and guards by "operating" on the corns and calluses on their feet. In the summer of 1944, he witnessed the murder of all of the Gypsies in Auschwitz.

Stabholz endured excruciating work, plagues of typhus and lice, and transfers to camps farther from the front lines. At one point he resigned himself to death, but a vision of his father and mother encouraged him and revived his will to live.

In April 1945 American troops fighting their way through southern Germany found Stabholz and some fellow prisoners who had escaped from the SS and hidden in the woods. After spending time in a displaced persons camp in Germany, Teddy came to the United States. He graduated from medical school and started a practice in Ohio. Dr. Stabholz's memoir of the Holocaust is called *Seven Hells*.

8

DEATH THROES AND KILLING
FRENZIES, 1944–1945

If the Germans were to lose the war, Hitler once said, they would bring down with them "a world in flames." Hitler kept that promise. The last stage of the war in Europe, from 1944 until May 1945, brought German retreat, defeat, and collapse, but the Nazi Empire remained bloody and destructive until its very end.

At the beginning of 1944, many Germans still expected to win the war. By the end of the year, few persisted in that hope. Germany was under assault—from the air, from the Red Army in the east, and, after D-Day in June, from the Allies in the west. Even internally there were some signs of weakening, but it still took until May 1945 for total collapse.

The death throes of the Third Reich were deadly themselves—far less for the privileged elite of the regime than for its victims. Even as defeat became ever more certain, killing went on in many settings. The Allies, both eastern and western, had to fight hard and suffer many casualties to advance. When a plot to assassinate Hitler and stage a coup failed in July 1944, the Nazi regime responded with a vicious crackdown on its own population.

Well into 1945, Nazi programs of mass murder continued in the ever-shrinking territories that Germany controlled. Most of the Gypsies in Auschwitz were gassed in 1944. The murder of almost four hundred thousand Hungarian Jews took place that summer too. Throughout the last year of the war, the Germans kept opening new labor camps. As they abandoned killing centers and camps in areas lost to Allied advances, guards sent the inmates still left alive on murderous treks known as death marches.

None of that killing halted the disintegration of German power, but it ensured that the defeat of Nazism was accompanied by the maximum amount of carnage. This chapter will survey developments in the last stage of the war. How did the Nazi Reich, the Holocaust, and the war in Europe end?

ATTACKS ON THE NAZI REGIME

The Soviet Advance

From late 1943, the Soviets remained on the offensive against Germany. The Red Army made rapid advances in 1944. On the third anniversary of Operation Barbarossa—in June 1944—the Soviets launched a massive offensive against the German Army Group Center.

By the end of 1944, odds on Germany's eastern front were heavily in favor of the Soviets. Against the total German strength of between 2 and 3.5 million men loomed 6 million Red Army soldiers. A German disadvantage of one German to every five Soviets was common; in some places the odds were closer to one to thirty or forty.

Still the Soviets fought at a tremendous cost. Even at the end of 1944, the Germans were still killing or wounding four Soviets for every casualty of their own. The huge Soviet advantage in replacements—and the need to send in wave after wave of those troops—itself implied the staggering death toll that the fighting took on the Red Army. It is estimated that the battle for Berlin alone cost half a million people their lives or their health. Small wonder that as soon as it could, the Soviet leadership would demand massive territorial gains and enormous reparations from the Germans.

Allied Bombing and Conditions in Germany

Air raids on Germany by the Royal Air Force and the U.S. air force peaked between January 1944 and January 1945. In the words of U.S. President Franklin Roosevelt, "Fortress Europe" had no roof. American planes alone made some 755,000 sorties that year and dropped 1.4 million tons of bombs on Germany and German-controlled territories. Much of that aerial bombing was inaccurate, so that planes often dropped their loads indiscriminately in and around major German cities. Allied bombing may have killed as many as five hundred thousand German civilians.

Attacks from the air hit the petroleum and chemical industries hard. By September the Germans could supply only 10 percent of their needs in aviation fuel. By early 1945, the flow of fuel and ammunition to the German fronts had almost stopped.

Nevertheless the German war machine demonstrated remarkable resilience to the assault from the air. Electric power stations continued to function, and German war production persisted during the last stage of the war. Of course a regime obsessed with public opinion ensured that these achievements were accompanied by massive "armaments propaganda." Did manufacturing of fighter planes peak in late 1944? Was total German military output in 1944 really more than the country's 1939 level? Eager to depict Germany as invincible in the face of economically superior enemies, Goebbels and his minions exaggerated and celebrated the triumphs of mass production and trumpeted the imminent appearance of new miracle weapons.

Such claims were encouraged and supported by Albert Speer (1905–1981), Hitler's minister of armaments and war production from 1942. A trained architect and a friend and confidante of Hitler, Speer also indulged the Führer's passion for designing giant buildings for the Nazi world of the future. The Allies captured Speer at the end of the war and brought him to trial for his role in German crimes against foreign labor. He served twenty years in prison. Speer published memoirs and a diary. Unlike almost all of his Nazi counterparts, it appears that by the end of his life Speer was repentant toward the victims of the Third Reich and regretted his role in German crimes.

The real key to German wartime production was the massive use of slave labor. In 1939 there were about three hundred thousand forced laborers in Germany. By 1944 that number had skyrocketed to 7.5 million. It was above all these non-Germans—from Russia, Ukraine, Belorussia, Poland, France, the Netherlands, Italy, Hungary, and elsewhere—who bore the tremendously high human cost involved in outfitting the German war machine.

The impact of the attack from the air on the morale of German civilians is hard to gauge. Certainly air raids alone did not destroy German support of Hitler's regime, although it is possible that the destruction of German cities made it easier for Germans to recognize defeat and surrender at the end of the war. Much easier to measure was the physical impact of the bombing. Allied raids destroyed between 4.5 and 5 million habitations, so that Germans experienced an incredible shortage of housing in the last stages of the war. Production of consumer goods fell dramatically at the same time.

By 1944 the German economy was in serious trouble. Hitler's insistence on protecting the home front from the costs of war meant deficit financing on a huge scale. The idea, of course, was that the vanquished would pay for the war. As long as the Germans were victorious they supported themselves through theft and plunder. Once the tide of the war turned, however, they were left with the hollowness of their own economy. Printing large amounts of money sparked inflation. Rapidly rising prices, in conjunction with stringent wage and price controls, led—as that particular combination always does—to the emergence of an active black market. In the German case, even before the war was over cigarettes began to overtake the official currency as the preferred medium of exchange.

D-Day—Allied Invasion from the West

On 6 June 1944, in a massive action with the code name Operation Overlord, the western Allies landed in Normandy in northwestern France. D-Day, as it became known, was the greatest amphibious assault ever. The numbers alone are staggering. More than 4,000 Allied ships landed 176,000 troops after 10,000 aircraft dropped 10,000 tons of explosives on the German defenders of the French coast.

By the end of July, after hard fighting and heavy casualties, Allied forces broke out of the beachheads and began to drive the Germans eastward. In August 1944 the Allies liberated Paris. The next month the western Allies under General Dwight Eisenhower crossed the German border. Germany's new "wonder weapons"—the V-1 and V-2 rockets—were deadly enough for those targeted, but they were no match for the onslaught of Soviet, British, and American artillery and tanks during 1944.

In the wake of D-Day and the Soviet offensive of June 1944, Hitler named Goebbels the Reich plenipotentiary for total war. Together the Führer and his loyal associate painted a gruesome picture for the Germans of what lay in store if they were defeated. Germans could expect only the harshest of treatment from the vengeful Allies, they warned. Their scare tactics assumed widespread knowledge of the atrocities that Germans had committed throughout the preceding years, especially in the east. It was as if Hitler and Goebbels were taunting the German public with its complicity—we Germans are all in this together, they insisted, and all of us will have to pay the price if we surrender.

Meanwhile Hitler and Goebbels instructed the German press to keep blaming the Jews for the war. U.S. President Roosevelt held out to Europeans the promise of the four freedoms: freedom of speech, freedom of worship, freedom from want, and freedom from fear. Hitler, for his part, threatened the German public with his own version of what Allied victory would mean:

"Jewish poison, Bolshevik slaughter, capitalist exploitation, and Anglo-American Imperialism."

It was not love for his people that motivated Hitler's raving but an obsessive fixation on his own goals of race and space. "I will shed no tears for the German people," he had once said in contemplating what defeat would mean. According to Hitler's logic, any people that allowed itself to be conquered proved its own unworthiness to wear the mantle of the master race.

Marion Kaufmann, later Cassirer (center), a Jewish girl from Berlin, with the Gypsy family that hid her for a month in the Netherlands in late 1944, after the area had been liberated by the Canadians only to be reoccupied by the Germans. Marion had fled Germany with her mother in 1942, but they were separated and not reunited until 1945.

The Plot of 20 July 1944

Not internal dissension but military defeat eventually brought down the Nazi regime. Nevertheless there was one important attack from within Germany during the last year of the war: the plot of 20 July 1944.

The plot was the work of a fairly disparate network of opponents of Hitler's regime. The conspirators included high-ranking military men who resented the way Hitler was conducting the war effort. Some of them hoped to overthrow his government and then join up with the western Allies against the Communist Soviet Union. Others more loosely involved in the plan had moral and humanitarian motivations. Appalled by German crimes against civilians in the east, such people saw no option but overthrow of the dictator if Germany's soul was to be saved.

Typical of the humanistic side of the opposition to Hitler was Count Helmuth James von Moltke (1907–1945), a lawyer and devoted Christian who, from 1939 to 1944, was a war administration counselor in the international law section of the German Armed Forces Supreme Command. Moltke organized a group of anti-Nazi friends and like-minded individuals who met during the war to make plans for a new, democratic Germany. Moltke, who struggled with issues of violence, did not support assassination, but he did urge military leaders to overthrow Hitler. Arrested already in January 1944, Moltke was hanged in Berlin-Plötzensee a year later.

Anti-Communists, conservatives, liberals, monarchists, and dedicated Christians all numbered among those who hoped to see Hitler assassinated or at least removed in July 1944. Although their visions for a reorganized Germany differed, they all saw the need to replace Hitler's rule with a government that would seek peace with the Allies and introduce reforms at home.

The plan for 20 July 1944 itself was straightforward. A high-ranking General Staff officer named Colonel Claus Schenck von Stauffenberg (1907–1944) would plant a bomb at a meeting in the "Wolf's Lair," Hitler's East Prussian headquarters. The death of Hitler would then give the signal for a coup d'état in Berlin.

The plan failed. Stauffenberg set the bomb in his briefcase, placed it under the table around which the meeting was taking place, and then left the building. As he drove toward Berlin he heard the explosion and assumed Hitler had been killed. In fact only part of the explosives went off, and Hitler was barely injured. Instead of a successful coup the conspirators experienced the Führer's terrible revenge.

Stauffenberg was captured and shot by firing squad on the evening of

20 July 1944. He went to his death shouting, "Long live Germany!" Others accused of participation in the plot were hauled before the so-called People's Court, publicly humiliated, and sent to prison. Hitler had many of them killed, some immediately, others only after some months. The assassination attempt provided an excuse for a general crackdown within Germany on anyone suspected of opposition.

A WORLD IN FLAMES

The Volkssturm

In September 1944, Hitler ordered full deployment of Germany's resources against the enemy through creation of a *Volkssturm,* a "people's storm." The Volkssturm was to mobilize all men between the ages of fifteen and sixty, adding a total of 1.5 million men under arms. Not just intended for local defense, Volkssturm units were to close gaps in the regular Wehrmacht and engage the enemy in combat.

Some of the Volkssturm boys and men fought valiantly and desperately against the Red Army and the western Allies. Some Volkssturm units were well organized and fairly well equipped. Others were thrown together; thirteen-year-old boys stood on bridges expecting to take on men in tanks, and men in their sixties took up arms to try to hold their villages. Some units took appalling losses of life; others collapsed in the face of the Allied advance.

By early 1945 even Nazi true believers had to see that the war was lost. The German army was falling apart. Increasing numbers of men deserted, although military authorities continued to shoot those they caught and in many cases to arrest members of their families. Special courts-martial were set up with the intent of frightening the German troops into reckless resistance. Propaganda announced the existence of the Werewolf organization to continue Nazi efforts behind enemy lines. Roving SS units sought out and punished German civilians who expressed defeatism, advised surrender, or made contact with the enemy. None of these measures stopped the Allied advance, but they did reveal for anyone who had not yet noticed the heartless ruthlessness of National Socialism.

On 19 March 1945, Hitler gave what became known as the Nero Order. He instructed Germans fleeing before the advancing Allies to destroy everything they left behind and leave nothing for the enemy. The Nero Order called for the destruction of all installations serving military purposes, transportation, communication, industry, and supply. At the same time Hitler ordered the defense of German cities under threat of the death penalty for anyone disobeying his orders. When Speer suggested that the Germans too would starve if such measures were implemented, Hitler showed no concern.

The Warsaw Uprising

The unraveling of German power emboldened the regime's opponents in occupied Europe. Once again, as in 1943, the city of Warsaw was the site of a major revolt. By August 1944 the Red Army was approaching Warsaw from the east. Leaders of the Polish Home Army decided to try to liberate the city from the Germans themselves. The Home Army was the non-Communist wing of the Polish resistance linked to traditional Polish nationalists and the Polish government-in-exile. Drawing on an armed force of about twenty-five thousand people, Home Army leaders launched a large-scale uprising.

Instead of continuing their advance into Warsaw, Red Army units stopped on the east bank of the Vistula River and waited. Perhaps they did not want to risk confrontation with the Germans massing on Warsaw, or perhaps Stalin preferred to let German forces wipe out the anti-Communist elements inside the city to clear the way for his own takeover. Whatever the reason, the Soviets abandoned the Polish insurgents.

German forces outnumbered and vastly outgunned the struggling Poles. Throwing everything they had into the effort, the Germans crushed the revolt by 2 October 1944. In the process they killed some 170,000 people in Warsaw.

By the fall of 1944 the Germans' overall position was weak. Nevertheless they still had the might to wreak terrible destruction, especially on civilians. Soon after the Warsaw Uprising began, Hitler ordered the city leveled. German forces carried out the command. Unlike Moscow and Leningrad, which the Germans never conquered, or Paris, which they spared, Warsaw was flattened. It was an act of revenge unique even in the gory history of World War II, but typical of the killing frenzies of the last stage of Hitler's war.

Germany's Allies and the Jews of Hungary

The year 1944 also brought dramatic changes within those countries that had been partners in the German war effort. In September Finland signed an armistice with the Soviet Union and withdrew from the war. Finnish authorities had never handed over the small community of Jews in their country to the Germans to be killed. There had even been a few Finnish Jewish soldiers fighting alongside the Wehrmacht against the Soviet Union. The history of World War II and the Holocaust is full of such strange twists.

For some time already the authoritarian regimes in Romania and Hungary had been eager to get out of the war. By mid-1944 the Germans had to abandon hope of getting their hands on Romanian oil. By the fall of 1944 the Soviets occupied Romania and Bulgaria and were moving toward Hungary and Yugoslavia. Both Romania and Bulgaria signed armistices with the Soviet Union and declared war on Germany.

In March 1944 the Germans took steps to prevent Hungary from capitulating. That month German forces occupied Hungary, their ally, to keep control of the territory and safeguard access to its resources. In October 1944, when the Hungarian leader Admiral Miklos Horthy was caught trying to cut a deal with the Soviets, Hitler had him overthrown. The Germans installed a Hungarian Fascist regime dependent on their support.

Until the spring of 1944 the Jews of Hungary had managed to stay out of German hands. In March 1944, however, when German forces moved into Hungary, they brought with them experts like Adolf Eichmann who were intent on making sure that Hungarian Jews too would be annihilated.

In the summer of 1944, Germans and Hungarian collaborators worked together to deport a large proportion of Hungary's Jewish population to Auschwitz-Birkenau. In hindsight it is clear that the war was lost for the Germans. Nevertheless, they continued to pursue their goal of racial purification in those areas still in their control. Between 15 May and 9 July 1944, German and Hungarian police crammed some 437,000 Hungarian Jews into 147 transports and sent them north to Auschwitz. As usual, Roma from Hungary shared that fate.

One of those Gypsies was fifteen-year-old Karoly Lendvai, who came from a town near Budapest. Rounded up by Hungarian police, he and his family walked forty miles to an internment camp, where they stayed for two weeks. Decades later Lendvai remembers his hunger and the pits overflowing with corpses as typhus raged among the prisoners. Among his most vivid memories is the double-barreled curse a Hungarian guard shouted at him: "Rot, you Jew-Gypsy!"

Because of Germany's acute shortage of labor, German officials decided to postpone the killing of some of the Hungarian Jews until they had been exploited as slave workers. In 1944 Hitler allowed Himmler and Speer to bring some Jews into Germany to add to the labor force needed for military production. Under those terms, about one hundred thousand Hungarian Jews slated for killing were brought to German labor camps. There these men and women

Women and children on the ramp at Auschwitz-Birkenau in May 1944. From the "Auschwitz Album," which documented the arrival, selection, and processing of Jews from Subcarpathian Rus, then part of Hungary. The album was presented to the camp commandant and found after liberation in an SS barracks by Lili Jacob (later Zelmanovic, now Meier), who appears in one of the pictures. The boys on the cover of this book are her brothers.

were used to excavate underground bunkers and make armaments. Conditions were terrible, but they had at least a chance to live, something denied to their more than three hundred thousand relatives and friends sent directly to the gas at Auschwitz.

Why did the Germans persist in the slaughter of the Hungarian Jews? Some scholars have suggested that such determination even in the face of impending defeat showed just how deeply committed many Germans were to the project of annihilating the Jews. Many German functionaries, however, showed similar dedication in the last stages of the war in their efforts against other victim groups, for example, Polish gentiles, Slavic slave laborers, Soviet POWs, and homosexual men.

At least some of these last-minute brutalities were motivated by the common drive of self-preservation. By 1944 and 1945 the prospect of the front looked worse all the time. Many German guards, police, and officials of various kinds who were involved in attacks on civilians worked feverishly to prove how crucial their jobs were—jobs they could do in relative safety. Even in Nazi Germany, cowards were probably more common than fanatics.

Some Hungarian Jews survived within Hungary, thanks to rescue efforts on the part of many people, including foreign diplomats and international Jewish groups. The most famous rescuer in Hungary was Rauol Wallenberg. Wallenberg was a Swedish businessman and diplomat who rescued as many as one hundred thousand Hungarian Jews from deportation. Using money raised largely from the Jewish community in the United States, Wallenberg set up safe houses under the jurisdiction of the Swedish embassy, issued Swedish passports, bribed German and Hungarian officials, and even rescued some Jews from transports slated for Auschwitz.

At the end of the war Wallenberg wound up in Soviet hands. His fate is unknown, but it seems likely that he was sent to Siberia as a suspected spy and perished there.

Elie Wiesel is no doubt the best-known Jewish survivor from Hungary.

Women and children who have been selected for death walk toward the gas chambers at Auschwitz-Birkenau, May 1944. The 193 pictures in the Auschwitz album are a rare record of the killing process. Normally photography was forbidden inside the camp.

His book *Night* is probably the single most widely read personal account of the Holocaust. It recounts the experiences of Wiesel, at the time an adolescent boy, in the hell of Auschwitz in the deadly last months of the war.

Another Hungarian survivor is Judith Magyar Isaacson, who recorded her experiences in *Seed of Sarah*. Like Wiesel just a teenager in 1944, Judith Magyar landed in Auschwitz with her mother and a young aunt. Somehow the three women managed to stay together. Once, Judith faced down an SS man who tried to send her to one side of a selection, her mother to another. He let her go with her mother. Camp functionaries offered Judith a position as kapo, but she refused. Judith, her mother, and her aunt were among the Hungarian Jews taken out of Auschwitz and sent as slave laborers to Germany. Beaten, half-starved, and terrified of rape, Judith lived through the final stages of the war. Later she married an American soldier and moved to Maine, where she taught mathematics and served as dean of students at Bates College until she retired.

The Hungarians suspended transports of Jews to Auschwitz in July 1944, and it was only in November that the new Arrow Cross government installed by the German coup ordered the Jews remaining in Budapest into a closed ghetto. The Arrow Cross was brutal: over the next two months its men shot twenty thousand Jews and dumped their bodies into the Danube River. But it could not approach the efficiency of Auschwitz. When the Red Army liberated Budapest in February 1945, there were one hundred thousand Jews still alive in the city.

Auschwitz at the End of the War

The killing center of Auschwitz reached new records of destruction in the final phase of the war. In the summer of 1944, as the transports from Hungary poured in, camp functionaries murdered as many as twelve thousand Jews per day.

There was a large operation against Gypsies that summer too, in which the entire Gypsy "family camp" was wiped out in one night. Of the twenty-three thousand Gypsies sent to Auschwitz, almost twenty thousand died there. By 2 August 1944 more than thirteen thousand were already dead. That night the remaining six thousand Roma in the camp were gassed. Now that transports of Jews from Hungary had been suspended, camp functionaries had time to kill Gypsies. German military setbacks, however severe, did not save the lives of those thousands of Gypsies any more than they spared the Jews of Hungary.

The last year of the war also saw several important incidents of armed resistance within German camps and killing centers. In mid-May 1944, when

SS officers and women auxiliaries in 1944 in Solahütte, the SS retreat center outside of Auschwitz. Karl Hoecker, adjutant to the camp commandant, appears in the middle. This photograph was included in a photo album prepared by or for Hoecker in 1944, around the same time as the Auschwitz album.

SS and camp workers first tried to liquidate the Gypsy camp at Auschwitz-Birkenau, they encountered violent resistance. Roma inside the camp improvised weapons as best they could or fought with their bare hands. That defiance may have helped postpone killing of all the Gypsies in Auschwitz until early August 1944.

The most dramatic example of resistance within Auschwitz came in October 1944. Jewish Sonderkommando prisoners blew up and destroyed Crematorium IV. Some of the necessary explosives were provided by a young Polish Jewish woman named Roza Robota. Assigned to work in an ammunition factory, Robota, along with some other women, began to smuggle small amounts of explosives to the Sonderkommando. The SS arrested and tortured her, but she refused to divulge any information. Robota was hanged in January 1945, shortly before the arrival of the Red Army.

THE DEATH MARCHES

Beginning in the fall of 1944, as the Germans lost control of much of the territory they had occupied, they began to evacuate many of the camps and killing centers. At the same time, they opened new labor camps in areas still safe from Allied advance. On orders from Himmler, camp officials began to empty the camps of prisoners. They sent the inmates, under guard, marching in columns toward places farther from the ever-advancing front. Throughout late 1944 and early 1945, these trails of half-dead prisoners made their way through the Polish, German, and Czech countrysides. Because of the awful numbers killed and dying along the way, these treks have come to be known as death marches.

A few examples give some idea of this new form of torture and killing. In the late fall of 1944, Germans sent about a thousand Jewish women, many of them Hungarian, from Auschwitz to Gross-Rosen. There the women were forced to dig antitank ditches, in the snow, with little or nothing to eat, and often without shoes.

In early January 1945, as the front advanced, that camp too was evacuated. Guards forced the remaining 970 women to begin a new march. In eight or nine days they had covered only about sixty miles. One hundred and fifty of the women died along the way. Perhaps 20 succumbed to starvation; guards shot another 130.

They were soon evacuated again from their next destination, with about a thousand additional prisoners. The group was divided into two, with half of the women being marched toward Helmbrechts in Bavaria, a satellite camp of Flossenbürg. In the middle of winter the women walked about three hundred miles. After five weeks, 621 of them arrived at the camp. A few had escaped, and around 230 had remained at various camps along the way. Between 150 and 250 of the prisoners did not survive that march. Many were shot by guards.

The camp at Helmbrechts was quite new. Established in the summer of 1944, it housed women prisoners set to work for an armaments firm. As always, they suffered brutal beatings and deadly privation.

In April 1945 Helmbrechts too was emptied. German guards forced some eleven hundred women on yet another death march to nowhere. The group was about half Jewish and half gentile. Guards refused food and water and forbade inhabitants of the surrounding area to help the prisoners. By many accounts Jewish women received even worse treatment than the others. Another 175 to 275 of the Jewish women died during this stage of the march, just weeks before the war ended. Every one of them would have died had they not been rescued by American forces.

On 15 April 1945, the same day that British troops reached the concentration camp of Bergen-Belsen, SS and camp guards forced seventeen thousand women and forty thousand men to march westward from the concentration camps of Ravensbrück and Sachsenhausen into territories still in German hands. Hundreds of women died of exhaustion on the march from Ravens-brück. Retreating guards and SS men shot hundreds of others. Some were killed by Allied bombs. Having made it so long, thousands died by the roadside just days away from the end of the war. Death marches continued right up until the German surrender on 8 May 1945. In all, an estimated 250,000 to 375,000 people died in such forced marches.

FINAL COLLAPSE

On the military front too, Hitler's Germans exacted a high price from their enemies. At the end of December, Hungary finally completed the reversal of its allegiances. Declaration of war on Germany was followed a month later by an armistice with Moscow.

The Germans came back with a final onslaught in the west. The Ardennes Offensive, called the Battle of the Bulge by the Allies, began in December 1944. That grandiose effort failed, but only after it had cost many lives on both sides.

By early March 1945 the German front in the west had collapsed. U.S. and British forces were advancing in the north, center, and south. German authorities responded by lowering the age for the draft to include boys born in 1929.

In the last months things unraveled quickly. March brought a partisan offensive by Tito's forces against German troops in Yugoslavia. By April the Red Army was in Vienna, and German forces in Italy capitulated at the end of that month. In early May, Czechs revolted against German occupation in Prague. In this climate, even the death of U.S. President Roosevelt on 12 April 1945 did not weaken the Allies' demand for Germany's unconditional sur-render.

Finally, in the last stage of the war, many Germans came to feel something of the reality of the conflict their leadership had inflicted on Europe. More Germans died in bombings, expulsions, and the collapse of the military fronts in the last six months of war than in the previous four years together. Approxi-mately 160,000 German soldiers died in 1940–1941. In 1944 that number increased almost fourfold to some 600,000. The all-or-nothing mentality of Hitler's Social Darwinism made all lives cheap, including those of the German people.

If you look at textbooks on Nazi Germany you will notice that many of them label the last days of the Third Reich the *Götterdämmerung*, or "twilight of the gods." The reference is to the end of the ring cycle, a group of operas by Richard Wagner. Hitler loved those operas, and the massive, tragic cataclysm at the end fit his own obsession with heroic death. That morbid fascination came to the fore in the last months of Hitler's regime.

In his poem "The Wasteland" (1922), T. S. Eliot wrote the following lines: "This is the way the world ends, not with a bang but a whimper." Eliot's description could be applied to the Third Reich, which ended with both an explosion of death and destruction and a whimper of cowardice and defeat.

In a small way, Hitler reaped what he had sown with the principle of divide and conquer when it came to the behavior of his inner circle in the last days. Whimpering treachery turned out to be more characteristic of Hitler's henchmen than that iron loyalty they had loved to espouse. Everyone, it turns out, seemed to have a plan as to how to salvage the Reich—and of course, save his own neck. In February 1945, Goebbels suggested that Hitler should remain head of state but appoint a new chancellor and foreign minister. Goebbels's preferred candidate for the job: himself, obviously. In deference to Himmler's control of the SS empire, Goebbels proposed Himmler for minister of war.

Himmler himself had toyed for a long time already with the idea of a separate peace with Britain. He used his contacts to test the waters, but they were icy cold. Efforts on the part of Luftwaffe commander Göring and German foreign minister Ribbentrop to negotiate a separate peace with the western powers also failed.

Hitler was determined to continue the fight, but on 22 April 1945, two days after his birthday, he fell into depression. Hitler realized that the war was lost, and he knew he could not negotiate a peace himself. Göring, he decided, was the man for the job.

When Göring heard about Hitler's remarks he decided it meant he was to take over. Outraged by that presumption, Hitler denounced Göring as a traitor, dismissed him from his many posts, and had him arrested by the SS. Göring would eventually be captured and brought to trial at Nuremberg, where he committed suicide before his scheduled execution.

Just days after he dismissed Göring, Hitler got word of Himmler's treachery. Furious, he ordered the arrest of the SS leader as well, but Himmler slipped through his hands. Himmler too would manage to kill himself before the Allies could exact justice. In the last days of April, Hitler swung briefly from depression into a kind of manic activity. He ordered a massive counterattack to drive the Soviets back from Berlin. He announced that the western Allies would soon be at war with the Soviet Union and that Germany would be saved. Nothing came of any of these notions.

On 29 April 1945, holed up in his bunker in Berlin, Hitler dictated one final document: his last will and political testament. In it he admonished Germans "punctiliously to observe the racial laws" and to fight on against "the poisoner of all the nations of the world, international Jewry." True to form he blamed the entire course of the lost war on "international Jewry and its helpers." Consistent to the end, Hitler described annihilation of the Jews of Europe as his greatest achievement.

That same day Hitler married Eva Braun. On 30 April the "first soldier of the German Reich" deserted by committing suicide in his bunker. Dead beside him by their own hands were his new wife, the loyal Goebbels, and Goebbels's wife and six children. Hitler's war would end as it had started— with a lie. His chosen successor, Admiral Karl Dönitz, reported by radio to the nation that its Führer had sustained "heroic death in battle." Two days later, the city of Berlin surrendered to the Soviets. Hitler's successors signed documents of unconditional surrender on 8 May 1945.

The reality of how Nazi rule ended sweeps away the myth of order that

Ruins of the Kovno ghetto, photographed in August 1944. In July 1944, the Germans transported over 6,000 Jews from Kovno to concentration camps. Aware that many people had not appeared for the roundups, German troops then razed the ghetto area, doused the ruins with gasoline, and incinerated thousands of people. Only about one hundred Jews survived the liquidation of Kovno.

has grown up around Hitler's regime. There was neither order nor glory to his demise. No heroic struggle marked his death, only cowardice, the ruin of his own people, and lies.

The Nazi revolution had promised a new awakening. Instead it brought destruction and death far beyond the borders of Germany. An estimated 55 million people died worldwide in World War II. Among them were more than 5 million German soldiers. At least 27 million Soviet citizens were dead, as well as millions of Poles, over a million Yugoslavs, and scores of other people from all over Europe. Close to 6 million Jews were murdered, and Jewish civilization was almost eradicated from Europe. The list could go on and on, and the world continues to feel the effects of hatreds sown for the Nazi goals of racial purification and territorial expansion.

Conclusion

THE LEGACIES OF ATROCITY

This account ends in May 1945, but the legacies of Nazism, World War II, and the Holocaust extend much further. Perhaps one story can begin to illustrate some of the personal and political repercussions of the history described in the previous eight chapters. Like many stories that end in death, the details can only be pieced together in a fragmentary way, but they are nonetheless significant.

This account begins in the mid-1930s in the Soviet Union. Frightened by manifestations of antisemitism under Stalin, a young Russian Jew whom we will call N. decided to leave his home and move west. He settled in France, where he built a life for himself until the Germans invaded in 1940, and his existence again became precarious.

For a while N. succeeded in evading the Nazi dragnet, but sometime in 1942 or 1943 German or French police rounded him up, along with many other foreign Jews living in France, and sent him east to a Nazi camp. Against terrible odds, N. survived more than a year as a prisoner and slave of Nazi Germany. In mid-April 1945, when British troops arrived at the concentration camp Bergen-Belsen, N. was one of the inmates liberated.

Under the terms of an Allied agreement, N., a citizen of the Soviet Union, was turned over to Soviet authorities. Instead of relief from years of torment at Nazi German hands, he soon found himself again on a deportation transport, this time to Siberia. Suspicious of the loyalty of Soviet citizens who had spent years outside the country, Stalin had tens of thousands of people like N.—Jews, POWs, forced laborers—sent directly from their "liberation" to labor camps and prisons in remote regions, where they toiled in massive industrialization projects.

Jewish youth liberated at Buchenwald lean out of a train in June 1945. Marked with the words, "Hitler kaput" (Hitler is finished), the train was en route to a children's home in France. This photograph comes from the collection of Romek Wajsman (now Robert Waisman) from Poland, one of 1,000 Jewish child survivors found by American troops when they arrived at Buchenwald in April 1945.

N. did not survive this second round of abuse. N.'s son, who lived through the war in France and later moved to New York, spent years trying to trace his father through the Red Cross and other international organizations. Decades after the war ended, he received the news he had long feared: his father had died in Siberia.

The fate of N. highlights several facts about the end of the Holocaust and World War II. The arrival of Allied forces and the collapse of Nazi Germany were not miracles that could undo or even stop the spirals of violence and misery unleashed by years of brutality. Although in hindsight it is easy to speak of liberation, for many individuals and groups of people, the end of the war meant continued and even new forms of misery. The defeat and total collapse of Hitler's Germany unleashed a movement of people within Europe, some of it voluntary, much of it coerced. Wartime atrocities created urgent demands for justice, even as the enormity of the crimes committed and the overwhelming death and destruction made any kind of restitution painfully inadequate and often impossible. Whether they had been victims, perpetrators, or bystanders in Nazi barbarity—and many Europeans had reason to count themselves in more than one of those categories—people faced the challenge of building lives for themselves and what was left of their families and communities with scarce resources and restricted freedom, and in a climate of distrust and grief.

As Allied troops moved into German-held territory in the last stages of the war, they encountered shocking scenes. The Soviets were the first to reach the major killing centers. Even they, many of whom had experienced and witnessed Nazi German brutality firsthand, were stunned by the horror of places like Auschwitz-Birkenau. Soldiers from the United States and Great Britain who fought their way into Germany from the west were even less prepared for what they found: mass graves, abandoned camps, boxcars full of corpses, and emaciated, dying prisoners.

On 15 April 1945, the first British tanks entered the concentration camp of Bergen-Belsen. Terrorized and enfeebled, inmates of the camp could not believe they were free. And in fact, freedom did not come easily. After initial contact, the British tanks moved on. For the next forty-eight hours, the camp was only nominally under British control. Hungarian soldiers whom the Ger-

German civilians conscripted by U.S. troops from the surrounding area dig mass graves for the dead found in Kaufering IV, a subcamp of Dachau in Bavaria. This photograph was taken on 30 April 1945.

mans had stationed there as guards remained in command. In two days they shot more than eighty Jews and non-Jews for such offenses as taking potato peels from the kitchen. Even after British troops entered Belsen in force, for more than two weeks three hundred inmates continued to die daily of typhus and starvation. Horror on the scale of the Holocaust did not simply disappear with the arrival of the Allied liberators.

The images captured on film by photographers and journalists who accompanied and followed Allied forces horrified people back home, just as the sights themselves stunned and sickened the soldiers who saw them first-hand. Decades later those images continue to haunt us and to shape the way we perceive and present atrocities in our own time. The questions they raise remain pressing even though they have almost become clichés: How could human beings do such things to other people? How can we go on living in a world where crimes and suffering of such magnitude are possible?

For those who survived, the end of World War II brought the realization of all that had been destroyed. Alone, without family or friends, often far from what had been their homes, many survivors, particularly Jews, had nowhere to go. Separated from their parents for years, some Jewish children no longer knew their birth names or even that they came from Jewish families. Many Jews had seen their gentile neighbors turn against them, denouncing them to Nazi officials and stealing their possessions. Could they now simply go back as if nothing had happened? In Poland, Ukraine, Hungary, and elsewhere, Jewish survivors who returned home to search for family members or reclaim their property were often met with violent hostility from the new "owners." Some Jews were attacked and beaten; some were killed.

Non-Jewish victims of Nazism faced their own problems as they discovered that true liberation was impossible in hostile surroundings. Gypsies who had managed to live through the Nazi assault were no more welcome in many places after May 1945 than they had been before or during the war. Few non-Gypsies realized or cared that Nazi Germany had singled out the Roma for particular abuse. Only decades after the war would Gypsies gradually begin to be acknowledged legally and unofficially as victims of Nazism. In some places—for example, in the western zones of occupied Germany—homosexual men were released from Nazi prisons and concentration camps only to be arrested again and incarcerated under old or new laws that criminalized homosexuality. Jehovah's Witnesses, thousands of whom endured imprisonment in Hitler's Germany, faced renewed persecution, especially under Communism, such as in the eastern zone of Germany, subsequently East Germany. Looking back at Nazism and the Holocaust, we often vow "never again," but for the

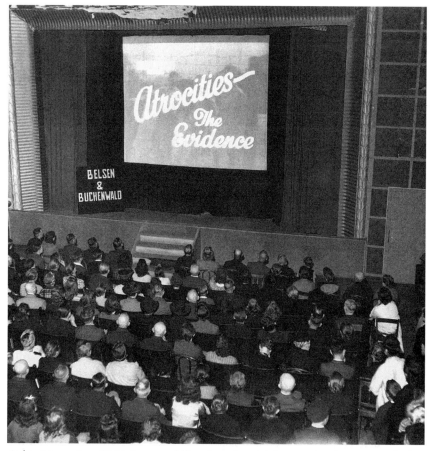

In late May or June 1945, German civilians from Burgsteinfurt watch a documentary in the local cinema about the atrocities of the Bergen-Belsen and Buchenwald concentration camps. When few residents showed up to see the film, British military authorities ordered all 4,000 townspeople to attend, assembled them, and marched them to the cinema.

Jews hounded out of Polish cities and towns by pogroms in 1945 and 1946, the Jehovah's Witnesses sitting in Communist jails in the 1950s, and the Gypsies crippled and left homeless by arson attacks in Romania in the 1990s, a more apt slogan might have been "Still?"

World War II sparked the movement of the largest number of people in the shortest period of time that the world had ever known. Refugees, fugitives, displaced persons, deportees, and expellees jammed the roadways and waterways of Europe and spilled over into Central Asia and the Americas. Hundreds

German civilians from Burgsteinfurt exit the cinema in their town where they were forced to see a film showing atrocities perpetrated in Buchenwald and Bergen-Belsen. This photograph was taken on 30 May 1945.

of thousands of people, like the Russian Jew N., were transported eastward, against their will, as prisoners and laborers of the Soviet Union. More of the wave of motion, however, was westward. An estimated 10 million refugees poured into the western zones of occupied Germany alone, those parts controlled by the United States, Britain, and France.

The motivations of those fleeing west varied. Some had experienced Communism in Stalin's Soviet Union and would risk anything to avoid a return to that misery. Some were ethnic Germans whose families had lived in eastern Europe for generations. Nazi authorities had begun evacuating them already before the war ended, aware that they would be targets for revenge. Many ethnic Germans had eagerly served the cause of race and space and benefited from the deprivation and expropriation of their neighbors. In some cases, Soviet and local authorities expelled ethnic Germans, both to remove potential troublemakers and to free up space for resettlement programs of their own. Ethnic Germans were forced out of western Poland, for example, at least partly because the Soviets needed homes for Poles they had pushed out of the eastern parts of the country, territories annexed to the Soviet Union after 1945.

Other east Europeans, who like many ethnic Germans had collaborated with Nazism, also had reasons to flee west, now that their German protectors had retreated. Fearing the wrath of their neighbors, they sought security or at least anonymity. The Red Army's horrific record of rape and plunder as its troops penetrated deeper into central Europe added another urgent reason for many people to try to escape westward.

Throughout 1945 masses of weary travelers crisscrossed Europe—Hungarian Jews trying to go home; ethnic Germans from the Sudetenland making their way north and west; demobilized soldiers, prisoners of war, former slave laborers from Ukraine and Poland. Amid the chaos it is no surprise that war criminals and other fugitives often found it easy to blend in and evade detection. Under such conditions, whose documentation was in order anyway? Who would know if a former SS man or high-ranking Nazi Party boss, or even Heinrich Himmler himself, had simply buried or burned his papers, put on old clothing, and assumed a new identity? Paradoxically, the Nazis, with their obsession with race, blood, and homeland, had created a situation where all of those identities were in flux.

Building on creation during the war of the U.N. Relief and Rehabilitation Administration, the United Nations tried to address some of the most pressing humanitarian concerns stemming from the refugee crisis. U.S. occupation authorities set up camps for displaced persons (DPs) in their zone, which became the first destination of many Jewish survivors. Initially DPs were organized by country of origin, so that Jews, ethnic Germans, and non-German collaborators might find themselves grouped together as Ukrainians, Poles, or Yugoslavians. Subsequently the Americans set up separate facilities for Jews, who had different needs and options from most gentiles.

By late 1946 more than 150,000 Jews lived in DP camps in the U.S. zone, bringing a Jewish presence to parts of Germany that previously had been home to relatively few Jews. Jewish DP camps were sites of Zionist activity, as survivors, especially young people, were urged to leave Europe for Palestine and, after 1948, Israel. Many Jews preferred to wait for visas to the United States, Canada, or Australia, and some accepted options that were often quicker, such as relocation to South Africa, South America, or the Caribbean. An estimated twenty thousand Jews remained in Germany even after the last Jewish DP camp finally closed in 1957. Some of them were too old or sick to travel or be granted visas; some had ties to Germany.

Jewish DP camps were more than just holding places for people waiting to exit. They developed an internal leadership and communal spirit, with cultural and religious activities, educational opportunities, and social and family life. The immediate postwar years saw a baby boom as the birthrate among Jewish DPs rose to remarkable heights, especially in contrast to the unusually low rates for other people in Germany. Those Jewish children must have represented faith in new beginnings and hope for life after so much death.

Despite the urgent demands of daily existence, many people in postwar Europe concerned themselves with questions of justice. Perpetrators and organizers of Nazi crimes went to immense lengths to avoid being brought to account for their deeds. They set up self-help networks and used connections in Turkey, the Middle East, South America, Canada, and the Vatican to get themselves to safety. For example, Franz Stangl, former T-4 operative and subsequently commandant of Sobibor and Treblinka, fled via Turkey and the Middle East to Argentina, where Hitler's expert on Jews and transportation/deportation, Adolf Eichmann, also found refuge. Josef Mengele, the doctor and medical scholar whose vicious experiments at Auschwitz killed thousands of people, made his way to Brazil, where he died in the 1980s.

Of course those victimized by Nazism had very different interests in justice. No acts of revenge or restitution could make up for the deaths of millions, the annihilation of Jewish life in much of Europe, the destruction of property, and the shattering of trust and coexistence. Nevertheless survivors had to begin new lives, and for that they required at least minimal material resources, some acknowledgment of their suffering, and a measure of confidence in the world around them. Seeing some key criminals brought to justice could begin to address those needs as well as combat the sense of meaninglessness that must have threatened to overwhelm many survivors.

Already during the war Allied leaders had agreed that the defeated Germany must be denazified and top perpetrators brought to justice. Doing so was necessary for postwar stability, at least some of them believed, because it would make it possible to effect some kind of separation between "Nazis," who needed to be punished, and "Germans," who could and should be integrated into a peaceable world. The International Military Tribunal with the Nuremberg Trials of 1945–1946, a joint effort of all the Allies, served this purpose.

Contrary to what detractors claimed, the trial of twenty-one major war criminals and a handful of central Nazi German organizations at Nuremberg was not sham "victors' justice" or a reflection of some Allied notion of German "collective guilt." Although the trials were not perfect, and Allied cooperation was severely strained at times, they were real legal proceedings, with witnesses, massive amounts of documentation, and counsels for the defense—

אומפארטייאישער אילוסטרירטער חודש זשורנאל פאר אלע יידן

צווייטער יארגאנג.   „JIDISZE BILDER"   מינכן, מאי 1948

דער סימבאל צייכנונג פון 3-טן קאָנגרעס פון דער שארית-הפליטה:
אן אונטערגעהאקטער בוים מיט בליענדע בלעטער פאן פון דער קארטע פון דער יידישער מדינה.
אין דער ערשטער רייַ: דאָס ערן פרעזידיום פון קאָנגרעס, אין דער צווייַמער רייַ: די מיטגלידער פון אפטרעטנדן 2-טן צ. ק.

Cover page of the publication Jidisze Bilder (Jewish Pictures) with a photograph of participants at a 1948 congress in Munich. Above the participants is a graphic of a branch growing from a chopped-down tree. This image of destruction and new life became a symbol of the survivors, the She'erith Hapleitah, "the saved remnant."

and without torture. Some individuals and organizations were acquitted, and those convicted received varying sentences, including death sentences in about half of the cases. The most famous defendant, Hitler's favorite, Hermann Göring, committed suicide in his cell before the order for his execution could be carried out.

The Nuremberg Trials were just one step. The occupying powers, and subsequently local authorities, including Germans and foreign governments—like Israel with the Eichmann trial in 1961—conducted their own hearings, trials, and deportation proceedings of camp guards, doctors, bureaucrats, members of the Einsatzgruppen, and former SS men accused of lying on their immigration applications to the United States, Canada, and elsewhere. Property of all kinds—art, gold, land, buildings, factories—has been grounds for other kinds of legal cases, commissions, and occasionally settlements. These processes are all important, although they can never bring closure to a past that remains an open wound despite remarkable—perhaps unprecedented—efforts by Germans to come to grips with their nation's cruel past.

This history has no happy ending, no uplifting message of redemption. It leaves us only with human beings, with their startling capacities for good and evil, and with an awareness of the complex ties that connect the fates of people and nations all over the world.

One final account may best express these points. This time the story begins in the Netherlands with the birth of a baby girl in 1943. When she was two weeks old, her Jewish parents and older brother were rounded up by German and Dutch police, sent to the transit camp of Westerbork, and from there to Sobibor, where they were murdered.

Somehow the baby escaped that fate. Perhaps her parents hid her or a sympathetic policeman took pity on her. Either way, someone brought her to a beauty parlor run by two young women with connections to the Dutch underground, including people who helped find hiding places for Jewish children.

Here the details become even blurrier. According to one version of events, the women found a family to take the baby, but the arrangement fell through, possibly because the couple would not promise to surrender the girl when the war was over. Meanwhile, the young women had fallen in love with the baby, and—after a coin toss to decide between them—one of them took the child herself and cared for her until 1947, when an uncle from New York managed to locate his niece. Although the Dutch woman could not bear to lose her daughter, she gave the girl up and never saw her again. Growing up in the United States, the girl remembered little from her early years, and her uncle and his wife discouraged all contact with her Dutch foster mother, who subsequently suffered severe emotional problems and died quite young. Only decades later would the twice-orphaned girl, now a mother and grandmother herself, find a way to restore contact with members of her Dutch family. In the process she met people who had known her parents and brother, saw photographs of them, and even was given a few of their belongings.

One could present this account as an inspirational example of heroism and miraculous luck, and those are indeed important messages to take away from a study of the Holocaust. At least as significant, however, are the crushing themes of loss and violence, and the unavoidable, heartbreaking decisions that no one should have to make, decisions the scholar Lawrence Langer has dubbed "choiceless choices." These are the realities of the Holocaust and its bitter legacy, a history specific and unique but at the same time firmly embedded in the all-too-familiar global experiences of war and genocide.

SOURCES AND SUGGESTIONS FOR FURTHER READING

Note: Books are listed in the first chapter(s) to which they directly relate. Many of the titles given in one chapter are relevant elsewhere too. To the extent possible, I have limited this list to materials available in English.

1. PRECONDITIONS: ANTISEMITISM, RACISM, AND COMMON PREJUDICES IN EARLY-TWENTIETH-CENTURY EUROPE

Bartlett, Roger, and Karen Schönwälder, eds. *The German Lands and Eastern Europe: Essays on the History of Their Social, Cultural and Political Relations.* New York: St. Martin's, 1999.

Bartov, Omer. *Mirrors of Destruction: War, Genocide, and Modern Identity.* New York: Oxford University Press, 2000.

Berenbaum, Michael. *A Mosaic of Victims.* New York: New York University Press, 1990.

Berenbaum, Michael, and Abraham J. Peck, eds. *The Holocaust and History: The Known, the Unknown, the Disputed, and the Reexamined.* Bloomington: Indiana University Press, 1998.

Botwinick, Rita Steinhardt. *A History of the Holocaust: From Ideology to Annihilation.* Upper Saddle River, N.J.: Prentice Hall, 1996.

Breitman, Richard. *The Architect of Genocide: Himmler and the Final Solution.* New York: Knopf, 1991.

Burleigh, Michael. *Death and Deliverance: "Euthanasia" in Germany c. 1900–1945.* New York: Cambridge University Press, 1997.

———. *The Third Reich: A New History.* New York: Hill and Wang, 2000.

Burleigh, Michael, and Wolfgang Wippermann. *The Racial State: Germany 1933–1945.* New York: Cambridge University Press, 1991.

Crowe, David, and John Kolsti, eds. *The Gypsies of Eastern Europe.* Armonk, N.Y.: Sharpe, 1991.

Evans, Richard J. *Rituals of Retribution: Capital Punishment in Germany 1600–1987.* Oxford: Oxford University Press, 1996.

Fout, John C. *Forbidden History: The State, Society, and the Regulation of Sexuality in Modern Europe.* Chicago: University of Chicago Press, 1992.

Friedlander, Henry. *The Origins of Nazi Genocide: From Euthanasia to the Final Solution.* Chapel Hill: University of North Carolina Press, 1995.

Gay, Peter. *My German Question: Growing Up in Nazi Berlin.* New Haven, Conn.: Yale University Press, 1998.

Gellately, Robert, and Nathan Stoltzfus, eds. *Social Outsiders in Nazi Germany.* Princeton, N.J.: Princeton University Press, 2001.

Gutman, Israel. *Encyclopedia of the Holocaust.* 3 vols. New York: Macmillan, 1990.

Hancock, Ian. "The Roots of Antigypsyism: To the Holocaust and After." In *Confronting the Holocaust: A Mandate for the 21st Century,* edited by C. Jan Colijn and Marcia Sachs Littell, 19–49. Studies in the Shoah 19. Lanham, Md.: University Press of America, 1997.

Hilberg, Raul. *The Destruction of the European Jews.* 3rd ed. 3 vols. New Haven, Conn.: Yale University Press, 2003.

Hull, Isabel. *Absolute Destruction: Military Culture and the Practices of War in Imperial Germany.* Ithaca, N.Y.: Cornell University Press, 2005.

Kenrick, Donald, and Grattan Puxon. *Gypsies under the Swastika.* Hatfield, U.K.: University of Hertfordshire Press, 1995.

King, Christine Elizabeth. *The Nazi State and the New Religions: Five Cases in Non-Conformity.* New York: Edwin Mellen, 1982.

Langmuir, Gavin I. *History, Religion, and Antisemitism.* Berkeley: University of California Press, 1990.

Levy, Richard S., ed. *Antisemitism in the Modern World: An Anthology of Texts.* Lexington, Mass.: Heath, 1991.

Marks, Sally. "Black Watch on the Rhine: A Study in Propaganda, Prejudice, and Prurience." *European Studies Review* 13, no. 3 (1983): 297–334.

———. *The Illusion of Peace.* New York: St. Martin's, 1976.

Milton, Sybil. "The Context of the Holocaust." *German Studies Review* 13, no. 2 (1990): 269–83.

Mosse, George. *Fallen Soldiers: Reshaping the Memory of the World Wars.* New York: Oxford University Press, 1990.

———. *The Nationalization of the Masses.* New York: Howard Fertig, 1975.

Müller-Hill, Benno. *Murderous Science: Elimination by Scientific Selection of Jews, Gypsies and Others in Germany, 1933–1945.* Translated by George R. Fraser. Plainview, N.Y.: Cold Spring Harbor Laboratory Press, 1998.

Naimark, Norman. *Fires of Hatred: Ethnic Cleansing in Twentieth-Century Europe.* Cambridge, Mass.: Harvard University Press, 2001.

Poliakov, Léon. *Harvest of Hate: The Nazi Program for the Destruction of the Jews of Europe.* New York: Holocaust Library, 1979.

Pomerantz, Jack, and Lyric Wallwork Winik. *Run East: Flight from the Holocaust.* Urbana: University of Illinois Press, 1997.

Siegal, Aranka. *Upon the Head of the Goat: A Childhood in Hungary, 1939–1944.* New York: Puffin, 1981.

Stern, Fritz. *The Politics of Cultural Despair.* Berkeley: University of California Press, 1961.

Stopes, Marie Carmichael, and Ruth E. Hall, eds. *Dear Dr. Stopes: Sex in the 1920s.* London: Deutsch, 1978.

Weinberg, Gerhard L. *Germany, Hitler, and World War II: Essays in Modern German and World History.* New York: Cambridge University Press, 1995.

Weiss, John. *Ideology of Death: Why the Holocaust Happened in Germany.* Chicago: Ivan R. Dee, 1996.

2. LEADERSHIP AND WILL: ADOLF HITLER, THE NATIONAL SOCIALIST GERMAN WORKERS' PARTY, AND NAZI IDEOLOGY

Allen, William Sheridan. *The Nazi Seizure of Power.* Rev. ed. New York: Watts, 1984.

Bessel, Richard. *Germany after the First World War.* Oxford: Clarendon, 1993.

Bukey, Evan Burr. *Hitler's Hometown.* Bloomington: Indiana University Press, 1986.

Bullock, Alan. *Hitler: A Study in Tyranny.* Rev. ed. New York: Bantam, 1962.

Burrin, Philippe. *Hitler and the Jews: The Genesis of the Holocaust.* Translated by Patsy Southgate. London: Arnold; New York: Routledge, Chapman and Hall, 1994.

Childers, Thomas. *The Nazi Voter: The Social Foundations of Fascism in Germany, 1919–1933.* Chapel Hill: University of North Carolina Press, 1983.

Eubank, Keith, ed. *World War II: Roots and Causes.* 2nd ed. Lexington, Mass.: Heath, 1992.

Fischer, Conan. *Stormtroopers: A Social, Economic and Ideological Analysis 1925–35.* London: Allen and Unwin, 1983.

Fischer, Klaus P. *Nazi Germany: A New History.* London: Continuum, 1995.

Friedländer, Saul. *Nazi Germany and the Jews.* Vol. 1, *The Years of Persecution.* New York: HarperCollins, 1997.

Haffner, Sebastian. *The Meaning of Hitler.* Translated by Ewald Osers. Cambridge, Mass.: Harvard University Press, 1983.

Hamann, Brigitte. *Hitler's Vienna.* Translated by Thomas Thornton. New York: Oxford University Press, 1999.

Hamilton, Richard F. *Who Voted for Hitler?* Princeton, N.J.: Princeton University Press, 1982.

Hitler's Table Talk, 1941–1944: His Private Conversations. 1953. New updated ed. Edited by Hugh R. Trevor-Roper. Introduction by Gerhard L. Weinberg. New York: Enigma, 2008.

Jäckel, Eberhard. *Hitler's World View: A Blueprint for Power.* Cambridge, Mass.: Harvard University Press, 1981.

Kater, Michael. *The Nazi Party: A Social Profile of Members and Leaders, 1919–1945.* Cambridge, Mass.: Harvard University Press, 1983.

Kershaw, Ian. *Hitler.* Vol. 1, *1889–1936: Hubris.* New York: Norton, 1998.

———. Vol. 2, *1936–1945: Nemesis.* New York: Norton, 2000.

Lochner, Louis P., ed. *The Goebbels Diaries 1942–43.* Garden City, N.Y.: Doubleday, 1948. (More complete editions of the diaries are available in German. See, for example, *Die Tagebücher von Joseph Goebbels. Sämtliche Fragmente, Teil I, Aufzeichnungen 1924–1941,* edited by Elke Fröhlich. 4 vols. Munich, 1987.)

Marks, Sally. "The Myths of Reparations." *Central European History* 11, no. 3 (1978): 231–35.

Marrus, Michael. *The Holocaust in History.* New York: Meridian, 1989.

Orlow, Dietrich. *The History of the Nazi Party.* 1 vol. ed. New York: Enigma, 2008.

Patch, William L., Jr. *Heinrich Brüning and the Dissolution of the Weimar Republic.* Cambridge, U.K.: Cambridge University Press, 1998.

Pauley, Bruce F. *Hitler and the Forgotten Nazis: A History of Austrian National Socialism.* Chapel Hill: University of North Carolina Press, 1981.

Reck-Malleczewen, Fritz Percy. *Diary of a Man in Despair.* Translated by Paul Ruebens. New York: Macmillan, 1971.

Sax, Benjamin, and Dieter Kuntz. *Inside Hitler's Germany.* Lexington, Mass.: Heath, 1992.

Turner, Henry Ashby, Jr. *Hitler's Thirty Days to Power: January 1933.* Reading, Mass.: Addison Wesley, 1996.

Weinberg, Gerhard L. *Germany, Hitler, and World War II: Essays in Modern German and World History.* New York: Cambridge University Press, 1995.

Wistrich, Robert S. *Hitler and the Holocaust.* New York: Modern Library, 2001.

3. FROM REVOLUTION TO ROUTINE: NAZI GERMANY, 1933–1938

Abel, Theodore. *Why Hitler Came into Power.* 1938. Reprint, Cambridge, Mass.: Harvard University Press, 1986.

Abrams, Alan. *Mischlinge: Special Treatment, the Untold Story of Hitler's Third Race.* Secaucus, N.J.: Lyle-Stuart, 1985.

Bankier, David. *The Germans and the Final Solution: Public Opinion under Nazism.* Cambridge, Mass.: Basil Blackwell, 1992.

Bergen, Doris L. *Twisted Cross: The German Christian Movement in the Third Reich.* Chapel Hill: University of North Carolina Press, 1996.

Caplan, Jane, ed. *Nazi Germany.* New York: Oxford University Press, 2008.

Engelmann, Bernd. *Inside Hitler's Germany.* Translated by Krishna Wilson. New York: Pantheon, 1985.

Friedländer, Saul. *Pius XII and the Third Reich: A Documentation.* New York: Knopf, 1960.

Fromm, Bella. *Blood and Banquets: A Social Diary.* New York: Harper and Brothers, 1942.

Giles, Geoffrey. " 'The Most Unkindest Cut of All': Castration, Homosexuality, and Nazi Justice." *Journal of Contemporary History* 27, no. 1 (1992): 41–61.

Grossmann, Atina. *Reforming Sex: The German Movement for Birth Control and Abortion Reform 1920–1950.* New York: Oxford University Press, 1995.

Heck, Alfons. *A Child of Hitler.* Frederick, Colo.: Renaissance House, 1985.

Jaskot, Paul. *The Architecture of Oppression.* London: Routledge, 2000.

Johnson, Eric A. *Nazi Terror: The Gestapo, Jews, and Ordinary Germans.* New York: Basic, 2000.

Kaplan, Marion. *Between Dignity and Despair: Jewish Life in Nazi Germany.* New York: Oxford University Press, 1998.

Kershaw, Ian. *The "Hitler Myth": Image and Reality in the Third Reich.* Oxford: Clarendon, 1987.

———. *The Nazi Dictatorship: Problems and Perspectives of Interpretation.* London: Arnold, 1993.

Klemperer, Victor. *I Will Bear Witness: A Diary of the Nazi Years, 1933–1941.* Vol. 1. Translated by Martin Chalmers. New York: Random House, 1998.

Koehn, Ilse. *Mischling, Second Degree: My Childhood in Nazi Germany.* New York: Bantam, 1977.

Koonz, Claudia. *Mothers in the Fatherland: Women, the Family, and Nazi Politics.* New York: St. Martin's, 1987.

———. *The Nazi Conscience.* Cambridge, Mass.: Harvard University Press, 2003.

Koshar, Rudy. *Social Life, Local Politics, and Nazism: Marburg, 1880–1935.* Chapel Hill: University of North Carolina Press, 1986.

Lewy, Guenter. *The Nazi Persecution of the Gypsies.* New York: Oxford University Press, 2000.

Maschmann, Melitta. *Account Rendered.* Translated by Geoffrey Strachan. London: Abelard-Schuman, 1964.

Merkl, Peter. *Political Violence under the Swastika.* Princeton, N.J.: Princeton University Press, 1975.

Mommsen, Hans. *From Weimar to Auschwitz: Essays in German History.* Translated by Philip O'Connor. Cambridge, Mass.: Polity Press; Oxford: Basil Blackwell, 1991.

Opitz, May, Katharina Oguntoye, and Dagmar Schultz, eds. *Showing Our Colors: Afro-German Women Speak Out.* Translated by Anne V. Adams. Amherst: University of Massachusetts Press, 1992.

Owings, Alison. *Frauen: German Women Recall the Third Reich.* New Brunswick, N.J.: Rutgers University Press, 1993.

Petropoulos, Jonathan. *Art as Politics in the Third Reich.* Chapel Hill: University of North Carolina Press, 1996.

Peukert, Detlev. *Inside Nazi Germany: Conformity, Opposition, and Racism in Everyday Life.* New Haven, Conn.: Yale University Press, 1987.

Plant, Richard. *The Pink Triangle.* New York: Henry Holt, 1986.

Rosenberg, Otto, as told to Ulrich Enzenberger, translated by Helmut Bögler. *A Gypsy in Auschwitz*. London: London House, 1999.

Steinweis, Alan. *Studying the Jew: Scholarly Antisemitism in Nazi Germany*. Cambridge, Mass.: Harvard University Press, 2006.

Thimme, Annelise. "Geprägt von der Geschichte. Eine Aussenseiterin." In *Erinnerungsstücke: Wege in die Vergangenheit*. Edited by Hartmut Lehmann and Gerhard Oexle, 153–223. Vienna: Boehlau, 1997.

Welch, David A. *The Third Reich: Politics and Propaganda*. London: Routledge, 1993.

4. OPEN AGGRESSION:
IN SEARCH OF WAR, 1938–1939

Bridenthal, Renate, Atina Grossmann, and Marion Kaplan, eds. *When Biology Became Destiny: Women in Weimar and Nazi Germany*. New York: Monthly Review Press, 1984.

Bukey, Evan Burr. *Hitler's Austria*. Chapel Hill: University of North Carolina Press, 2000.

Conway, John S. *The Nazi Persecution of the Churches 1933–45*. London: Westfield and Nicolson, 1968.

Ericksen, Robert P., and Susannah Heschel, eds. *Betrayal: German Churches and the Holocaust*. Minneapolis, Minn.: Fortress, 1999.

Friedlander, Henry. *The Origins of Nazi Genocide: From Euthanasia to the Final Solution*. Chapel Hill: University of North Carolina Press, 1995.

Friedländer, Saul. *When Memory Comes*. New York: Farrar, Straus, and Giroux, 1979.

Gellately, Robert. *The Gestapo and German Society: Enforcing Racial Policy, 1933–1945*. New York: Oxford University Press, 1990.

Grau, Günter, ed. *Hidden Holocaust? Gay and Lesbian Persecution in Germany, 1933–1945*. Translated by Patrick Camiller. London: Cassell, 1995.

Hayes, Peter. *Industry and Ideology: IG Farben in the Nazi Era*. New York: Cambridge University Press, 2000.

Heilbronner, Oded. *Catholicism, Political Culture, and the Countryside: A Social History of the Nazi Party in South Germany*. Ann Arbor: University of Michigan Press, 1998.

Hesse, Hans, ed. *Persecution and Resistance of Jehovah's Witnesses during the Nazi-Regime, 1933–1945*. Bremen, Germany: Edition Temmen, 2001.

Jehovah's Witnesses Stand Firm against Nazi Assault. 1 hr. 45 min. Watchtower Society, 1995. Videocassette.

Kluger, Ruth. *Still Alive: A Holocaust Girlhood Remembered*. New York: Feminist Press, 2001.

Opfermann, Charlotte. *The Ides of November*. Unpublished manuscript, 1999.

Phayer, Michael. *The Catholic Church and the Holocaust*. Bloomington: Indiana University Press, 2000.

Quack, Sibylle, ed. *Between Sorrow and Strength: Women Refugees of the Nazi Period*. Washington, D.C.: German Historical Institute; New York: Cambridge University Press, 1995.

Rigg, Bryan Mark. *Hitler's Jewish Soldiers*. Lawrence: University Press of Kansas, 2002.

Sofsky, Wolfgang. *The Order of Terror: The Concentration Camp.* Translated by William Templer. Princeton, N.J.: Princeton University Press, 1997.

Steinhoff, Johannes, Peter Pechel, and Dennis Showalter, eds. *Voices from the Third Reich.* Washington, D.C.: Regnery Gateway, 1989.

Weinberg, Gerhard L. *Germany, Hitler, and World War II: Essays in Modern German and World History.* New York: Cambridge University Press, 1995.

5. EXPERIMENTS IN BRUTALITY, 1939–1940: WAR AGAINST POLAND AND THE SO-CALLED EUTHANASIA PROGRAM

Adelson, Alan, and Robert Lapides, eds. *Lodz Ghetto: Inside a Community under Siege.* New York: Viking, 1989.

Aly, Götz. *"Final Solution": Nazi Population Policy and the Murder of the European Jews.* Translated by Belinda Cooper and Allison Brown. London: Arnold, 1999.

Arad, Yitzhak. *Ghetto in Flames.* New York: Holocaust Library, 1982.

Arendt, Hannah. *Eichmann in Jerusalem.* New York: Viking, 1963.

Bartov, Omer. *Hitler's Army: Soldiers, Nazis, and War in the Third Reich.* New York: Oxford University Press, 1991.

Bauman, Zygmunt. *Modernity and the Holocaust.* Ithaca, N.Y.: Cornell University Press, 1989.

Cornwell, John. *Hitler's Pope: The Secret History of Pius XII.* New York: Viking, 1999.

Dobroszycki, Lucien. *The Chronicle of the Lodz Ghetto, 1941–1944.* New Haven, Conn.: Yale University Press, 1984.

Gerlach, Christian. "Failure of Plans for an SS Extermination Camp in Mogilev, Belorussia." Translated by Deborah Cohen and Helmut Gerlach. *Holocaust and Genocide Studies* 11, no. 1 (1997): 60–78.

Gotfryd, Bernard. *Anton the Dove Fancier and Other Tales of the Holocaust.* New York: Washington Square Press, 1990.

Gross, Jan. *Neighbors: The Destruction of the Jewish Community in Jedwabne, Poland.* Princeton, N.J.: Princeton University Press, 2001.

Harvey, Elizabeth. *Women in the Nazi East: Agents and Witnesses of Germanization.* New Haven, Conn.: Yale University Press, 2003.

Hilberg, Raul. *The Destruction of the European Jews.* 3rd ed. 3 vols. New Haven, Conn.: Yale University Press, 2003.

Hilberg, Raul, Stanislaw Staron, and Josef Kermisz, eds. *The Warsaw Diary of Adam Czerniaków: Prelude to Doom.* Translated by Stanislaw Staron and the staff of Yad Vashem. New York: Stein and Day, 1979.

Klein, Gerda Weissmann. *All but My Life.* New York: Hill and Wang, 1995.

Knappe, Siegfried, and Ted Brusaw. *Soldat: Reflections of a German Soldier, 1936–1949.* New York: Orion Books, 1992.

Kogon, Eugen, Hermann Langbein, and Adalbert Rückerl, eds. *Nazi Mass Murder: A Documentary History of the Use of Poison Gas.* Translated by Mary Scott and Caroline Lloyd-Morris. New Haven, Conn.: Yale University Press, 1993.

Lukas, Richard C. *Did the Children Cry? Hitler's War against Jewish and Polish Children.* New York: Hippocrene, 1995.

————. *The Forgotten Holocaust: The Poles under German Occupation, 1939–1944.* Rev. ed. New York: Hippocrene, 1997.

————. *Out of the Inferno: Poles Remember the Holocaust.* Lexington: University Press of Kentucky, 1989.

Melson, Robert. *False Papers: Deception and Survival in the Holocaust.* Urbana: University of Illinois Press, 2000.

Noakes, Jeremy, and Geoffrey Pridham, eds. *Nazism 1919–1945: A Documentary Reader.* 4 vols. Exeter: University of Exeter Department of History and Archeology, 1983–1998.

Polonsky, Antony, ed. *"My Brother's Keeper?": Recent Polish Debates on the Holocaust.* London: Routledge, 1990.

Rossino, Alexander B. *Hitler Strikes Poland: Blitzkrieg, Ideology, and Atrocity.* Lawrence: University Press of Kansas, 2003.

Tec, Nechama. *Defiance: The Bielski Partisans.* New York: Oxford University Press, 1993.

Yahil, Leni. *The Holocaust: The Fate of European Jewry.* Translated by Ina Friedman and Haya Galai. New York: Oxford University Press, 1990.

6. EXPANSION AND SYSTEMATIZATION: EXPORTING WAR AND TERROR, 1940–1941

Aronson, Shlomo. *Hitler, the Allies, and the Jews.* New York: Cambridge University Press, 2004.

Bartoszewski, Wladyslaw. *The Warsaw Ghetto: A Christian's Testimony.* Translated by Stephen G. Cappellari. Boston: Beacon, 1987.

Bartov, Omer. *The Eastern Front, 1941–1945: German Troops and the Barbarisation of Warfare.* London: St. Martin's, 1985.

Borowski, Tadeusz. *This Way for the Gas, Ladies and Gentlemen.* Translated by Barbara Vedder. New York: Penguin, 1976.

Breitman, Richard. *The Architect of Genocide: Himmler and the Final Solution.* New York: Knopf, 1991.

————. *Official Secrets: What the Nazis Planned and What the British and Americans Knew.* New York: Hill and Wang, 1998.

Browning, Christopher. *Fateful Months: Essays on the Emergence of the Final Solution.* New York: Holmes and Meier, 1985.

Dallin, Alexander. *German Rule in Russia 1941–1945: A Study of Occupation Policies.* 2nd ed. London: Macmillan, 1981.

Dobroszycki, Lucjan, and Jeffrey S. Gurock, eds. *The Holocaust in the Soviet Union*. Armonk, N.Y.: Sharpe, 1993.

Dwork, Debórah. *Children with a Star: Jewish Youth in Nazi Europe*. New Haven, Conn.: Yale University Press, 1991.

Eliach, Yaffa. *Hasidic Tales of the Holocaust*. New York: Vintage, 1988.

Fonseca, Isabel. *Bury Me Standing: The Gypsies and Their Journey*. New York: Knopf, 1995.

Frank, Anne. *The Diary of a Young Girl*. New York: Doubleday, 1995.

Friedländer, Saul. *Nazi Germany and the Jews, 1939–1945: The Years of Extermination*. New York: HarperCollins, 2007.

———. *When Memory Comes*. New York: Farrar, Straus and Giroux, 1979.

Friedman, Henry. *I'm No Hero: Journeys of a Holocaust Survivor*. Seattle: University of Washington Press, 1999.

Gellately, Robert. *Backing Hitler: Consent and Coercion in Nazi Germany*. New York: Oxford University Press, 2001.

Goda, Norman J. W. *Tomorrow the World: Hitler, Northwest Africa, and the Path toward America*. College Station: Texas A&M University Press, 1998.

Herf, Jeffrey. *The Jewish Enemy: Nazi Propaganda during World War II and the Holocaust*. Cambridge, Mass.: Harvard University Press, 2006.

Hirschfeld, Gerhard, ed. *The Policies of Genocide: Jews and Soviet Prisoners of War in Nazi Germany*. London: Allen and Unwin, 1986.

Longerich, Peter. *The Unwritten Order: Hitler's Role in the Final Solution*. London: Tempus, 2003.

Mazower, Mark. *Inside Hitler's Greece: The Experience of Occupation, 1941–1944*. New Haven, Conn.: Yale University Press, 1993.

Megargee, Geoffrey. *Inside Hitler's High Command*. Lawrence: University Press of Kansas, 2000.

My Knees Were Jumping: Remembering the Kindertransports. Directed and produced by Melissa Hacker. 1 hr. 16 min. National Center for Jewish Film, 1996. Videocassette.

Ramras-Rauch, Gila. *Aharon Appelfeld: The Holocaust and Beyond*. Bloomington: Indiana University Press, 1994.

Sachse, William L. *English History in the Making: Readings from the Sources*. Vol. 2 *Since 1689*. New York: Wiley, 1970.

Scheck, Raffael. *Hitler's African Victims: The German Army Massacres of Black French Soldiers in 1940*. New York: Cambridge University Press, 2006.

Schulte, Theo J. *The German Army and Nazi Policies in Occupied Russia*. Oxford: St. Martin's, 1989.

Steinberg, Jonathan. *All or Nothing: The Axis and the Holocaust: 1941–1943*. London: Routledge, 1990.

Steinert, Marlis. *Hitler's War and the Germans: Public Mood and Attitude during the Second World War*. Athens: Ohio University Press, 1977.

Tec, Nechama. *Dry Tears*. New York: Oxford University Press, 1982.

Toll, Nelly S. *Behind the Secret Window: A Memoir of a Hidden Childhood during World War Two*. New York: Dial, 1993.

Tolstoy, Nikolai. *Stalin's Secret War*. New York: Holt, Rinehart and Winston, 1982.

Weinberg, Gerhard L. *A World at Arms: A Global History of World War II*. 2nd ed. New York: Cambridge University Press, 2005.

7. THE PEAK YEARS OF KILLING: 1942 AND 1943

Améry, Jean. *At the Mind's Limits: Contemplations by a Survivor on Auschwitz and Its Realities*. New York: Schocken, 1986.

Bauer, Yehuda. *A History of the Holocaust*. New York: F. Watts, 1982.

Blatt, Thomas (Toivi). *Sobibor: The Forgotten Revolt*. Issaquah, Wash.: H.E.P., 1998.

Browning, Christopher R. *Nazi Policy, Jewish Labor, German Killers*. Cambridge, U.K.: Cambridge University Press, 2000.

———. *Ordinary Men: Reserve Police Battalion 101 and the Final Solution in Poland*. New York: HarperCollins, 1992.

Cesarani, David, ed. *The Final Solution: Origins and Implementation*. London: Routledge, 1994.

Dean, Martin. *Collaboration in the Holocaust: Crimes of the Local Police in Belorussia and Ukraine, 1941–1944*. New York: St. Martin's, 2000.

Delbo, Charlotte. *None of Us Will Return*. Translated by John Githens. Boston: Beacon, 1967.

Donat, Alexander, ed. *The Death Camp Treblinka: A Documentary*. New York: Holocaust Library, 1979.

Felstiner, Mary Lowenthal. *To Paint Her Life: Charlotte Salomon in the Nazi Era*. New York: HarperCollins, 1995.

Fenelon, Fania. *Playing for Time*. Edited by Marcelle Routier. Translated by Judith Landry. Syracuse, N.Y.: Syracuse University Press, 1976.

Friedländer, Saul. *Kurt Gerstein: The Ambiguity of Good*. Translated by Charles Fullman. New York: Knopf, 1969.

Ginaite-Rubinson, Sara. *Resistance and Survival: The Jewish Community in Kaunas, 1941–1944*. Oakville, Ont.: Mosaic, 2005.

Goda, Norman J. W. "Black Marks: Hitler's Bribery of His Senior Officers during World War II." *Journal of Modern History* 72, no. 2 (2000): 413–52.

Goldenberg, Myrna. "Different Horrors, Same Hell: Women Remembering the Holocaust." In *Thinking the Unthinkable: Meanings of the Holocaust*, edited by Roger Gottlieb. New York: Paulist Press, 1990.

Greif, Gideon. *We Wept without Tears: Testimonies of the Jewish Sonderkommando from Auschwitz*. New Haven, Conn.: Yale University Press, 2005.

Hackett, David A. *The Buchenwald Report*. Boulder, Colo.: Westview, 1995.

Heger, Heinz. *The Men with the Pink Triangle*. Translated by David Fernbach. Boston: Alyson Publications, 1980.

Herbermann, Nanda. *The Blessed Abyss: Inmate #6582 in Ravensbrück Concentration Camp for Women*. Edited by Hester Baer and Elizabeth R. Baer. Translated by Hester Baer. Detroit: Wayne State University Press, 2000.

Herbert, Ulrich, ed. *National Socialist Extermination Policies: Contemporary German Perspectives and Controversies*. New York: Berghahn Books, 2000.

Hilberg, Raul, Stanislaw Staron, and Josef Kermisz, eds. *The Warsaw Diary of Adam Czerniakow: Prelude to Doom*. Translated by Stanislaw Staron and the staff of Yad Vashem. New York: Stein and Day, 1979.

Hillesum, Etty. *An Interrupted Life: The Diary of Etty Hillesum*. New York: Pocket Books, 1981.

———. *Letters from Westerbork*. New York: Pantheon, 1986.

Hoess, Rudolf. *Commandant of Auschwitz*. Translated by Andrew Pollinger. Buffalo, N.Y.: Prometheus, 1992.

Hoffmann, Peter. *The History of the German Resistance, 1933–1945*. 3rd ed. Montreal: McGill-Queen's University Publishing, 1996.

Horwitz, Gordon J. *In the Shadow of Death: Living outside the Gates of Mauthausen*. New York: Free Press, 1990.

Klee, Ernst, Willi Dressen, and Volker Reiss, eds. *The Good Old Days: The Holocaust as Seen by Its Perpetrators and Bystanders*. Translated by Deborah Burnstone. New York: Simon & Schuster, 1991.

Klemperer, Victor. *I Will Bear Witness: A Diary of the Nazi Years, 1941–1945*. Vol. 2. Translated by Martin Chalmers. New York: Random House, 1999.

Korczak, Janusz. *Ghetto Diary*. Edited and translated by H. Goldsmitz. New York: Holocaust Library, 1978.

Laks, Szymon. *Music of Another World*. Translated by Chester A. Kisiel. Evanston, Ill.: Northwestern University Press, 1989.

Lanzmann, Claude. *Shoah: An Oral History of the Holocaust, The Complete Text of the Film*. New York: Pantheon, 1985.

Laska, Vera. *Women in the Resistance and the Holocaust*. Westport, Conn.: Greenwood, 1983.

Levi, Primo. *Survival in Auschwitz*. New York: Collier, 1958.

Lindeman, Yehudi, ed. *Shards of Memory: Narratives of Holocaust Survival*. Westport, Conn.: Praeger, 2007.

Lower, Wendy. *Nazi Empire-Building and the Holocaust in Ukraine*. Chapel Hill: University of North Carolina Press, 2005.

Millu, Liana. *Smoke over Birkenau*. Translated by Lynne Sharon Schwartz. Evanston, Ill.: Northwestern University Press, 1991.

Muller, Filip. *Eyewitness Auschwitz*. Edited and translated by Susanne Flatauer. Chicago: Ivan R. Dee, in association with the U.S. Holocaust Memorial Museum, 1999.

Noakes, Jeremy, and Geoffrey Pridham, eds. *Nazism 1919–1945: A Documentary Reader*. 4 vols. Exeter: University of Exeter Department of History and Archeology, 1983–1998.

Nomberg-Przytyk, Sara. *Auschwitz: True Tales from a Grotesque Land*. Translated by Roslyn Hirsch. Chapel Hill: University of North Carolina Press, 1985.

Przyrembel, Alexandra. "Transfixed by an Image: Ilse Koch, the 'Kommandeuse of Buchenwald.'" Translated by Pamela Selwyn. *German History* 19, no. 3 (2001): 369–99.

Ringelheim, Joan. "Women and the Holocaust: A Reconsideration of Research." *Signs* 10 (1985): 741–61.

Rittner, Carol, and John Roth, eds. *Different Voices: Women and the Holocaust.* New York: Paragon, 1993.

Scholl, Inge. *The White Rose.* 2nd ed. Translated by Arthur R. Schultz. Hanover, N.H.: Wesleyan University Press, 1983.

Scrase, David, and Wolfgang Mieder, eds. *The Holocaust: Introductory Essays.* Burlington: Center for Holocaust Studies at the University of Vermont, 1996.

Sereny, Gitta. *Into That Darkness: An Examination of Conscience.* New York: Vintage, 1983.

Shoah. Produced by Les Films Aleph and Historia Films. Directed by Claude Lanzmann. 9 hrs. 30 min. Paramount Home Video, 1986. Videocassette.

Spiegelman, Art. *Maus: A Survivor's Tale.* 2 vols. New York: Pantheon, 1986.

Stabholz, Thaddeus. *Seven Hells.* Translated by Jacques Grunblatt and Hilda R. Grunblatt. New York: Holocaust Library, 1990.

Steinbacher, Sybille. *Auschwitz: A History.* Translated by Shaun Whiteside. New York: HarperCollins, 2006.

Stoltzfus, Nathan. *Resistance of the Heart: Intermarriage and the Rosenstrasse Protest in Nazi Germany.* New York: Norton, 1996.

Szwajger, Adina Blady. *I Remember Nothing More.* Translated by Tasja Darowska. New York: Pantheon, 1990.

Tec, Nechama. *When Light Pierced the Darkness.* New York: Oxford University Press, 1985.

Troller, Norbert. *Theresienstadt: Hitler's Gift to the Jews.* Chapel Hill: University of North Carolina Press, 1991.

Tydor, Judith Baumel. *Double Jeopardy: Gender and the Holocaust.* London: Vallentine-Mitchell, 1998.

Weinberg, Gerhard L. *A World at Arms: A Global History of World War II.* 2nd New York: Cambridge University Press, 2005.

Wood, E. Thomas, and Stanislaw M. Jankowski. *Karski: How One Man Tried to Stop the Holocaust.* New York: Wiley, 1994.

8. DEATH THROES AND KILLING FRENZIES, 1944–1945

Aly, Götz. *Hitler's Beneficiaries: Plunder, Racial War, and the Nazi Welfare State.* Translated by Jefferson Chase. New York: Henry Holt, 2008.

Braham, Randolph L. *The Politics of Genocide: The Holocaust in Hungary.* Condensed ed. Detroit: Wayne State University Press, 2000.

Braham, Randolph L., and Scott Miller, eds. *The Nazis' Last Victims: The Holocaust in Hungary.* Detroit: Wayne State University Press, 1998.

Elias, Ruth. *Triumph of Hope: From Theresienstadt and Auschwitz to Israel.* Translated by Margot Bettauer Dembo. New York: Wiley, 1998.

Fein, Helen. *Accounting for Genocide: National Responses and Jewish Victimization during the Holocaust.* Chicago: University of Chicago Press, 1984.

Fritz, Stephen G. *Endkampf: Soldiers, Civilians, and the Death of the Third Reich.* Lexington: University Press of Kentucky, 2004.

Goldhagen, Daniel Jonah. *Hitler's Willing Executioners.* New York: Knopf, 1996.

Gutman, Israel, and Michael Berenbaum, eds. *Anatomy of the Auschwitz Death Camp.* Bloomington: Indiana University Press, 1994.

Hellman, Peter, Lili Meier, and Serge Klarsfeld. *The Auschwitz Album: A Book Based upon an Album Discovered by a Concentration Camp Survivor.* New York: Random House, 1981.

Hoffmann, Peter. *Stauffenberg: A Family History, 1904–1944.* Cambridge, U.K.: Cambridge University Press, 1995.

Ioanid, Radu. *The Holocaust in Romania: The Destruction of Jews and Gypsies under the Antonescu Regime, 1940–1944.* Chicago: Ivan R. Dee, 2000.

Isaacson, Judith Magyar. *Seed of Sarah: Memoirs of a Survivor.* Urbana: University of Illinois Press, 1990.

Klein, Gerda Weissmann. *All but My Life.* New York: Hill and Wang, 1957.

Moltke, Helmuth James von. *Letters to Freya 1939–1945.* Edited and translated by Beate Ruhm von Oppen. New York: Knopf, 1990.

Perel, Solomon. *Europa, Europa.* Translated by Margot Bettauer Dembo. New York: Wiley, in association with the U.S. Holocaust Memorial Museum, 1997.

Rotem, Simha. "Kazik." In *Memoirs of a Warsaw Ghetto Fighter,* translated by Barbara Harshav. New Haven, Conn.: Yale University Press, 1994.

Sereny, Gitta. *Albert Speer: His Battle with Truth.* New York: Knopf, 1995.

Siegal, Aranka. *Grace in the Wilderness.* New York: Puffin, 1985.

Speer, Albert. *Inside the Third Reich: Memoirs.* Translated by Richard Winston and Clara Winston. New York: Macmillan, 1970.

Tooze, Adam. *The Wages of Destruction: The Making and Breaking of the Nazi Economy.* London: Allen Lane, 2006.

Volavkova, Hana, ed. *I Never Saw Another Butterfly: Children's Drawings and Poems from Terezin Concentration Camp, 1942–1944.* 2nd ed. New York: Pantheon, 1994.

Wallenberg, Raoul. *Letters and Dispatches: 1924–1944.* Translated by Kjersti Board. New York: Arcade, 1995.

Weinberg, Gerhard L. *Visions of Victory: The Hopes of Eight World War II Leaders.* New York: Cambridge University Press, 2005.

Wells, Leon Welickzer. *The Janowska Road.* New York: Macmillan, 1999.

Wiesel, Elie. *Night.* Translated by Stella Rodway. New York: Bantam, 1960.

CONCLUSION: THE LEGACIES OF ATROCITY

Abzug, Robert H. *Inside the Vicious Heart: Americans and the Liberation of Nazi Concentration Camps.* New York: Oxford University Press, 1985.

Baldwin, Peter, ed. *Reworking the Past: Hitler, the Holocaust and the Historians' Debate.* Boston: Beacon, 1990.

Bartov, Omer. *Erased: Vanishing Traces of Jewish Galicia in Present-Day Ukraine.* Princeton, N.J.: Princeton University Press, 2007.

Brenner, Michael. *After the Holocaust: Rebuilding Jewish Lives in Postwar Germany.* Princeton, N.J.: Princeton University Press, 1997.

Dinnerstein, Leonard. *America and the Survivors of the Holocaust.* New York: Columbia University Press, 1982.

Friedländer, Saul. *Reflections on Nazism: An Essay on Kitsch and Death.* New York: Harper and Row, 1982.

Gross, Jan T. *Fear: Anti-Semitism in Poland after Auschwitz.* New York: Random House, 2006.

Herzog, Dagmar. *Sex after Fascism: Memory and Morality in Twentieth-Century Germany.* Princeton, N.J.: Princeton University Press, 2005.

Langer, Lawrence. *Holocaust Testimonies: Ruins of Memory.* New Haven, Conn.: Yale University Press, 1991.

———. *Preempting the Holocaust.* New Haven, Conn.: Yale University Press, 1998.

Levi, Primo. *The Drowned and the Saved.* Translated by Raymond Rosenthal. New York: Summit, 1988.

Mankowitz, Zeev W. *The Survivors of the Holocaust in Occupied Germany.* New York: Cambridge University Press, 2002.

Marrus, Michael. *The Nuremberg War Crimes Trial 1945–46: A Documentary History.* Boston: Bedford Books, 1997.

Miller, Judith. *One, by One, by One: Facing the Holocaust.* New York: Simon and Schuster, 1990.

Myers, Margarete. "The Jewish Displaced Persons: Reconstructing Individual and Community in the U.S. Zone of Occupied Germany." *Leo Baeck Institute Yearbook* 42 (1997): 302–24.

Naimark, Norman. *The Russians in Germany: A History of the Soviet Zone of Occupation, 1945–1949.* Cambridge, Mass.: Belknap, 1995.

Niewyk, Donald. *Fresh Wounds: Early Narratives of Holocaust Survival.* Chapel Hill: University of North Carolina Press, 1998.

Novick, Peter. *The Holocaust in American Life.* Boston: Houghton Mifflin, 1999.

Rubenstein, Richard. *After Auschwitz.* Baltimore: Johns Hopkins University Press, 1992.

Trials of War Criminals before the Nuremberg Military Tribunals under Control Council Law No. 10, October 1946–April 1949. 42 vols. Nuremberg: U.S. Government Printing Office, 1947–1949.

PHOTO CREDITS

Note: USHMM is the United States Holocaust Memorial Museum.

CHAPTER 1

Page 9: USHMM Photo Archives, courtesy of Marilka (Mairanz) Ben Naim, Ita (Mairanz) Mond and Tuvia Mairanz
Page 21: USHMM Photo Archives, courtesy of Museum Purchase
Page 22: USHMM Photo Archives Photo Archives, courtesy of Schwules Museum
Page 24: Watercolor by Johannes Steyer from Hans Hesse, ed., *Persecution and Resistance of Jehovah's Witnesses during the Nazi Regime 1933–1945.* Bremen, Germany: Edition Temmen, 2000. Used with permission
Page 25: USHMM Photo Archives, courtesy of Hans Pauli

CHAPTER 2

Page 35: USHMM Photo Archives, courtesy of Richard Freimark
Page 41: USHMM Photo Archives, courtesy of James Sanders
Page 43: Alfred Eisenstaedt/Pix Inc./TimePix

CHAPTER 3

Page 54: John Heartfield, 1933
Page 57: USHMM Photo Archives, courtesy of Bezirkskrankenhaus Kaufbeuren

Page 59: USHMM Photo Archives, courtesy of Der Stuermer Archive, Stadtarchiv Nuremberg

Page 63: USHMM Photo Archives, courtesy of Foto-Willinger Collection, Hoover Institution Archives

Page 65: USHMM Photo Archives, courtesy of KZ Gedenkstaette Dachau

CHAPTER 4

Page 82: Bundesarchiv Koblenz (146/87/111/21)

Page 86: USHMM Photo Archives, courtesy of Michael Irving Ashe

Page 88: USHMM Photo Archives, courtesy of Trudy Isenberg. Photographer: Georg Schmidt

Page 90: USHMM Photo Archives, courtesy of Lydia Chagoll

Page 95: USHMM Photo Archives, courtesy of Stadtarchiv Neustadt

Page 96: USHMM Photo Archives, courtesy of Stadtarchiv Singen am Hohentwiel

Page 97: USHMM Photo Archives, courtesy of Joseph Fiszman

CHAPTER 5

Page 105: USHMM Photo Archives, courtesy of the Main Commission for the Prosecution of the Crimes against the Polish Nation

Page 107: USHMM Photo Archives, courtesy of the Main Commission for the Prosecution of the Crimes against the Polish Nation

Page 113: USHMM Photo Archives

Page 114: USHMM Photo Archives, courtesy of Juedisches Museum der Stadt Frankfurt. Photographer: Walter Genewein

Page 115: USHMM Photo Archives, courtesy of Chaya Lifshitz Waxman

Page 120: Beit Lohamei Haghetaot. Photographer: Mendel Grosman

Page 122: USHMM Photo Archives, courtesy of the Dokumentationsarchiv des Oesterreichischen Widerstandes

Page 126: USHMM Photo Archives, courtesy of the Dokumentationsarchiv des Oesterreichischen Widerstandes

Page 129: Stiftung Liebenau, Ressort Kommunikation [neg. 10564]

Page 131: Archiv Diakonie Neuendettelsau

CHAPTER 6

Page 138: USHMM Photo Archives, courtesy of Instytut Pamieci Narodowej
Page 140: USHMM Photo Archives, courtesy of Instytut Pamieci Narodowej
Page 141: USHMM Photo Archives, courtesy of Jacqueline Levy
Page 148: USHMM Photo Archives, courtesy of Mrs. John Titak III
Page 156: USHMM Photo Archives, courtesy of Dokumentationsarchiv des Oesterreichischen Widerstandes
Page 159: USHMM Photo Archives, courtesy of Dokumentationsarchiv des Oesterreichischen Widerstandes
Page 162: USHMM Photo Archives, courtesy of Archiwum Dokumentacji Mechanicznej. Photographer: Heinrich Hoffmann/Studio of H. Hoffmann

CHAPTER 7

Page 177: USHMM Photo Archives
Page 181: Bundesarchiv Koblenz (179/1575/15)
Page 184: USHMM Photo Archives, courtesy of Leopold Page Photographic Collection
Page 186: USHMM Photo Archives
Page 192: USHMM Photo Archives, courtesy of Halina Olomucki
Page 195: USHMM Photo Archives, courtesy of Henia Wisgardisky Lewin
Page 197: USHMM Photo Archives, courtesy of Anna Hassa Jarosky and Peter Hassa
Page 201: USHMM Photo Archives, courtesy of Archiwum Dokumentocji Mechanizney
Page 205: USHMM Photo Archives, courtesy of Muzej Revolucije Narodnosti Jugoslavije
Page 206: USHMM Photo Archives, courtesy of Toni Boumans
Page 208: USHMM Photo Archives, courtesy of Sara Ginaite
Page 210: USHMM Photo Archives, courtesy of Yad Vashem Photo Archives. Photographer: Rudolf Werner Breslauer
Page 213: USHMM Photo Archives, courtesy of Jewish Historical Museum of Yugoslavia

CHAPTER 8

Page 219: USHMM Photo Archives, courtesy of Marion I. Cassirer
Page 224: USHMM Photo Archives, courtesy of Yad Vashem (Public Domain). Photographer: Bernhardt Walter/Ernst Hofmann
Page 225: USHMM Photo Archives, courtesy of Yad Vashem (Public Domain). Photographer: Bernhardt Walter/Ernst Hofmann
Page 227: USHMM Photo Archives, courtesy of Anonymous Donor
Page 231: USHMM Photo Archives, courtesy of George Kadish/Zvi Kadushin. Photographer: George Kadish/Zvi Kadushin

CONCLUSION

Page 234: USHMM Photo Archives, courtesy of Robert Waisman
Page 235: USHMM Photo Archives, courtesy of William O. McWorkman; Photographer: William O. McWorkman
Page 237: USHMM Photo Archives, courtesy of Imperial War Museum
Page 238: USHMM Photo Archives, courtesy of Imperial War Museum
Page 241: USHMM Photo Archives, courtesy of Jack Sutin. Photographer: Jack Sutin

INDEX

Abel, Theodore, 63

Africa, 16–18, 56–57, 111, 178; North Africa, 178–79

African soldiers, in occupation of Germany after World War I, 17–18; as victims of killings in 1940, 139, *140*

Afro-Germans, x, 7, 17–18, 33, 56–58, 73

Against the Jews and Their Lies (Luther), 6

air raids: Allied, 158, 174, 216–17, 229; German, 138, 143–44. *See also* Blitzkrieg; Luftwaffe

Albania, 180

Algeria, 178

Allied forces/Allies, 137, 138, 139, 142–44; and Jews, 172–73, 175–76, 204–7; in last year of war, 212, 215, 218–19, 220, 221–22, 229; in postwar, 217, 233, 234–35, 240. *See also* Britain; Soviet Union; United States; World War II

Alsace-Lorraine, 27

Alten, Mark, 116–17

Americans. *See* United States

Amsterdam, 138, 206

Ansbach, *131*

Anschluss (annexation of Austria), 81–83, 87, 146–47. *See also* Austria; Germany

anti-Gypsyism, 13–16

antisemitism, 1, 3, 10–11, 95, 96, 108; as center of Nazi ideology, x, 4; history of, 4–7; Hitler's, 37–38; linked to other Nazi prejudices, 14, 20, 25; outside Germany, 81–82, 119–21, 123–25, 159–61, 233; redemptive, x, 38

anti-Slavic attitudes, 18–20, 123, 153, 163

Antonescu, Ion, 160, 161

appeasement, 83–84

Appelfeld, Aharon, 160

Ardennes Offensive (Battle of the Bulge), 229

Arendt, Hannah, 115, 125

Argentina, 240

armistice agreement, German-French, 139–40

Arondeus, Willem, *206*

Article 48, Weimar Constitution, 49

Article 231, Treaty of Versailles, 27

"Aryans," 168; as a constructed category, 36–37, 72, 149–50, 169, 174–75, 200–201

"asocials," 20–21, 55, 62, 185; in concentration camps, 196–97, 199

Augspurg, Anita, 95–96

Auschwitz (and Auschwitz-Birkenau), 118, 165, 189–91, *192*, 199, *210*, 240; at end of war, 226–27, 228, 235; Hungarian Jews in, 108, 191, 223–26; Jews in, 112, 118, 139, 144, 180–82, 214; resistance in, 207–8; Roma and Soviet POWs, 163, 215. *See also* killing centers

Australia, 61, 88, 98, 142, 239

Austria, 27, 47–48, 65, 120; Anschluss, 108–10; Jews from, 136, 171, 256

Austria-Hungary, 19

Axis, Rome-Berlin, 93, 179–80

Babinska, Bogumila (Jasiuk), *197*

Babi Yar, 156–57

Baden-Baden, *90*

Badoglio, Pietro, 179–80

Baeck, Rabbi Leo, 61

Balkans, 147–50, 167. *See also* Greece; Yugoslavia

Baltic States, 93, 108, 145–46, 151. *See also* Estonia; Latvia; Lithuania

Bartov, Omer, 150

Battle of Britain, 142–44

Battle of Omdurman, 16–17

Battle of Stalingrad, 173–78

Battle of the Bulge (Ardennes Offensive), 229

Bavaria, 34, 228

Beer Hall Putsch, 34, 40, 48, 85

Belaya Tserkov, 157–58

Belgium, 45, 135, 137, 139, 167

Belgrade, 148

Belorussia, 109, 119, 123, 126–27, 151, 154, 169, 217. *See also* Soviet Union

Belzec, 185–87, 189, *201*, 204. *See also* killing centers

Bergen-Belsen, 139, 197, 228, 233, 235–36, *237*, *238*. *See also* concentration camps

Berk, Shoshana Bluma (Sarid), *195*

Berlin, 44, 164, 186, 216, 220, 231; concentration camps nearby, 89, 91; gay community of, 22–23, 55, 203; Hitler

and, 104, 231; Jews in, 92, 98, 142, 174–75, *219*; T-4 program, 128–30

Berlin-Plötzensee, 220

Bessarabia, 145

Bialystok, 114, 207

Bielski, Tuvia, 126–27

Bielski partisans, 126

Binding, Karl, 12–13

Bismarck, Otto von, 136

black market, postwar, 218

Blaskowitz, Johannes, 110–11

Blitzkrieg, 102–3, 136. *See also* Germany; Poland

Blomberg, Werner von, 77–78

Bolsheviks/Bolshevism, 19–20, *21*, 39, 40, 123, 163, 219. *See also* Communism; Communists; Russia; Soviet Union

Bosnia, 148–49. *See also* Yugoslavia

Bouhler, Philipp, 99–100, 128, 130

boycott, anti-Jewish, 58–60

Brandt, Karl, 99–100, 128, 130

Brauchitsch, Walter von, 77

Braun, Eva, 231

Braunau am Inn, 31

Brazil, 240

Brecht, Bertolt, 64, 95

Breitman, Richard, 42–43

Brest Litovsk, Treaty of, 27

Britain, 60, 146, 148, 164; Battle of, 142–44; final stages of war, 228–30, 233, 235; as imperial power, 16–17, 142; Jews and, 98–99, 142–43, 172–73, 204; navy, 93, 136, 143; as occupying power, 238; partisans and, 148; prewar relations with Germany, 83–84, 93; World War I and, 27, 46, 75; World War II and, 103, 135–44, 162, 178

brothels, 106, 190, 198, 203

Bruckberg care facility, *131*

Brüning, Heinrich, 49

Buchenwald, 89, 197–99, 203, *234*, *237*, *238*. *See also* concentration camps

Budapest, 223, 226
Bug River, 160
Bukovina, 145
Bulgaria, 144, 148, 223
Buna rubber works, 189
Burgsteinfurt, *237, 238*
Bydgoszcz (Bromberg), *105*, 130

Canada, 142, 206; as destination for refugees and fugitives, 61, 88, 98, *208*, 239–40, 242
Caribbean, 16, 98, 239
Catholic Church, 31, 152, 153; in Germany, 24, 56, 66, 90; protest against and legitimation of Nazi measures, 62, 105, 109, 132–33, 157–58, 171–72, 193. *See also* Christianity; Galen; Pius XII; protest and nonprotest; Vatican
Caucasus, 173
Center Party, 52
Chamberlain, Neville, 83–84
chaplains, military, 157–58, 171–72
Chelmno (Kulmhof), 114, 182–85, 193. *See also* killing centers
children: of concentration camp personnel, 190; Germanization of, 169–70, 211; Jehovah's Witnesses', taken away, 91; Jewish, killed, 157–58, 171–72, 188, 190, 194, *225*; Jewish, postwar, 236, 240; Jewish, rescued and hidden, 142–43, 194–96, 207, 242–43; Roma, killed, 200, *201*; in Volkssturm, 221–22
China, 96–98
Christianity, 11, 16, 123, 143, 174; antisemitism and Jews and, 4–6, 72; Nazi suspicion of, 40, 90, 171, 185; role in protests against Nazi measures, 132–33, 202, 220. *See also* Catholic Church; Protestant church in Germany
Churchill, Winston, *21*, 143, 204
circumcision, 8, 194
code-breaking, 136, 206

collaboration, 135–36, 137, 212; against Jews and Gypsies, 155, 156, 176–77, 194, 223; postwar fate of collaborators, 239, 240
Communism, 20, 52–53, 77, 151, 238; Hitler and, 39, 93–94; Jews and Jehovah's Witnesses and, 124, 236–37; papacy and, 66, 109. *See also* Communist Party; Communists; Soviet Union; Stalin
Communist Party, German, 20, 48–49, 50, 70; attacked under Nazism, 52–53, 64, 90; resistance and obstacles, 94–95, 209–10. *See also* Communism; Communists
Communists, 3, 19, 47, 60, 149, 160; resistance by, 140, 203; Soviet purges of, 95; as targets of Nazism, x, 64, 154, 196–97, 199, 200. *See also* Communism; Communist Party; Soviet Union
concentration camps, 17; in prewar Germany, 64, 70, 73, 86, 89–92; in World War II, 102, 106, 146, 185, 196–203
Concordat, with Vatican, 66, 90, 93. *See also* Catholic Church; Pius XII
Conti, Leonardo, 128
conversion/converts, from Judaism to Christianity, 8, 58–59, 60, 80, 118
Coventry, 144
Cracow. *See* Krakow
Crimea, 171
criminals, imprisoned in concentration camps, 196–97, 199. *See also* "asocials"
Croatia, 144, 148–49, 198. *See also* Yugoslavia
Cuba, 88, 98
Czechoslovakia, 46, 83–84, 169; German minority in, 19, 83; Jews from, 108, 141, 142, 187; resistance in, 211, 229; Sudetenland crisis, 83–84
Czerniaków, Adam, 118, 194

Dachau, 53, 64, *65*, 89, 90–91, *90*, 188, 189, 198, *235*. *See also* concentration camps

Dante Alighieri, 200
Danzig (Gdansk), 104
D-Day, 215, 218
death marches, 215, 227–29
de Gaulle, Charles, 140
dehumanization, 182
Denmark, 93, 123, 135, 137, 167; rescue of Jews from, 144
denunciations, 74–75, 155, 202, 207, 236
deportations, 108, 145, 182, 233. *See also* ghetto/ghettoization; killing centers; resettlement schemes
deserters, Wehrmacht, 172, 174, 203, 221
Dietrich, Marlene, 95
Dirlewanger, penal battalion, 203
disabled (handicapped), 1, 15; 1933 and 1935 laws, 61–62, 73; attitudes toward, 11–13; children killed, 99–100; as first victims of killing program, x, 163–64; killed in T-4 program, by Einsatzgruppen, and in gas vans, 101–2, 127–33, 154, 183; protests against killing, 132–33, 187
displaced persons, 214, 237–40
displaced persons camps, 239–40
Divine Comedy (Dante), 200
Dniester River, 160
Dönitz, Karl, 231
Dora-Mittelbau, 198
Dresden, 69, 79
Dubno, 155
Dunkirk, 139, 143

East Prussia, 96, 220
East Germany (German Democratic Republic), 236
Egypt, 13
Eichmann, Adolf, 108, 164, 223, 240, 242; visits to killing centers, 188–89
Einsatzgruppen, 154–57, 160, 164, 242. *See also* Order Police; SS
Einstein, Albert, 64, 95

Eisenhower, Dwight D., 178, 218
Eisenstaedt, Alfred, *43*
Eisysky (Eishyshok), 155
El Alamein, 178
Eliach, Yaffa, 155
Eliot, T. S., 230
Enabling Law, 53
Engelmann, Bernd, 67
Estonia, 93, 108, 145, 151
Ethiopia, 178
ethnic Germans, 19, 169; as beneficiaries of Nazi measures, 125, 130, 155; involved in persecution and killing, 117, 154, 160, 198; in Poland, 94, 102, 105, 107; postwar displacement, 238–39; resettlement plans for, 106–8, 201; in Sudetenland, 83–84
eugenics, 12–13
Eulenburg-Hertefeld, Philip zu, 22–23
"Euthanasia" Program, x, 101–2, 127–33; children's, 99–100, 128. *See also* disabled; T-4 program
exiles, 95
experiments, Nazi medical, 189–90, 197, 203, 240

Fascists, Italian, 179. *See also* Italy; Mussolini
Filipovic, Stjepan, *205. See also* partisans; Yugoslavia
Finland, 144, 146, 222
Fiszman, Joseph, *97*
Flossenbürg, 163, 197, 228
Fonseca, Isabel, 160
Foreign Office, German, 111, 164
Four-Year Plan, 42, 76, 104
France, 83, 143, 146, 167; invaded, 135, 139–40; Jews and Gypsies in, 15, 99, *141*, 144, 189, 233; killing of black soldiers in, 139, *140*; postwar, 186, 238; resistance in, 142, 203, 212; Rhineland and, 18, 56, 76; World War I and, 26–27, 45, 49, 75; World War II and, 103, 136, 137, 178, 180, 218

Franco, Francisco, 77
Frank, Anne, 138–39
Frank, Hans, 104, 109, 164, 185. *See also*
    General Government
Frank, Otto, 139
Frankfurt, 138
Frankfurter, Felix, 205
Free French forces, 140
Freemasons, 20, 25–26
Freikorps (Free Corps), 19
Frick, Wilhelm, 52, 62
Friedländer, Saul, x, 38, 141, 144
Fritsch, Werner von, 77–78
Führer principle, 39–40
functionalists, 30

Galen, Clemens August von, 132–33, 187
Galicia, 152
gas, use of poison: on disabled, 129–30; on
    Jews, 164–65, 185–86, 188–90, 193; on
    Soviet POWs, 163–64, 189; vans, 130,
    183, 185, 188
Gay, Peter (Fröhlich), 9, 87
Gellately, Robert, 75, 146
General Government, 104, 108–9, 123,
    164, 185, 207. *See also* Poland
General Plan East, 168–69
genocide, x, 2, 17, 172, 193
Gens, Jacob, 119
German Africa Corps, 178
Germanization, 123, 169, 183, 211
Germans, popular opinion among: in 1935
    and 1936, 72, 74–75, 76; in 1938, 82–
    83, 87; during war's end and postwar,
    215, 229, 232, 242, *237*, *238*; Nazi sen-
    sitivity toward, 55, 87, 170; programs
    against disabled, 99–100, 132–33;
    regarding homosexuals, 56; regarding
    Nazi revolution, 67–68, 69, 71, 78; and
    war, 82–83, 102, 146–47, 172, 174, 217
German-Soviet Non-Aggression Pact. *See*
    Hitler-Stalin Pact

Germany, 2, 9, 10, 21, 144; anti-black and
    anti-Slavic attitudes in, 18–20; before
    Hitler, 44–47; declarations of war on,
    103, 136, 142, 180, 223, 229; East Ger-
    many (German Democratic Republic),
    236; as imperial power in Africa, 17;
    Jews in, 7, 88, 182, 188, 240; Nazi revo-
    lution and routinization in, 51–75;
    occupied, 236–38; prewar expansion,
    81, 84; rearmament, 67, 75–78; wartime
    conditions in, 146–47, 169, 216–18;
    World War I and, 20, 26–28. *See also*
    East Germany; Germans; West Ger-
    many; World War II
Gerstein, Kurt, 185–87
Gestapo, 42, 70, 75, 143; roles outside Ger-
    many, 115, 118, 153, 172, 211
ghettos/ghettoization, 5, 153, 172, 191,
    194; Jewish Councils and Jewish police
    in, 114–19; in Poland, 111–14, 193;
    resistance in, 207, 211; Roma and Sinti
    in, 114, 201–2
Ginaite, Sara, *208*
Gleichschaltung (coordination), 62
Globocnik, Odilo, 194
Goebbels, Helga, *35*
Goebbels, Joseph, 39, 40, 42, *43*, 230; death
    of, 231; jokes about, 37, 74; propaganda
    efforts of, 64, 76, 85, 87, 170–71, 174–
    75, 217–18. *See also* propaganda
Goebbels, Magda, *35*, 42, 231
Goldenberg, Myrna, 191
Göring, Hermann, 37, 40–42, 52, *54*, 77;
    Four-Year Plan and, 42, 76, 104, 109;
    Luftwaffe and, 42, 136, 143; war's end
    and suicide, 230, 242
Gotfryd, Bernard, 127
Gotthold, Helene, 92
Göttingen, 198
Graebe, Hermann, 155
Graf, Willi, 210–11
Grafeneck, 129

Grand Mufti of Jerusalem (Hajj Amin al-Husayni), 179
Great Britain. See Britain
Great Depression, 44, 48, 61
Greece, 135, 147–50, 180, 203; murder of Jews from, 180, 181, 187–88, 193
Grese, Irma, 199
Grosman, Mendel, 120
Grosman, Shmuel, 120
Gross, Jan, 121
Gross-Rosen, 163, 197, 228
Grynszpan, Herschel, 85
guards, camp, 176, 190, 198; at killing centers, 181, 183, 187, 204, 214; at war's end, 215, 223, 224–25, 228–29, 236. See also concentration camps; killing centers
Gürtner, Franz, 71
Gypsies. See Roma; Sinti

Habsburg Empire, 19, 46
Hacker, Melissa, 143
Hadamar, 129–30. See also "Euthanasia" Program; T-4 program
handicapped. See disabled
Harvest Festival, 176–77
Hasidism, 8
Heck, Alfons, 73, 78, 79–80, 86, 147
Helmbrechts, 228
Herero, 17, 41
Herzegovina, 149
Heuaktion (hay action), 169
Heydrich, Reinhard, 70, 211; and deportation and resettlement schemes, 105, 108; and Einsatzgruppen, 154; and Wannsee Conference, 164, 187
Heymann, Lida Gustava, 95–96
Himmler, Heinrich, 42–43, 64, 105, 109, 171, 223; as architect of genocide, 154, 163, 185, 189–90; attacks on Jehovah's Witnesses, homosexuals, and Roma, 55, 92, 201–2; SS and, 64, 68–69, 70, 104; at war's end, 228, 230, 239. See also SS

Hindenburg, Paul von, 27, 47, 49–50, 69, 70–71
Hirschfeld, Magnus, 23, 56
Hitler, Adolf, 3, 7, 10, 27, 42, 74; biographical information, 31–36, 44, 174; consolidation of power, 52–55, 68–69; inner circle, 40–44, 217; murder of disabled and, 128, 131, 132, 147; plot to assassinate, 220–21; preparing for war, 71, 77, 80, 83, 93–94, 102; prewar foreign policy, 66–67, 75–78; progress of war and, 136, 139, 153–54, 178; promise to annihilate Jews, 94, 147, 179; response to protests, 109, 172, 175; rise to power, 44, 47–50; significance of, 29–30, 51; Stalin compared to, 145–46; at war's end, 215, 218–19, 221–22, 229–32; worldview, x, 36–40, 101, 150–51, 171
Hitler, Alois, 31
Hitler, Klara, 31
Hitler-Stalin Pact, 80, 93, 103, 151
Hitler Youth (Hitler Jugend, HJ), 73, 78, 79, 147
Hoche, Alfred, 13
Hoecker, Karl, 227
Hoess, Rudolf, 163, 189, 190
Holland. See Netherlands
Holocaust, ix, x, 2; legacies of, 234–43
Home Army, Polish (AK), 125–26, 222. See also Poland; underground; Warsaw uprising
homosexuality/homosexuals: accusations used to discredit, 69, 77–78; in concentration camps, 90, 196, 199, 202–3; Nazi measures against, x, 42, 55–56, 64, 73; prejudices against, 3, 20–23, 236; resistance and, 206
Horthy, Miklos, 223
Huber, Kurt, 210–11
Hungary, 27, 144, 148, 153, 191; Jews in, 10, 108, 215, 222–26, 236, 239; Roma in, 15; war after Stalingrad and, 175–76, 222–23, 228, 229, 235

IG Farben, 189
imperialism, 16–17, 57–58
incorporated territories, from Poland into
  Germany, 103–4, 108, 119, 123, 183.
  See also Poland
India, 13, 16, 37, 98, 142, 201
inflation, 26, 45–46, 218
intentionalists, 30
International Military Tribunal, 240
International Red Cross, 234
international responses to Nazism, 82, 86–
  87, 204–5. *See also* Allied forces
Ioannina, Greece, *181*
Irish Free State (Eire), 142, 164
Isaacson, Judith Magyar, 226
Israel, 60, 108, 125, 160, 179, 239, 242
Italy, 48, 81; Jews and, 200; military cooper-
  ation with Germany, 77, 93, 144, 147–
  49, 178; war in, 122, 179, 179–82, 229

Jacob, Israel, *cover photo*
Jacob, Lili (Zelmanovic, now Meier), *224*
Jacob, Zelig, *cover photo*
Japan, 96, *97*, 144
Jedwabne, 121
Jehovah's Witnesses, x, 2, 3, 20, 23–25, 56,
  70, 236–37; in Nazi concentration
  camps, 89–92, 196, 199, 203
Jewish Councils (Judenräte), 114–19, 185,
  193–94. *See also* ghettos
Jewish Fighting Organization, Warsaw
  (ZOB), 208–9, 211. *See also* resistance
Jews, ix, 1, 201, 222–23; 1933–1935 situation in Germany, 58–61, 71–73; in Austria after Anschluss, 81–83; in
  concentration and labor camps, 198,
  199–200; defined and marked, 37–38,
  71–72, 147, 182; diversity among, 7–11;
  in ghettos, 111–19, 151–53; in hiding,
  194–96, *219*, 242–43; history of, 4–7;
  Hitler, Nazi ideology and, 36, 39, 94,
  168–69; Hungarian Jews killed, 215,

222–26; killed by Einsatzgruppen, 135,
  153–61, 171–72; killing centers and,
  163–65, 183–90, 193–94; Kristallnacht
  and, 84–89, 92; linked to Communism,
  20, 124; as partisans, 126–27; in Poland,
  104–5, 106, 109, 119–25, 127; postwar,
  232, 233–40; as refugees, 95–96, 140–
  41, 142–43, 144; repercussions of war
  on, 179, 180; resistance among, 207–9,
  211, 227; saved remnant (She'erith
  Hapleitah), *241*; in Yugoslavia, 149, *159*
Jidisze Bilder (Jewish Pictures), *241*
Judaism, 4–8, 10, 24, 58–59, 72, 80, 85,
  115, 171
justice, postwar, 240–42
Justin, Eva, 89

kapos, 127, 199–200, 226
Karski, Jan, 204–6
Katyn Forest massacre, 174
Kaufmann, Marion (Cassirer), *219*
Kershaw, Ian, 39
KGB (People's Commissariat for State
  Security), 145
Kiev, 156
killing centers, 61, 176, 235; described,
  182–91; knowledge of, 191–94;
  opened, 163–65; transports from ghettos
  to, 191, 209. *See also* Auschwitz; Belzec;
  Chelmno; Majdanek; Sobibor;
  Treblinka
Kindertransports, 142–43
Klemperer, Victor, 69, 79–80
Kluger, Ruth, 83
Knappe, Siegfried, 136
Knauer baby, 99
Koch, Ilse, 199
Koch, Karl, 199
Kovno, 194, *195*, *208*, *231*
Krakow, 104, 106, 163
Kristallnacht pogrom, 84–89, 92, *95*
Kusserow, Wolfgang, 92

labor camps, 111, 117, 145, 197–98; combined with killing centers, 188–89; Jews in, 209, 223–24; new in last year of war, 215, 228; in Poland, 106, 191
Lang, Fritz, 95
Langer, Lawrence, 243
Latter-Day Saints, Church of Jesus Christ of the, 91
Latvia, 93, 108, 151, 154, 198; Soviet takeover, 145
Laval, Pierre, 140
Law for the Prevention of Hereditarily Diseased Offspring (Sterilization Law), 62, 90. *See also* disabled; eugenics; sterilization
Law for the Protection of German Blood and Honor. *See* Nuremberg Laws
League of German Girls (Bund deutscher Mädel, BDM), 63
League of Nations, 45, 67
Lebensraum, 36, 101, 150, 154, 168
Leipelt, Hans, 210–11
Leitner, Isabella, 191
Lendvai, Karoly, 223
Lenin, Vladimir Ilyich, 19–20, 46
Leningrad, 222
lesbians, 22–23, *22*, 55, 95, 198. *See also* asocials; homosexuals; women
Levi, Elda, *181*
Levi, Primo, 180–82, 200
Libya, 178
Lidice, 211
Liebenau institution for mentally disabled people, *129*
Lifszyc, Rabbi David, *115*
Linz, 32
Lithuania, 93, 119, 151, 155, *156*, 194–95; Jewish partisans in, 156, 207, *208*; Soviet takeover, 145
Lodz, 104, 106, 152, 182–83; ghetto in, *9*, 112–14, 115, 118, 119, *120*, 177, *184*, 185

London, 61, 131, 140, 144; governments-in-exile in, 103, *107*, 125, 137, 204
London, Jack, 64
Lublin, 10, 104, 106, 108, 111, 194; ghettos in, 114, 116–17; killing operations near, 163, 176, 185, 188
Ludendorff, Erich, 27, 34, 47
Lueger, Karl, 7, 32
Luftwaffe (German air force), 42, 77, 103, 148; use of, in the west, 136, 138, 143
Luther, Martin, 6
Luxembourg, 114, 135, 136, 137
Lvov (Lwow, Lemberg, L'viv), 151–53, 157, 185

Macva, *159*
Madagascar plan, 111
Majdanek, 106, 127, 163, 176, 188–89, *192*, 213–14
Majranc, Tsvi, *9*
Malicious Practices Act, 74
Mann, Heinrich, 64
Mann, Thomas, 64, 95
Marx, Karl, 8
Marxism, 30. *See also* Communism
Marzahn, 74, 79, 89, 91. *See also* concentration camps; Roma
Maschmann, Melitta, 63
Masons. *See* Freemasons
Mauthausen, 92, 163
May, Karl, 34
medical doctors, 99–100, 128–30, 189–90, 242
Mein Kampf (Hitler), 31, 32, 34, 69, *90*; and Hitler's antisemitism, 38, 55; and Hitler's view of Lebensraum in east, 150, 154
Mengele, Josef, 189–90, 240
Mennonites, 155
Merin, Moishe, 118
Michalowsky, Zvi, 155–56
Middle East, 144, 240. *See also* Egypt; Grand Mufti of Jerusalem; Israel; Palestine

Minsk, 119
Mischlinge, 72, 175
mixed marriages, Jewish-Christian, 174–75. *See also* Klemperer; Rosenstrasse incident
Mokotow prison, *107*
Molotov-Ribbentrop Pact. *See* Hitler-Stalin Pact
Moltke, Helmuth James von, 220
Monowitz, 190. *See also* Auschwitz
Montgomery, Bernard L., 178
Morley, Ruth, 143
Morocco, 178
Moscow, 222
Munich, 33–36, 53, 64, 70, 210–11, *241*
Munich Conference, 83–84
Münster, 132
Mussolini, Benito, 48, 77, 81, 147, 149, 178; collapse of Fascist regime and, 179–80

Nama, 17, 41
Namibia. *See* Southwest Africa
Naples, 179
Napoleon, 6, 47, 150
National Socialist German Worker's Party (NSDAP, Nazi Party), 1, 3, 20–21, 41, 42, 70; in 1920s, 33–34, 47–49; in 1930s, 49–50, 52, 54, 73–74; in wartime, 164, 174
Naval Agreement, German-British, 93
Nazi ideology, 137, 167; centered on anti-semitism, x, 4; and concentration camps, 89, 196; homosexuals in, 202–3; Jewish-ness considered "race," 60, 71–72, 175; Roma and Sinti in, 200–201; Slavs in, 123, 169. *See also* Hitler; race and space; war
Nazi Party. *See* National Socialist German Workers' Party
Nazi revolution, 52–69, 82, 90, 146
Nazism: German criticism of, 78, 110–11,

210–11; in immediate postwar, 239–40; links to World War I, 27, 28; Marxist interpretation of, 30; relationship to Stalinism, 145; and war, 147. *See also* Hitler; National Socialist German Workers' Party; Nazi ideology
Nazi terminology, 36, 200
Nero Order, 221–22
Netherlands, 7, 123, 151, 167, *206*; German conquest of, 135, 137–39, 142; Jews in, 99, 187, 195–96, *219*, 242–43
Neurath, Constantin von, 77
Neustadt, *95*
New Zealand, 142
Nietzsche, Friedrich, 33
Night of Long Knives. *See* Röhm Putsch
Nisko, 108
NKGB. *See* KGB
NKVD (People's Commissariat for Internal Affairs), 145. *See also* Soviet Union
Nomberg-Przytyk, Sara, 200
non-aggression pacts, 66, 93
"non-Aryans," 128. *See also* Afro-Germans; Jews; Nuremberg Laws; Roma; Slavic peoples
Normandy, 218. *See also* D-Day
North Africa, 178–79
Norway, 123, 135, 137, 139, 142, 167
Nuremberg, 73, 75
Nuremberg Laws, 71–73, 90
Nuremberg Trials, 230, 240, 242

Ober Ramstadt, *88*
Odessa, 160
Olomucki, Halina (Olszewski), *192*
Olympic Games, 1936 in Berlin, 74, 76, 90
Omdurman, Battle of, 16–17
Operation Barbarossa, 150–51, 216
Operation Overlord, 218
Operation Reinhard, 187. *See also* killing centers
Operation Sea Lion, 143

Operation Torch, 178

orchestras, in camps, 198

Order Police, German, 154–55, 157, 176–77, 206. *See also* Einsatzgruppen

Oswiecim, 189. *See also* Auschwitz

Pact of Steel, 93

Pale of Settlement, 8

Palestine, 4, 61, 88, 127, 179, 239

Pan-Germanism, 32

Papen, Franz von, 50

Paragraph 175 (German criminal code), 55, 73. *See also* homosexuality/homosexuals

Paris, 85, 139, 145, 218, 222

partisans, 126–27, 158, 170, 171, 180; Jewish, 177, 207–9, 211, *213*; Yugoslavian, 148–50, *205*, *213*, 229

Pauli, Harry, 203

Paulus, Friedrich, 173

Pavelic, Ante, 149

Pawiak prison, *107*

penal units, 203

Penner, Ilona, 142

Penner, Kurt, 142

Pétain, Henri Philippe, 140

"phony war," 136

photographs, uses of, *59*, *107*, *208*, 236; from killing sites, *148*, 149, *156*, *159*

pink triangle, 199. *See also* homosexuality/homosexuals

Piotrków Trybunalski, 118, 193

Pius XII, 109, 132. *See also* Catholic Church

Plaschow, 106

plot of 20 July 1944, 215, 220–21

Plymouth, 144

Podchlebnik, Mordechai, 184

pogroms, 5, 7, 10, 80, 84–89, 92, 117, 152, 155, 160, 237

Poland, 45, 152, 167, 183; effects of war in, 232, 239; established as state after World War I, 19, 46; German crimes against, 104–6, 109–11, 150; German invasion and occupation of, 101–4, 136, 150; German plans for, 36, 106–9, 169, 185; German-Soviet arrangement regarding, 93–94, 151; government-in-exile, *107*, 125, 142, 204, 222; disabled murdered in, 130, 132; Jews in, 7, 8, 10, 111–21, *122*, 124–25, 152, 185, 194, 200, 204–5, 236; particularities of situation in, 122–24; prewar relations with Germany, 66, 85, 93; rescue of Jews and resistance, *107*, 125, 153, 194, 204–7; Soviet crimes against, 174, 239; underground army in, 103, 125–27, 222

Pomerantz, Jack (Yankel), 10–11, 103, 124

Portugal, 144

Prague, 61, 141, 203, 211, 229

priests: Roman Catholic, 66, 69, 84, 90, 105, 109–10, 132, 152, 157, 171–72, 195; Ukrainian Catholic, 153. *See also* Catholic Church

prisoners of war, 103, 140, 162, 180, 188, 204; black POWs shot by Germans, 139; captured by Allies, 178; Soviet POWs, 8, 161–64, 186, 257, 258, 303

Probst, Christoph, 210–11

propaganda, Nazi German, *21*, 62, 64, 73, 85, 93; and German war effort, 147, 174, *177*, 218–19, 221

protest and nonprotest, against killing: the disabled, 132–33, 187; Jews, 180, 186–87; Polish priests, 109–10; Roma, 202. *See also* Germans; international responses to Nazism; resistance

Protestant church in Germany, 24, 56, 59, 84; conflict and cooperation with Nazi regime, 92, *129*, 132, 157, 171. *See also* Christianity

Protestant Reformation, 6

Quisling, Vidkun, 137

race and space, ideology of, ix–x, 2, 36–40, 80–81; implemented in war, 94, 102,

110, 112, 130, 154, 176, 190, 219, 238. *See also* Hitler; Nazi ideology; war

Racial Hygiene and Population Research Center, *82*, 201

racism: antiblack, 17–18, 56–58; and killing of French black soldiers, 139; against Jews, 37–38. *See also* Afro-Germans; antisemitism; Nazi ideology

Radom, 127

Radu, Drina, 160–61

Radzyn, 10, 103

Rassenschande, 90

Raubal, Geli, 34–35

Ravensbrück, 79, 89, 197–99, 228–29. *See also* concentration camps; women

Reck-Malleczewen, Fritz Percy, 34, 50

Red Army, 124, 145, 170, 178–79, *208*; advancing, in 1944–1945, 181, 212, 215, 216, 221, 222, 223, 229; Battle of Stalingrad and, 173–74, 175; prisoners of war from, 161–64; at war's end, 239; Warsaw uprising and, 222

refugees, *86*, 98–99, 116, 140–41, 144, 237–39. *See also* displaced persons

Reich Citizenship Law. *See* Nuremberg Laws

Reich Committee for Scientific Registration of Serious Hereditarily and Congenitally Based Illnesses, 99

Reich Department of Health, Racial Hygiene and Population Biology Research. *See* Racial Hygiene and Population Research Center

Reichenau, Walter von, 158

Reich Representation of the German Jews, 61

Reich Security Main Office (RSHA), 105, 108

Reichstag, 42, 49–50, 52–53, 76, 94; Reichstag fire, 53–54, 64, 78

Reiprich, Doris, 56–58

Remarque, Erich Maria, 174

reparations, post–World War I, 26–27, 45. *See also* Article 231, Treaty of Versailles

reprisals, German use of, in World War II, 149, 171, 211

rescue: of Danish Jews, 144; hiding Jews, 194–96; of Hungarian Jews, 225–26; of Jews in Poland, 125. *See also* protest and nonprotest; resistance

resettlement schemes, 104–5, 123, 168; of ethnic Germans, 106–8, 113; Soviet postwar plans, 238–39

resistance, 156, 170, 171, 203–12; in camps and killing centers, 187, 188, 197, 226–27; gay, *206*; in Germany, 209–11, 220–21; Jewish, 118, 207–9, 213; obstacles to, 211–12; in Poland, 125–27; among Roma and Sinti, 226–27. *See also* partisans; protest and nonprotest

Rhineland, 18, 56, 76

Ribbentrop, Joachim von, 77, 230

Riefenstahl, Leni, 73

Riga, 118

Ritter, Robert, 89

Rivesaltes internment camp, *141*

Robota, Roza, 227

Röhm, Ernst, 68. *See also* Stormtroopers

Röhm Putsch, 68–69, 71

Roma (Gypsies), x, 149, *219*; in concentration camps, 198, 198–99, 200–202; Einsatzgruppen killings and, 154, 155, 157, *159*, 161; in ghettos and internment camps, 74, 79, 114, 117, *141*, 223; history of, 13–16; in killing centers, 183, 185, 187, 189, 190–91, 214, 215, 226–27; postwar problems, 236; prejudices against, 1, 3, 12, 21, 42, 56; prewar measures against, in Germany, 62, 72, 74, *82*, 89, 90–91; resistance, 226–27

Roman Catholic Church. *See* Catholic Church

Romania, 144, 145, 148; Gypsies in, 15, 237; Jews from, 119, 159–161; after Stalingrad, 173, 175–76, 223

Romani language, 16, 201. *See also* Roma
Rome, 77, 93, 180; ancient, 4, 37
Rommel, Erwin, 178
Roosevelt, Franklin D., *21*, 204, 216, 218, 229
Rosenberg, Otto, 74, 79, 89
Rosenstrasse incident, 175, 202. *See also* Germans; mixed marriages; protest and nonprotest; resistance
Rotterdam, 138
Royal Air Force, 143, 216
Rumkowski, Chaim, 118–19, 185
Russia, 5, 8, 16, 18, 19–20, 27, 46, 47, 150. *See also* Soviet Union
Russian Revolution, 20, 28

Sachsenhausen, 79, 89, 203, 228
Sartre, Jean-Paul, 119
Schieder, Theodor, 168
Schleicher, Kurt, 69
Schmidt, Georg, *88*
Schmorell, Alexander, 210–11
Scholl, Hans, 210–11
Scholl, Sophie, 210–11
Schuschnigg, Kurt von, 81
Scientific Registration of Serious Hereditarily and Congenitally Based Illnesses, Reich Committee for, 99
secrecy, of mass killing operations, 188, 191, 193–94, 205–7
Security Service (SD), 70, 75, 174
Serbia, *148*, 149, 198, *205*. *See also* Yugoslavia
Sevastopol, 171
sexual slavery, 198. *See also* brothels
Shanghai, 96–98
Sheptytsky, Andreas, 152–53
Siberia, 95, 123, 145, 152, 225, 233–34
Sicily, 179
Siegal, Aranka (Piri Dawidowitz), 10–11
Silesia, 108, 118
Singen am Hohentwiel, *96*

Sinti, 13, 56, 62, 74, 89. *See also* Roma
slave labor, 170, 180, 197, 217; Jews as, 190, 223–24; postwar situation, 233, 238
Slavic peoples, x, 3, 36, 167–68; anti-Slavic attitudes, 18–20, 123, 153, 163. *See also* Poland; Soviet Union; Ukraine
Slovakia, 46, 84, 144, 180, 189
Sobibor, 187, 188, 193, 207, 240, 242
Social Darwinism, 7, 12, 33, 40, 229. *See also* Nazi ideology
Social Democrats, German, 48, 53–54, 89
Solahütte SS retreat center, *227*
soldiers. *See* Allies; Red Army; Wehrmacht
Sonderkommandos, Jewish, 183–84, 188, 227. *See also* killing centers
Sosnowski, Piotr, *105*
South Africa, 142, 239
Southwest Africa (later Namibia), 17, 41–42, 56
Soviet Union, 45, 46, 77, 142, 178–79; Baltic states and, 145; Communist exiles in, 60, 94–95; German invasion of, 135, 144, 148, 150–51; German plans for, 36, 39, 108; Jews and, 123–24, 172, 187, 206, 233; nature of war in, 153–59, 167; Poland and, 93–94, 103, 121, 152, 174, 239; prisoners of war from, x, 135, 154, 161–64; resistance, 203; slave laborers from, 170; war's end, 220, 222–23, 225, 229, 230, 232, 235, 238–39
Spain, 5, 7, 144; civil war in, 77, 79, 140, *141*
Special Operations Executive, 203, 211
Speer, Albert, 217, 222, 223
Spielberg, Steven, 106
SS (Schutzstaffel), 42, 64, 66, 68, 169, *227*; concentration camps and, 89, 198–99; ghettos and, 209, 213; at killing centers, 183–84, 185–86, 188, 189–90, 207, 226; mass killings and, 130, 157–58, 163, 164, 171; in Poland, 104, 106, *107*, 109; at war's end, 176, 228–29, 230, 239, 242. *See also* Himmler

St. Louis (ship), 98–99
Stabholz, Thaddeus, 212–14
stab-in-the-back myth, 28, 47, 55, 85, 137. *See also* World War I
Stalin, Josef, *21*, 150–51, 173, 178–79; abuses of regime, 94–95, 145–46, 170, 222, 233; pact with Hitler, 80, 93–94, 103, 123. *See also* Soviet Union
Stalingrad, 173; Battle of, 173–78
Stangl, Franz, 187, 188, 193, 240
Stangl, Teresa, 193
Stauffenberg, Claus Schenck von, 220. *See also* plot of 20 July 1944
sterilization, 12, 56, 58, 61–62, 66, 73, 89–90, 169, 200. *See also* Law for the Prevention of Hereditarily Diseased Offspring
Steyer, Johannes, *24*
Stoltzfus, Nathan, 175
Stopes, Marie, 12
Stormtroopers (Sturmabteilung, SA), 48, 52, 65, 66; attacks by, on homosexuals, Jews, and Poles, 56, 58, 85, *90*, 106; Röhm Putsch and, 68–69, 70, 77
Strasser, Gregor, 69
Strength through Joy (agency), 64, 112
Stutthof, 197. *See also* concentration camps
Subcarpathian Rus, *224*
Sudan, 17–18
Sudetenland, 83–84, 92, 146–47, 239. *See also* Czechoslovakia
Suwalki, *115*
Sweden, 10, 137, 144, 164, 186; Jews and, 144, 225
Switzerland, 96, 144, 180, 206
Szerynski, Josef, 118

T-4 Program, 128–33, 163–64, 183, 187, 193, 240. *See also* disabled; "Euthanasia" Program
Tec, Nechama, 127
Theresienstadt (Terezin), 61

Thimme, Annelise, 104
Thimme, Friedrich, 78
Third Reich, 51. *See also* Germany; Hitler
Three-Power Pact, 144–45
Thuringia, 48
Tirailleurs Sénégalais, *140*
Tiso, Josef, 84
Tito, Josip Broz, 143, 229
Tokyo, 77
Toll, Nelly, 151–53
Torah scrolls, *115*
Transnistria, 159–61
Treaty of Versailles, 27, 67, 75–76, 81–82, 84
Treblinka, 176, 187–88, 193, 207–8, 213, 240
Triumph of the Will (film), 73
tuberculosis, 113, 185
Tucholsky, Kurt, 64
Tunis, 178–79
Tunisia, 178
Turin, 180
Turkey, 27, 89, 144, 164, 240
twins, experiments on, 190

Ukraine, 10, 18, 104, 109, 123, 151, 175, 202; camp guards from, 183, 198–99; mass killings in, 119, 125, 152–53, 154, 155, 156–58, 160, 171–72; postwar, 236, 239; slave laborers from, 217. *See also* Soviet Union
unconditional surrender, 229, 231
underground: Czech, 211; Dutch, 242; Jewish, 118, 126–27, 203–4; Polish, *107*, 125–26, 204. *See also* resistance
United Nations, 239
United Nations Relief and Rehabilitation Administration, 239
United States, 12, 49, 75–76, 142, 162; destination for refugees and exiles, 10, 60, 95, 98, 142–43, 153; and Jehovah's Witnesses, 24, 91; and Jews, 172, 204–7,

225, 228, 239; as occupying power, 238; and World War II, 93, 179, 214, 229, 235, 242
United States Air Force, 216
United States Holocaust Memorial Museum, 99
universities, German, 59
Ural Mountains, 169
Ustasha, 149. *See also* Croatia; Yugoslavia

Vajs, Bigula, *213*
van der Lubbe, Marinus, 53
Vatican, 66, 90, 93, 109, 186, 240. *See also* Catholic Church
Versailles, Treaty of, 27, 66, 67, 75, 76, 81, 82, 84, 93. *See also* World War I
Vichy, 140
Vichy France, 140, 178, 180. *See also* France
Vienna, 32–33, 36, 77, *82*, 108, 229; Jews in, 82–83, 143
Vilna (Vilnius), *97*, 119, *208*, 211
Vistula River, 222
Volga River, 173
Volksdeutschen. *See* ethnic Germans
Volkssturm, 221–22
Volkswagen, 64
Voltaire, 6
V-weapons, 198, 218

Wagner, Richard, 32, 230
Wajsman, Romek (Robert Waisman), *234*
Wallenberg, Raoul, 225
Wannsee Conference, 164–65, 175; construction of killing centers and, 182, 183, 185, 187, 189
war: accelerating dynamic of, 167; cover for killing of disabled, 130, 147; German preparations for, 79, 83–84, 94; in Hitler's worldview, 38, 80, 136, 168; outbreak in September 1939, 101–3. *See also* Hitler; Nazi ideology; race and space; World War II

war criminals, 144, 186, 217, 239
Warsaw, *97*, 104, *107*, 126, 152, 187, *192*, 212; uprising (1944), 222
Warsaw ghetto, 112, 114, 118, 187, 194, 204, 207, 212; uprising (1943), 208–9, 213; Wehrmacht (German military), 76, 84, 106, 107, 113, 173–74; bribery of officers, 172; chaplains in, 157–58, 171–72; at end of war, 216, 221–22, 229; establishment and nazification of, 67, 71, 77–78; invading, 102–4, 139–41, 148–50, 150–51; mass killings and, 154, 157–59; morale in, 110, 133; target groups and, 72, 152, 162, 164, 203, 222–23. *See also* Germany; Luftwaffe; World War II
Weimar, *41*, 44, 89
Weimar Constitution, 49
Weimar Republic, *22*, 23, 44–46, 47–49, 68
Weinberg, Gerhard, 153
Werewolf Organization, 221
Wessel, Horst, 65, *90*
Westerbork, 139, *210*, 242
West Germany (Federal Republic of Germany), 203
White Rose, 210–11. *See also* resistance
Wiesel, Elie, 225–26
Wilhelm II, Kaiser, 23
Winter War, 146
Wirth, Christian, 186
Wisgardisky, Henia, *195*
women: gentile, as victims, 89, 95–96, 106, 169–70, 211, 228; Germanization and, 169–70; Jewish, 153, 157, 158, 171, 190, 191, 226, 228; Nazi ideas about, 39, 55; Nazi racial laws and, 58, 71, 73; as partisans, 126, *208*; as partners and beneficiaries of Nazism, 43, 146, 149, 190, 198–99; as rescuers, 174–75, 242–43; sexual abuse of, 106, 110, 198; vote and, 45. *See also* Germans; Jews; lesbians; resistance

World War I, 13, 140; effects of German
defeat in, 3, 18, 45, 81, 163; Hitler's
experience in, 33; impact on Europe,
19, 75; Jewish veterans of, 9, 68, 80; as
precondition for Nazism, 26–28. *See also*
stab-in-the-back myth; Treaty of Versailles
World War II, 167; final phase, 221–32;
impact in Germany, 146–47; in Italy,
179–82; legacies of, 231–32, 233–43; in
North Africa, 178–79; in northern and
western Europe, 136–44; outbreak of, in
Poland, 102–3; relationship to Holocaust, ix; in Soviet Union, 150–51,
173–78; in Yugoslavia and Greece, 147–
50. *See also* Allies; Germany; Jews;
Poland; Red Army; Roma; Soviet
Union; Wehrmacht

Yad Vashem, 125
Yiddish language, 8, 10
Yugoslavia, 135, 148–49, *159*, 180, 199;
end of war for, 223, 232, 239; partisans
and resistance in, 202, 203, *213*, 229

Zacharias, Karin (Pardo), 96, 98
Zbaszyn refugee camp, *86*
Zegota, 125. *See also* Poland; rescue
Zionism, 61, 91, 118, 239
Zyklon B pesticide (hydrogen cyanide),
163, 186, 189, 214

ABOUT THE AUTHOR

Doris L. Bergen is Chancellor Rose and Ray Wolfe Professor of Holocaust Studies at the University of Toronto, where she teaches in the Department of History. Bergen received her Ph.D. from the University of North Carolina, Chapel Hill, in 1991 and taught from 1991 to 1996 at the University of Vermont and from 1996 to 2007 at the University of Notre Dame. She has also been a visiting instructor at the University of Tuzla in Bosnia, the University of Pristina in Kosovo, and Warsaw University in Poland.

Bergen's research focuses on issues of religion, ethnicity, gender, and violence in Europe in the Nazi era. She is the author of *Twisted Cross: The German Christian Movement in the Third Reich* (1996) and numerous articles and essays on aspects of the Holocaust, comparative genocide, Christian antisemitism, and the Volksdeutschen (ethnic Germans) of eastern Europe during World War II. Bergen has edited two volumes of essays: *The Sword of the Lord: Military Chaplains from the First to the Twenty-First Century* (2003) and *Lessons and Legacies VIII: From Generation to Generation* (2008). She is a member of the Academic Advisory Committee of the Center for Advanced Holocaust Studies at the United States Holocaust Memorial Museum in Washington, D.C.